Hiking
Colorado Wilderness Areas

Dave Muller

Westcliffe Publishers
BOULDER

Published by Westcliffe Publishers
a Big Earth Publishing company
3005 Center Green Drive, Suite 225
Boulder, Colorado 80301
1-800-258-5830
E-mail: books@bigearthpublishing.com
www.bigearthpublishing.com

Cover and text design: D.K. Luraas
Cover photos: D.K. Luraas
Production Manager: Mira Perrizo

9   8   7   6   5   4   3   2   1

ISBN 978-1-56579-664-5
Library of Congress Control Number: 2015937632

Printed in Korea

Please Note: Risk is always a factor in backcountry and high-mountain travel. Many of the activities described in this book can be dangerous, especially when weather is adverse or unpredictable, and when unforeseen events or conditions create a hazardous situation. The author has done his best to provide the reader with accurate information about backcountry travel, as well as to point out some of its potential hazards. It is the responsibility of the users of this guide to learn the necessary skills for safe backcountry travel, and to exercise caution in potentially hazardous areas, especially on glaciers and avalanche-prone terrain. The author and publisher disclaim any liability for injury or other damage caused by backcountry traveling or performing any other activity described in this book.

Contents

Acknowledgments

This book would not be possible without the help of my many hiking companions, numerous hiking guidebooks, Mira Perrizo, Julie Heins, and Kari Luraas from Big Earth Publishing, and especially my loving wife, Jackie, and the Source which has provided this marvelous natural world and made Colorado such a wonderful playground.

Introduction

Why produce another Colorado hiking guidebook? Even though books seem to be a vanishing species, another documented collection of Colorado hikes with many specifics can be a valuable resource and promote the enjoyment of hiking for many—now and into the future.

This is my eighth Colorado outdoor guidebook. Most of these hikes do not appear in the previous books. However, a few hikes, which are especially interesting and enjoyable, are repeated. All descriptions are first-hand.

There are at present forty-four Colorado Wilderness Areas with more to come. The Wilderness Act of 1964 was an inspired piece of legislation.

Hiking Times: These are times of the author over the past decades. They are listed to provide points of reference only.

Elevation Gain: This figure includes elevation losses on the ascent as the trail declines and some ascending parts of the trail on the descent. Those are the extra feet that are included.

Relevant Maps: The most useful usually is the Trails Illustrated Map. The greatest detail is provided by the 7½ minute U.S.G.S. Maps. The schematic map with each hike will usually suffice.

Caution: Mountain terrain can be dangerous with falls, bad weather, and getting lost. Be sure to carry a compass, adequate water, clothing, a cell phone if possible, and a map. Leave word with someone about your destination and anticipated time of return.

Guide to Wilderness Areas

General Wilderness Prohibitions

Motorized equipment and equipment used for mechanical transport is generally prohibited on all federal lands designated as wilderness. This includes the use of motor vehicles, motorboats, motorized equipment, bicycles, hang gliders, wagons, carts, portage wheels, and the landing of aircraft including helicopters, unless provided for in specific legislation. In a few areas some exceptions allowing the use of motorized equipment or mechanical transport are described in the special regulations in effect for a specific area. Contact the Forest Service office or visit the websites listed below for more specific information.

These general prohibitions have been implemented for all national forest wildernesses in order to implement the provisions of the Wilderness Act of 1964. The Wilderness Act requires management of human-caused impacts and protection of the area's wilderness character to ensure that it is "unimpaired for the future use and enjoyment as wilderness."

All Visitors

Campfires are prohibited. Camp stoves are allowed.

Maximum group size allowed in the Wilderness is twelve people or a combined total of twelve people and livestock.

Pets must be on a hand-held leash at all times.

Overnight Visitors

Camping is prohibited within 100 feet of lakes, streams, and trails.

Stock Users

Hobbled, tethered, or picketed livestock are prohibited within 100 feet of lakes, streams, or trails. Grazing livestock within 100 feet of lakes, streams, or developed trails is prohibited.

Only pelletized or steam-rolled feed grains, or certified weed-free hay, straw, or mulch are allowed in the Wilderness.

General Things to Consider When Planning a Trip to Any Wilderness

The information here gives general guidance about trip planning in any Wilderness. Be sure to check whether specific regulations exist for the area you plan on visiting, and be sure to contact the area's managing office for additional recommendations on trip planning.

Leave No Trace Principles

Plan Ahead and Prepare
- Know the regulations and special concerns for the area you'll visit.
- Prepare for extreme weather, hazards, and emergencies.
- Schedule your trip to avoid times of high use.
- Visit in small groups; split larger parties into smaller groups.
- Repackage food to minimize waste.
- Use a map and compass to eliminate the use of marking paint, rock cairns, or flagging.

Travel and Camp on Durable Surfaces
- Durable surfaces include established trails and campsites, rock, gravel, dry grasses or snow.
- Obey camping setbacks from lakes, streams, trails, other campsites, and historic and cultural sites and structures.
- Good campsites are found, not made. Altering a site is not necessary.
- In popular areas:
  - Concentrate use on existing trails and campsites.
  - Walk single file in the middle of the trail, even when wet or muddy.
  - Keep campsites small. Focus activity in areas where vegetation is absent.
- In pristine areas:
  - Disperse use to prevent the creation of campsites and trails.
  - Avoid places where impacts are just beginning.

Dispose of Waste Properly
- Pack it in, pack it out. Inspect your campsite and rest areas for trash or spilled foods. Pack out all trash, leftover food, and litter.
- Deposit solid human waste in catholes dug 6 to 8 inches deep at least 200 feet from water, camp, and trails. Cover and disguise the cathole when finished.

- Pack out toilet paper and hygiene products.
- To wash yourself or your dishes, carry water 200 feet away from streams or lakes and use small amounts of biodegradable soap. Scatter strained dishwater.

Leave What You Find

- Preserve the past: examine, but do not touch, cultural or historic structures and artifacts.
- Leave rocks, plants and other natural objects as you find them.
- Avoid introducing or transporting non-native species.
- Do not build structures, furniture, or dig trenches.

Minimize Campfire Impacts

- Campfires can cause lasting impacts to the backcountry. Instead, consider using a lightweight stove for cooking and a candle lantern for light.
- If fires are permitted:
  - Use established fire rings, fire pans, or mound fires.
  - Keep fires small. Only use sticks from the ground that can be broken by hand.
  - Burn all wood and coals to ash, put out campfires completely, then scatter cool ashes.

Respect Wildlife

- Observe wildlife from a distance. Do not follow or approach them.
- Never feed animals. Feeding wildlife damages their health, alters natural behaviors, and exposes them to predators and other dangers.
- Protect wildlife and your food by storing rations and trash securely.
- Control pets at all times, or leave them at home.
- Avoid wildlife during sensitive times: mating, nesting, raising young, or winter.

Be Considerate of Other Visitors

- Respect other visitors and protect the quality of their experience.
- Be courteous. Yield to other users on the trail.
- Step to the downhill side of the trail when encountering pack stock.
- Take breaks and camp away from trails and other visitors.
- Let nature's sounds prevail. Avoid loud voices and noises.

The above information is adapted from the Leave No Trace: Center for Outdoor Ethics.

23 Colorado 14ers included in this book

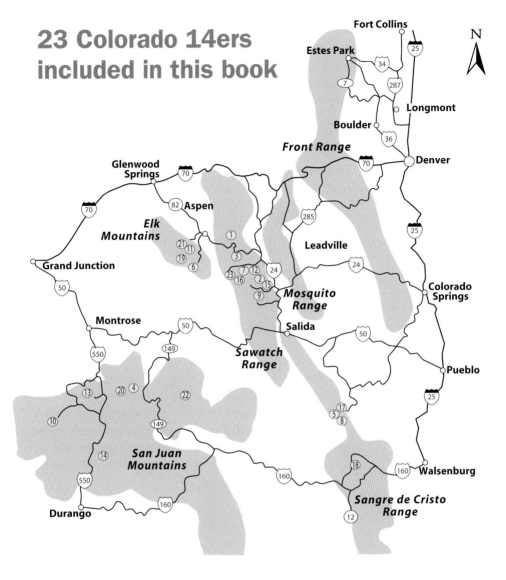

1. Mount Massive	14,421		13. Mount Sneffels	14,150
2. Mount Harvard	14,420		14. Mount Eolus	14,083
3. La Plata Peak	14,336		15. Mount Columbia	14,073
4. Uncompahgre Peak	14,309		16. Missouri Mountain	14,067
5. Crestone Peak	14,294		17. Humboldt Peak	14,064
6. Castle Peak	14,265		18. Mount Lindsey	14,042
7. Mount Belford	14,197		19. Pyramid Peak	14,018
8. Crestone Needle	14,197		20. Wetterhorn Peak	14,017
9. Mount Yale	14,196		21. North Maroon Peak	14,014
10. El Diente Peak	14,159		22. San Luis Peak	14,014
11. Maroon Peak	14,156		23. Huron Peak	14,003
12. Mount Oxford	14,153			

Neighboring towns: Fairplay, Buena Vista
Size: 43,410 acres
Elevation: 9,200 to 13,300 feet
Miles of trails: 18

One of Colorado's newest Wilderness Areas congressionally designated in 1993, Buffalo Peaks offers an enjoyable alternative to nearby areas thronged by crowds pursuing fourteener summits. It gets its name from the thirteen thousand-foot Buffalo Peaks located 15 miles southwest of Fairplay, Colorado. East (13,300 feet) and West (13,326 feet) Buffalo Peaks are two, high-domed mountains plainly visible from throughout South Park and the Arkansas Valley. The peaks mark the southern terminus of the Mosquito Range, a large faulted anticline.

Beaver, elk, mule deer, and one of Colorado's largest herds of bighorn sheep (150 individuals) call the Buffalo Peaks Wilderness home, but human visitors are relatively few.

Unlike the dramatic sculpted landscape of the Collegiate Peaks immediately west across the Arkansas Valley, Buffalo Peaks contains no deep glaciated valleys and no lakes other than impressive beaver ponds. Gentle forests, extensive meadows, and fewer visitors reward hikers who venture here. Several fine stands of bristlecone pine grace the area's southerly slopes.

Buffalo Meadows via Salt Creek Trail

Buffalo Meadows from the Tumble Creek Trail

Hike Distance: 3.7 miles each way
Hiking Time: Up in 104 minutes. Down in 89 minutes (senior time)
Starting Elevation: 10,382 feet
Lowest Elevation: 10,150 feet
Highest Elevation: 11,130 feet
Elevation Gain: 1,558 feet (includes 578 extra feet)
Trail: All the way
Difficulty: Moderate
Relevant Maps: Trails Illustrated 110; South Peak 7½ minute; Jones Hill 7½
minute; Park County Three; Pike National Forest

Getting There: From U.S. 285, 13.1 miles south of Fairplay, turn west on the Buffalo Peaks Road (Road 431) and stay on this good road for 8.8 miles and park, as the road ends at the Lynch Creek Trailhead.

Comment: This is another way to enter the Buffalo Peaks Wilderness and leads to the vast, open Buffalo Meadows.

The Hike: Begin northwest at the Lynch Creek Trailhead on the Salt Creek Trail and descend 1.1 miles to the Wilderness boundary, Tumble Creek, and a trail junction. Take the Tumble Creek Trail (617) on the left and ascend through the forest, cross Tumble Creek and reach open terrain. The trail becomes more level and gradually rises to a signed fork with the Tumble Creek Trail going up Buffalo Meadows on the left and the Rich Creek Trail continuing straight. This is the turnaround point. Enjoy the setting before retracing your route back to the Lynch Creek Trailhead.

Buffalo Meadows via Salt Creek

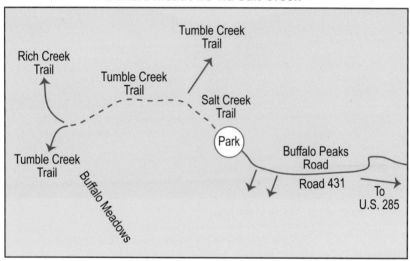

Rich Creek—Tumble Creek Loop

Hike Distance: 12 miles (total loop)
Hiking Time: 372 minutes (senior time)
Starting Elevation: 9,950 feet
Highest Elevation: 11,250 feet
Elevation Gain: 1,877 feet (includes 577 extra feet)
Trail: All the way
Difficulty: More difficult
Relevant Maps: Trails Illustrated 110; Jones Hill 7½ minute; South Peak 7½ minute; Park County Three; Pike National Forest

Ascending the Rich Creek Trail from the north

Getting There: From U.S. 285 south of Fairplay drive west on County Road 5 toward Weston Pass. After 7 miles meet Road 22 and keep right for 2.8 miles and park on the left at the Rich Creek Trailhead.

Comment: This beautiful loop hike lies mostly within the Buffalo Peaks Wilderness. In June the creeks are rushing and in September the aspen are spectacular. A counterclockwise route on the clear well-marked trail is recommended.

The Hike: Begin southeast over Rich Creek on a bridge and go right at the sign. After 0.6 mile begin the loop—avoid the trail on the left—and go straight on Trail 616 that rises to a vast high meadow. The trail continues along the left side of the drainage and the bushes, and enters the trees to the highest point of the loop. Then gradually descend to a signed fork with Buffalo Meadows on the right. Continue straight on Trail 617 and descend with Tumble Creek on the right. Reach a junction with the Salt Creek Trail on the right and go left and leave the Wilderness at a sign on the left for the final quarter of the loop. Cross Tumble Creek that will now be on the right with several beaver ponds. After some gentle ascending areas, descend to the end of the loop. Pass down to the right on Trail 616 and quickly reach the Rich Creek Trailhead and your starting point.

Rich Creek—Tumble Creek Loop

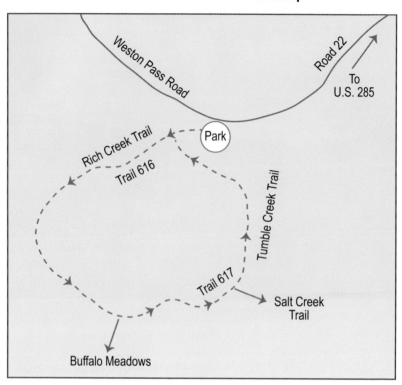

The Buffalo Peaks

Hike Distance: 8.5 miles total loop. 3.5 miles up to West Buffalo Peak.

Hiking Time: Up to West Buffalo Peak in 150 minutes. Over to East Buffalo Peak in 50 minutes. Down in 130 minutes (Total 330 minutes.)

Starting Elevation: 10,640 feet

Highest Elevation: 13,300 feet

Elevation Gain: 3,466 feet (includes 650 feet between the peaks and an extra 65 feet each way)

Trail: Initial and final 2.4 miles

Difficulty: More difficult

Relevant Maps: Trails Illustrated numbers 110 and 129 or 148 (partial); Jones Hill 7½ minute; Marmot Peak 7½ minute; Park County Number Three; Pike National Forest

Views from the summit:

From West Buffalo Peak:

 N to Mount Silverheels and Little Baldy Mountain
 NNW to Weston Pass and Ptarmigan Peak
 E to Pikes Peak
 ESE to East Buffalo Peak
 S to Mount Antero and Mount Princeton
 SSE to Buena Vista
 SW to La Plata Peak, Mount Elbert, and Mount Massive

From East Buffalo Peak:

 N to Mount Silverheels and Little Baldy Mountain
 NNW to Weston Pass and Ptarmigan Peak
 E to Pikes Peak
 S to Mount Antero
 SSW to Mount Princeton
 SW to La Plata Peak, Mount Elbert, and Mount Massive
 WNW to West Buffalo Peak

West Buffalo Peak

Getting There: Drive on U.S. 285 13.1 miles south of Fairplay and turn west onto Buffalo Peaks Road (431). Follow this good, dirt road 8.2 miles to a fork and go left on Road 431.2D and park at road end. En route to this point always stay on the main road (431). Keep straight at 0.7 mile, left at 3.3 miles, right at 5.4 miles, left at 6 miles and again at 7.5 miles. You will park with an open meadow on your right. Regular cars can come this far.

Comment: The Buffalo Peaks are distinctive and can be seen from South Park along U.S. 285 between Kenosha Pass and Trout Creek Pass. Their ascent is similar in terrain and difficulty to many "fourteeners." The several trails and old roads weaving through the basin below timberline make a **compass and map essential on this hike.**

The Hike: Begin to the south-southwest on the trail. Follow the trail as it curves southward. Continue south up the valley on a faint trail along a small creek and in 0.5 mile from the trailhead join an old road and ascend south to the right. In 1.6 more miles a fork is reached. Take the right fork and continue up into the basin below the two Buffalo Peaks. If you lose the trail, bushwhack up to the southwest. Within 0.25 mile leave the trail and angle southwest toward the ridge to the right of West Buffalo Peak. Soon you will reach some open areas and cross tundra and eventually talus above timberline to gain the ridge. Then proceed southeast over rocks to a summit cairn and trail register atop West Buffalo Peak.

Continue your loop hike by descending east to the saddle and then up to the unmarked small cairn on the summit of East Buffalo Peak. The loop continues

The Buffalo Peaks

north-northeast and then northwest down past timberline. Use the treeless areas to proceed as low and northward as possible before bushwhacking northwest to re-gain the ascent trail back to the trailhead. Be sure to keep Lynch Creek well to your left (west). This regaining of the trail will be the most difficult part of this hike so use your compass and maps carefully here.

Buffalo Peaks

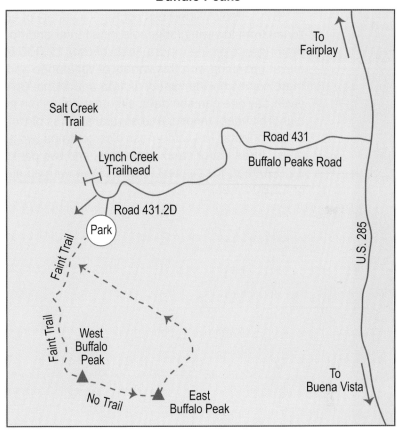

Neighboring towns: Fraser, Empire
Size: 8,913 acres
Elevation: 9,200 to 12,800 feet
Miles of trails: 23

The Byers Peak Wilderness was established by Congress in 1993. Byers Peak was named after William N. Byers, founder of Colorado's first newspaper, the *Rocky Mountain News*. He was also the first mayor of Hot Sulphur Springs.

Byers Peak Wilderness contains a variety of eco-zones from low-lying lodgepole pine forest and riparian drainages to alpine tundra fields of over 12,000 feet in elevation. Along with this variety of vegetation and climate comes a wide variety of flora and fauna. On any given day one can see deer, elk, bear, mountain goats, bighorn sheep, moose, and several species of trout and small rodents. The wilderness also contains two glacial lakes, three major creek drainages, and two peaks over 12,500 feet. The highest is Byers Peak with an elevation of 12,804 feet.

Byers Peak

Hike Distance: 5.3 miles each way
Hiking Time: Up in 157 minutes. Down in 107 minutes.
Starting Elevation: 9,885 feet
Highest Elevation: 12,804 feet
Elevation Gain: 3,229 feet (includes 155 extra feet each way)
Trail: All the way
Relevant Maps: Trails Illustrated 103; Bottle Pass 7½ minute; Byers Peak 7½
   minute; Grand County 4; Arapahoe National Forest
Views from the Summit:
   NNE to Bottle Peak
   NNW to Ptarmigan Peak
   SSE to Saint Louis Peak
   SW to Torreys Peak
   SW to Bills Peak

Byers Peak from the east

Getting There: From the traffic light in Fraser on U.S. 40 set your odometer to zero and turn left onto Road 72. Take the right fork after 0.3 mile. At mile 1.0 go left on Road 73, the Saint Louis Creek Road. Stay on the good, main road. At mile 5.2 continue straight at a four-way intersection. At mile 6.8 continue straight and avoid the King Creek Road on the left. At mile 7.9 take the right fork. Turn left at mile 9.8 and park at mile 10.8. This is the Byers Peak Trailhead.

Comment: The hike to Byers Peak became longer when the trailhead was moved lower. Great views await you on the top.

The Hike: Begin northwest from the signboard up the blocked road. (Bicycles can only proceed 1.8 miles on this road.) Follow the wide road as it curves and passes the Bottle Peak Trailhead after 1.3 miles. Another 0.5 mile brings you to the old Byers Peak Trailhead and the end of the road. Continue east-southeast on the trail, which gets steeper just before treeline. Follow the ridge to the south end and pass the trail to Bottle Pass on the right. A benchmark and rock pile greet you at the summit.

Byers Peak

Neighboring towns: Buena Vista, Crested Butte, Aspen
Size: 166,938 acres
Elevation: 8,500 to 14,420 feet
Miles of trails: 105

Collegiate Peaks is one of the ten largest Wilderness Areas in the state. Within its boundaries are more fourteeners and high peaks than any other Wilderness Area in Colorado or the lower 48 states.

Eight peaks exceeding 14,000 feet are found here, including the state's third and fifth highest summits, Mount Harvard and La Plata Peak. In addition, another half-dozen peaks soar over 13,800 feet.

The popularity of climbing fourteeners, combined with proximity to Denver and the Front Range, means the Collegiates receive crowds on summer weekends. For more solitude, plan to visit during the week or in the fall.

Wide U-shaped valleys open onto beautiful mountain scenery, including dozens of alpine lakes. About 40 miles of the Continental Divide crosses the area.

Collegiate Peaks Wilderness Area

Browns Pass and Browns Cabin

Hike Distance: 4.1 miles each way
Hiking Time: Out in 140 minutes. Back in 106 minutes.
Starting Elevation: 9,900 feet
Highest Elevation: 12,020 feet
Elevation Gain: 2,632 feet (includes 512 extra feet)
Trail: All the way
Difficulty: Moderate
Relevant Maps: Trails Illustrated Number 129 or 148; Mount Yale 7½ minute; Chaffee County Number Two; Gunnison County Number Three; San Isabel National Forest; Gunnison National Forest

Getting There: From U.S. 24 in central Buena Vista drive west on Main Street (Chaffee County Road 306), which becomes the Cottonwood Pass Road, for 11.8 miles and park on the right at the Denny Creek Trailhead.

Comment: Most hikers use the Denny Creek Trail to climb Mount Yale, one of Colorado's fourteeners and a "Collegiate Peak." There are, however, other destinations above the cutoff to Mount Yale. Hartenstein Lake is one and Browns Pass on the Continental Divide is another.

North from Browns Pass

This hike to the pass enjoys a clear, gradually ascending trail with several creek crossings. At the pass, there are further options. One trail descends north to Texas Creek and passes the ruins of Browns Cabin, which collapsed a few years ago. Another trail continues east to Kroenke Lake and the North Cottonwood Creek Trail. The panorama from Browns Pass to the north is breathtaking. Missouri Mountain to the north-northwest is one of many visible peaks.

The Hike: From the parking area, begin to the northwest and quickly pass a signboard, a register, and a Collegiate Peaks Wilderness sign. The wide trail is initially steep and reaches a signed fork with the Mount Yale Trail on the right at mile 1.3. Continue northwest by the left fork as the terrain becomes more open. At mile 2 there is another signed fork just beyond a single tall, bare tree, known as a "snag." The left trail leads to Hartenstein Lake but you continue up the trail on the right (north-northwest) another 2 miles to Browns Pass at timberline. Enjoy the vistas and if time and energy permit, descend the Texas Creek Trail north 0.4 mile and 300 feet to the collapsed, and once two-story, Browns Cabin. En route, there is a small wooden shack off trail on the right. To return, retrace your route on this delightful trail.

Browns Pass and Browns Cabin

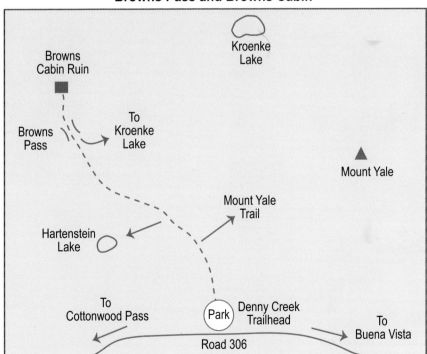

Grizzly Peak

Hike Distance: 5.3 miles each way
Hiking Time: up in 170 minutes. Down in 142 minutes.
Starting Elevation: 10,760 feet
Highest Elevation: 13,988 feet
Elevation Gain: 3,628 feet (includes 200 extra feet each way)
Trail: Initial 2.3 miles and last 1.0 mile
Difficulty: More difficult
Relevant Maps: Trails Illustrated number 127 or 148; Independence Pass 7½
  minute; Chaffee County Number One; San Isabel National Forest
Views from the Summit:
  NE to Mount Elbert
  ESE to LaPlata Peak
  SSE to Mount Garfield
  SSW to Anderson Lake
  SE to Red Mountain
  WNW to Truro Lake

Grizzly Peak

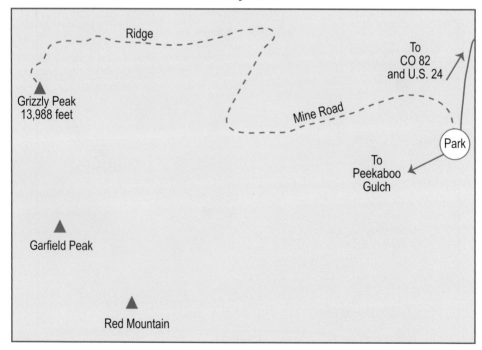

Getting There: From U.S. 24 between Leadville and Buena Vista, drive west on Colorado 82 for 14.5 miles and turn left onto the South Fork Lake Creek Road. Follow this rough road for 2.6 miles and take the right fork at a sign. (The left road leads to Sayres Gulch.) Drive 0.6 mile up the right fork and park off the road at another road junction. Many regular cars with high clearance can reach this point. (Four-wheel drive is required for the next 1.25-mile segment of McNasser Gulch to a road barrier.)

Comment: There are several Grizzly Peaks in Colorado and this is the highest one. In fact, it was once considered a fourteener. The trailhead lies in out-of-the-way McNasser Gulch. The trail is, at first, an old road to an abandoned mine. Then, without trail, you ascend to a ridge trail on the Continental Divide. This approach to the ridge requires some route finding and is the key to the hike.

The Hike: Start your hike up the right fork into McNasser Gulch. After 1.25 miles pass around a metal gate past a trail register and continue another mile above timberline to an abandoned mine. From here angle up to the northwest 0.5 mile without a trail and then turn north and ascend grassy slopes to the ridge. Avoid scree and talus as much as possible. At the ridge, turn left (west) and quickly reach an orange tinged saddle. The ridge up to the top of Grizzly Peak looks more difficult than it is from this saddle. Follow a faint ridge trail from this saddle for 0.8 mile to a ridge crossing and the final trail segment on the west side of the peak. A register and a small rock pile mark the highest point. Enjoy the extensive views before returning by your ascent route. (An alternate return is by way of an easy chute down to the southeast into the basin after 0.75 mile from the top on your ascent route. From the basin proceed east back to the mine and road.)

Huron Peak

Hike Distance: 5.1 miles each way
Hiking Time: Up in 192 minutes. Down in 136 minutes.
Starting Elevation: 10,250 feet
Highest Elevation: 14,003 feet
Elevation Gain: 4,623 feet (includes 435 feet each way)
Trail: First 60 percent and last 20 percent
Difficulty: More difficult
Relevant Maps: Trails Illustrated Number 129 or 148; Winfield 7½ minute; Chaffee County Number One; San Isabel National Forest

Views from the Summit:
N to Mount Hope
NNW to Browns Peak and Mount Elbert
NE to Mount Belford
NW to LaPlata Peak and Mount Massive
E to Mount Harvard
ENE to Missouri Mountain

Huron Peak from Lake Ann

Getting There: From the intersection of U.S. 24 and Colorado 82 south of Lead-ville, drive south on U.S. 24 for 4.3 miles and turn right onto Chaffee County Road 390, which goes past the Clear Creek Reservoir on your left. Follow this good main dirt road for 11.7 miles to the old mining town of Winfield. Turn left at a fork and after 0.2 more miles park off the road. Regular cars can drive this far. The road con-tinues another 2 miles alongside Clear Creek before it is blocked but four-wheel drive and high clearance are needed for this final segment.

Comment: There are usually several hiking routes to the top of a Colorado four-teener. With each different way to the summit, the mountain has a different aspect. This trail description to Huron Peak in the Sawatch Range proceeds south on a four-wheel drive road and then steeply ascends to the east and southeast, crosses a grassy basin and then resumes steeply to the top of one of the 54 mountains in Colorado with an elevation of over 14,000 feet, Huron Peak, at the boundary of the Collegiate Peaks Wilderness.

Huron Peak

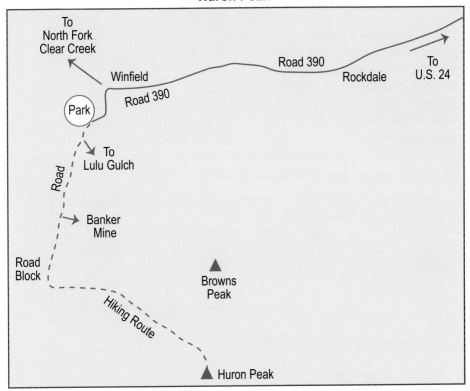

The Hike: Begin southwest from your parking spot on the rocky, dirt road. After 0.5 mile keep straight as a road ascends to the left up into Lulu Gulch. After another mile reach a four-way intersection. The ruins of the Banker Mine will be above on your left. Continue straight up the valley for 0.4 mile to a trail register and sign at a road barrier. Go around the barrier and stay on the road another few hundred yards. Then ascend steeply left at a cairn and leave the road. Follow this trail east and then southeast up into a grassy basin. Around timberline Huron Peak comes impressively into view to the east-southeast. The trail becomes unclear at times around treeline.

　　Then continue east and steeply up into the basin on a trail that eventually fades away. Persist up to the ridge between Browns Peak on the left and Huron Peak on the right. Then follow a rough ridge trail up to the south over a false summit to a rock pile and a register cylinder at the high point of Huron Peak. On a clear day many high summits can be seen. Take it all in before you return on your ascent route. The descent is a steep one and will stress your knees. Be careful with your footing.

Kroenke Lake

Hike Distance: 4.2 miles
Hiking Time: Up in 114 minutes. Down in 84 minutes.
Starting Elevation: 9,840 feet
Highest Elevation: 11,530 feet
Elevation Gain: 2,200 feet (includes 510 extra feet)
Trail: All the way
Difficulty: Moderate
Relevant Maps: Trails Illustrated Number 129 or 148; Mount Yale 7½ minute; Chaffee County Number Two; San Isabel National Forest

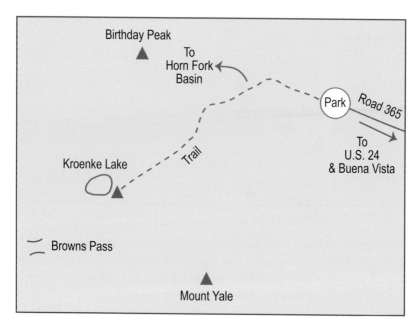

Getting There: From the middle of Buena Vista at the intersection of U.S. 24 and Chaffee County Road 306, drive north on U.S. 24 for 0.4 mile and turn left (west) on Crossman Avenue, which is County Road 350. After 2.1 straight miles on this road, turn right onto Road 361. After 0.9 mile on road 361 turn sharply left onto Road 365. Follow this main dirt road for 5.2 miles and park near the trailhead sign-board at the end of the road. Regular cars can reach this point on the occasionally rough road. (Road 361 and Road 365 can also be reached from Road 306 and several other connecting county roads west of U.S. 24.)

Comment: Kroenke Lake lies close to three fourteeners in the Collegiate Peaks Wilderness: Mount Yale, Mount Harvard, and Mount Columbia. This popular hike begins at the North Cottonwood Creek Trailhead and proceeds up to a fork. The left fork leads to Kroenke Lake and Browns Pass and the trail on the right leads to lovely Horn Basin, Bear Lake, and Mount Harvard.

The Hike: Begin walking west on the good path that quickly passes a trail register and follows North Cottonwood Creek. A bridge crossing occurs before you arrive at a sign and a fork after almost 2 miles from the trailhead. Take the left fork to the west as the right fork ascends into Horn Fork Basin. The trail becomes somewhat steeper as it rises through the forest and makes two creek crossings. The second creek drains the basin below Birthday Peak.

The final approach becomes more gradual before Kroenke Lake comes into view. A short descent brings you to the edge of the lake, which has an island in its center. The trail continues southwest up to Browns Pass and beyond. The high peaks around Kroenke Lake are impressive. Mount Yale is prominent to the southeast and Birthday Peak can barely be seen to the north. Take your time at this scenic lake before your return.

Lake Ann

Hike Distance: 6.0 miles each way
Hiking Time: Up in 150 minutes. Down in 122 minutes.
Starting Elevation: 10,250 feet
Highest Elevation: 11,805 feet
Elevation Gain: 2,825 feet (includes 635 extra feet each way)
Trail: All the way
Difficulty: Moderate
Relevant Maps: Trails Illustrated Number 129 or 148; Winfield 7½ minute;
    Chaffee County Number One; San Isabel National Forest

Getting There: From the intersection with Colorado 82 south of Leadville, drive south on U.S. 24 for 4.2 miles and turn right onto Chaffee Road 390. Pass the Clear Creek Reservoir on the left and drive on this good, dirt road for 11.7 miles to the former town site of Winfield. Turn left at a fork, cross Clear Creek, and after 0.2 mile from Winfield, park on the right. (The road is blocked after 2 more miles and high clearance and four-wheel drive are advised for this final road segment.)

Comment: Lake Ann is located high in a remote basin of the Collegiate Peaks Wilderness beneath the Continental Divide. Rock peaks ring the lake, many of them unnamed. Remnants of Colorado mining history abound along the route to Lake Ann. Driving to the trailhead, you pass the former mining towns of Vicksburg, Rockdale, and Winfield. On the hiking trail you pass the former Banker Mine on the left and walk through an open area where the town of Hamilton once stood.

The Hike: Hike south from your parking area and at mile 1.5 pass the Banker Mine on the left and keep straight at a four-way intersection. Persist on the rough road another 0.5 mile to a trailhead sign and register where the road is blocked. Continue on the road and within 100 yards from the roadblock reach a Wilderness sign and a trail on the left. This footpath on the left leads to Huron Peak, a fourteener. You continue straight on the South Fork Clear Creek Trail. At mile 2.9 pass a small Wilderness sign. At mile 3.6 cross a meadow, which was once occupied by the mining town of Hamilton. The formidable mountains known as The Three Apostles are visible on your left. Go right here at a signed fork. The left fork ascends to Apostle Basin.

A Continental Divide Trail symbol marks the right (south) fork that you follow across a sturdy bridge over the South Fork of Clear Creek. Follow this good trail as it steepens for another mile to a crucial fork. The right fork is marked by another Continental Divide Trail symbol and the left fork is unmarked. Go left (south-southeast) on this adequate trail that soon crosses the creek on three logs and in 1.4 miles reaches circular Lake Ann at the far southern end of the basin at timberline under the Continental Divide. If you lose the trail, follow the creek up to the lake. Huron Peak can be seen to the northeast and the rugged South Apostle to the east. Granite Peak is the closest mountain to the north-northwest. Enjoy and then retrace your ascent route back to the trailhead.

Lake Ann

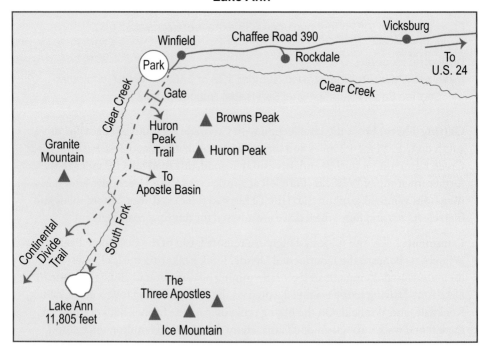

La Plata Peak

Hike Distance: 6.1 miles each way
Hiking Time: Up in 245 minutes. Down in 192 minutes.
Starting Elevation: 10,358 feet
Highest Elevation: 14,336 feet
Elevation Gain: 4,458 feet (includes 240 extra feet each way)
Trail: Initial half plus faint ridge trail over last mile
Difficulty: More difficult
Relevant Maps: Trails Illustrated Numbers 127 and 129 or 148; Winfield 7½ minute; Mount Elbert 7½ minute; Chaffee County Number One; San Isabel National Forest
Views from the Summit:
    N to Mount Elbert
    NNW to Mount Massive
    NE to Parry Peak
    E to Mount Hope
    ESE to Mount Oxford, Mount Belford, and Mount Harvard
    SSE to Huron Peak and The Three Apostles
    SE to Crystal Lake and Missouri Mountain
    W to Snowmass Mountain
    WNW to Capitol Peak and Mount Sopris

La Plata Peak from Mount Massive

La Plata Peak

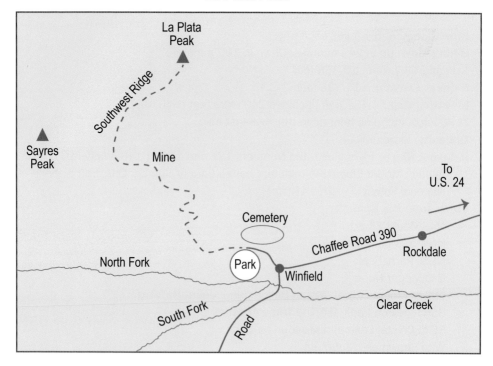

Getting There: Drive on U.S. 24 either 4.2 miles south of its junction with Colorado 82 or 15.3 miles north of the stoplight in the center of Buena Vista. Then turn west onto Chaffee County Road 390. Follow this good dirt road up the valley for 11.6 miles to the ghost town of Winfield. En route to Winfield keep right at mile 3.4. At Winfield take two successive right forks within 100 yards and continue 0.4 mile farther on the rough but passable road to Winfield Cemetery on the right. Park around here off the road since high clearance or four-wheel drive may be required farther on.

Comment: La Plata Peak, in the Sawatch Range, is the fifth highest in Colorado and a strenuous effort is needed to reach its summit. This route from the south is less used than the trail from the north up La Plata Basin. You will traverse a lovely, unnamed basin before reaching the southwest ridge leading over several false summits to the top, deep within the Collegiate Peaks Wilderness.

The Hike: Begin west on the rough road taking the left fork just past the cemetery and then the right fork after 0.6 mile. You then enter an open valley and in 0.5 mile farther take a right fork up a road that becomes overgrown and less defined as it switchbacks upward to reach a metal road barrier in 0.2 mile from the previous fork. Continue east-northeast on the road, which turns to the northwest and in 1.8 miles from the road barrier you will reach road end at an abandoned mine near timberline. Continue west from the mine, stay around timberline and curve in a clockwise direction farther up into the large basin.

Do not lose any elevation and keep well to the right (east) of the drainage. As you enter the upper basin, keep right and ascend a brief steeper section to the north to reach the southwest ridge. Then turn right (north-northeast) and ascend the talus on a faint trail past the first of several false summits. The true summit will now be visible and the ascent from here is more gradual on the ridge. A cairn, rock shelter, and register cylinder can be found at the high point. The views are spectacular. Return as you came up, but be careful to find the same way back down into the upper basin.

Missouri Mountain

Hike Distance: 7.0 miles each way
Hiking Time: Up in 266 minutes. Down in 152 minutes (loop).
Starting Elevation: 9,940 feet
Highest Elevation: 14,067 feet
Elevation Gain: 4,802 feet (includes 675 extra feet)
Trail: Initial 5 miles and last 1.5 miles on ascent. First 1.5 mile and last 5 miles on descent.
Difficulty: More difficult
Relevant Maps: Trails Illustrated Number 129 or 148; Winfield 7½ minute; Chaffee County Number One; San Isabel National Forest
Views from the Summit:
NNE to Mount Belford
NW to Mount Elbert
E to Pikes Peak
ENE to Mount Oxford
ESE to Mount Harvard
SSE to Mount Yale, Silver King Lake, and Emerald Mountain
SSW to Iowa Peak
SE to Mount Columbia
SW to Ice Mountain
W to Browns Peak
WNW to La Plata Peak
WSW to Mount Huron

Missouri Mountain from Iowa Peak

Getting There: On U.S. 24 south of Leadville, drive 4.2 miles south of the Colorado 82 intersection and turn right onto Chaffee County Road 390. (This turnoff is 15 miles north of the intersection of U.S. 24 and Chaffee Road 306 in Buena Vista.) Follow Road 390 for 9.8 miles and turn left onto an unmarked road. Pass several old cabins and avoid a road on the right before reaching the first of two crossings of Clear Creek. Park off the road. (Only four-wheel drive vehicles will carry you over the two creek crossings and then up the rough road for 3 miles to a road barrier and parking.)

Comment: Missouri Mountain is usually climbed either from the southwest and Clohesy Lake or from Vicksburg and Missouri Gulch on the northwest. This southern route requires a foot-soaking crossing of Clear Creek at the beginning (unless you use four-wheel drive) and entering the Collegiate Peaks Wilderness near privately-owned Clohesy Lake. The ridge then leads to a summit with great vistas. Late summer is the best time for this climb due to the creek crossing.

The Hike: Start to the east and cross two segments of Clear Creek. Then follow the rough road up to the south with the Lake Fork of Clear Creek always on the right. The valley is largely open and scenic as you ascend. At mile 2.9 pass a trail register on the right and shortly thereafter the Huron Peak Trail on the right. Follow the road another 0.3 mile and walk around a road barrier. Soon Clohesy Lake will come into view and you will leave the road on a trail to the left (south). Follow this trail as it rises to enter the basin to the southeast. A subpeak of Iowa Peak lies ahead of you to the south-southeast. The trail reaches the basin around timberline

Missouri Mountain

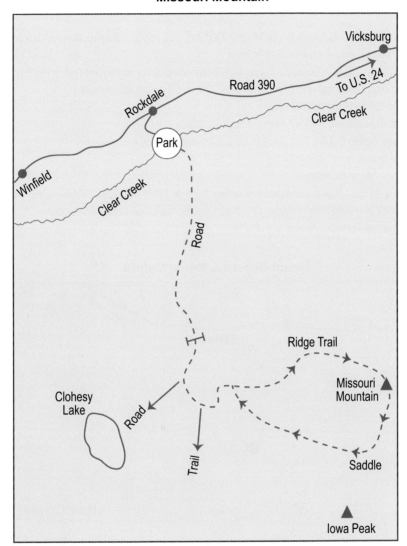

and Missouri Mountain now comes into view to the left of the saddle at the head of the basin. The best route leads without trail directly up to a ridge. Then follow a clear trail on and close to the ridge all the way to the Missouri Summit. Red-tufted markers occasionally line the trail. There is a short down-climb to the right of the ridge that requires some careful hand and foot work shortly before the summit. At the high point there is a trail register, rock shelter, and a great panorama of peaks.

To descend most easily, proceed south to the saddle before Iowa Peak. Then descend to the right (west) down an easy scree slope back to the basin floor to reconnect with the ascent route.

Mount Belford and Mount Oxford

Hike Distance: 4.6 miles up to Mount Belford. 1.7 more miles to Mount Oxford (Total one way distance 6.3 miles)

Hiking Time: Up to Mount Belford in 190 minutes. Over to Mount Oxford in 50 minutes. Total up time 240 minutes. Down time in 180 minutes.

Starting Elevation: 9,669 feet

Highest Elevation: 14,197 feet (Mount Belford)

Elevation Gain: 6,148 feet (includes 1,620 extra feet)

Trail: All the way

Difficulty: More difficult

Relevant Maps: Trails Illustrated number 129 or 148; Winfield 7½ minute; Mount Harvard 7½ minute; Chaffee County Number Two; San Isabel National Forest

Mount Belford & Mount Oxford

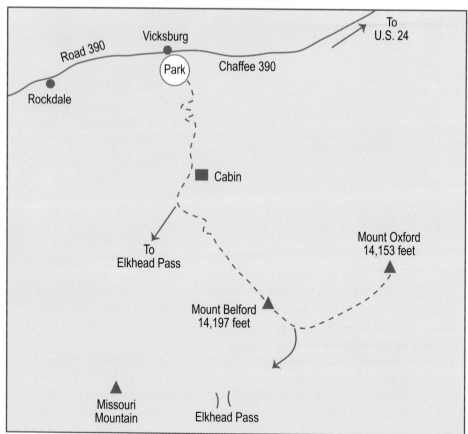

Mount Belford

Views from the Summit of Mount Belford:
NNW to Pecks Peak
NW to Mount Hope and Mount Elbert
ENE to Mount Oxford
S to Elkhead Pass
SSW to Missouri Mountain
SE to Mount Harvard

Getting There: On U.S. 24 south of Leadville and north of Buena Vista, drive south from the intersection with Colorado 82 (the Independence Pass Road to Aspen) for 4.3 miles, or north from the stoplight in Buena Vista for 15.3 miles and turn west onto Chaffee Road Number 390. Follow this good, wide, dirt road for 7.7 miles to the former townsite of Vicksburg and park in the large lot on the left at the Missouri Gulch Trailhead.

Comment: This long, steep hike to two of Colorado's fourteeners takes you up into lovely Missouri Gulch with Missouri Mountain, another fourteener, on the right and Mounts Belford and Oxford on the left. Mount Belford is named after the first Colorado member of the U.S. House of Representatives. Oxford is named after the British university and is one of the so-called "Collegiate Peaks."

Extensive improvements on the trail up Mount Belford make this a more pleasant hike. Solid rocks and many switchbacks are easier on the legs.

The Hike: Begin south from the parking area down to a trail register and a bridge over Clear Creek. The good trail soon passes the marked grave of baby William

Huffman, who died of pneumonia at the age of one month in 1884. Continue steeply through the trees and after 1.5 miles from the trailhead cross the main creek. A cabin ruin at 11,280 feet lies on the left in the last stand of trees before Missouri Gulch opens up. Another 0.75 mile brings you to a sign and trail junction just below treeline. Two false summits of Mount Belford loom above on the left. Ascend the left fork on the excellent trail up the ridge. The trail to the right ascends to Elkhead Pass and down into the Pine Creek Basin.

Hike up the long ridge with great scenery to the west. At the summit ridge the trail curves left and rises to a rock pile and a flat area before the rocky, accessible summit of Belford. A benchmark and register cylinder signify the high point. You will return to this summit on your way back. Continue down southwest by trail and soon take a left fork to a saddle and then up to Mount Oxford. Savor it all before your long return by way of your ascent route. Stay on the trail and avoid shortcutting. This not only prevents erosion but also avoids unwelcome surprises such as steep drop-offs and becoming lost.

Mount Oxford from Mount Belford

Mount Columbia

Hike Distance: 7.2 miles each way
Hiking Time: Up in 255 minutes. Down in 170 minutes.
Starting Elevation: 8,600 feet
Highest Elevation: 14, 073 feet
Elevation Gain: 6,323 feet (includes 425 extra feet each way)
Trail: Initial 5 miles
Difficulty: More difficult
Relevant Maps: Trails Illustrated Number 129 or 148; Harvard Lakes 7½
    minute; Mount Harvard 7½ minute; Chaffee County Number One; San Isabel
    National Forest
Views from the Summit:
    NE to the Buffalo Peaks
    NW to Mount Harvard
    ENE to Pikes Peak
    ESE to Buena Vista
    S to Mount Yale
    SE to Mount Princeton and Mount Antero
    W to Bear Lake
    WSW to Taylor Park Reservoir

Mount Columbia

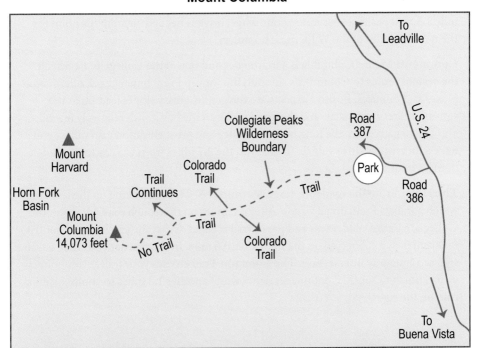

Mount Columbia from Mount Harvard

Getting There: From its intersection with Colorado 82, south of Leadville, drive south on U.S. 24 for 11.9 miles and turn right onto Chaffee County Road 386. After 100 yards on this dirt road keep left and on the main road at an intersection, and then right at mile 0.4. Pass through an open gate at mile 0.5 and park on the left at mile 1.5, just past another fork. (Four-wheel drive is needed beyond this point for the next 2.2 miles to the Wilderness boundary.)

Comment: Mount Columbia is a fourteener and one of the Collegiate Peaks. Of the several routes to Columbia's summit, the way up Frenchman Creek offers some pluses and minuses. Positive aspects are the gentle, grassy slopes leading to the summit ridge, great vistas, and the good trail into the basin with relatively few hikers. The negatives are the long hiking distance and great elevation gain unless you have a four-wheel drive vehicle to take you the 3.7 miles from U.S. 24 to the Wilderness boundary.

The Hike: From the road fork 1.5 miles from U.S. 24, begin hiking up the left fork, which parallels Frenchman Creek. After 2.2 miles on this rough road you enter the Collegiate Peaks Wilderness and pass a trail register. Cross the creek in another 0.5 mile and pass a cabin ruin on the right after 0.6 mile. In short order you reach a trail sign at a four-way intersection. The Colorado Trail crosses your trail at this point as it runs north to south. Continue straight (west) another 1.3 miles to another cabin ruin on the right.

Follow the good trail another 0.3 mile to an elevation of 11,600 feet. The grassy slopes of Mount Columbia will be seen on your left. Leave the trail here and work your way through and around the willows, ascending 0.5 mile to the south. You can continue south up to the ridge but I recommend turning west another 0.5 mile before ascending the last grassy ridge leading to the summit ridge. (To proceed directly southwest toward the summit involves you with considerable scree and talus.)

Once on the summit ridge, turn right and continue southeast up to a benchmark, register cylinder, and small rock shelter at the top. Drink in the wonderful panorama from Columbia's summit.

An alternative to retracing your ascent route is to descend from the top directly north to the grassy basin and then turn east to intersect with the route you took when you left the trail.

Mount Harvard

Hike Distance: 5.2 miles to Bear Lake. 1.7 miles from Bear Lake to Mount Harvard. 6.5 miles from Mount Harvard to trailhead.
Hiking Time: Trailhead to Bear Lake in 104 minutes. Bear Lake to Mount Harvard in 100 minutes. Down in 187 minutes.
Starting Elevation: 9,840 feet
Highest Elevation: 14,420 feet
Elevation Gain: 5,180 feet (includes 300 extra feet each way)
Trail: All the way

Mount Harvard and Mount Columbia from Mount Yale

Difficulty: More difficult

Relevant Maps: Trails Illustrated Number 129 or 148; Mount Harvard 7½
minute; Mount Yale 7½ minute; Chaffee County Numbers One and Two;
San Isabel National Forest

Views from the Summit:

NW to Mount Belford and Mount Oxford

S to Birthday Peak

SSE to Mount Princeton, Mount Antero, Mount Shavano, Tabeguache Peak,
Mount Yale, and Bear Lake

SE to Mount Columbia

W to Huron Peak

WNW to Missouri Mountain

Getting There: From the center of Buena Vista at the intersection of U.S. 24 and
Chaffee County Road 306 (the Cottonwood Pass Road), drive north on U.S. 24
for 0.4 mile and turn left (west) on Crossman Avenue, which is County Road 350.
After 2.1 straight miles on this road turn right at a T onto County Road 361. After
0.9 mile on Road 361, turn sharply left onto County Road 365. Follow this main
dirt road for 5.2 miles and park at the trailhead.

En route to the trailhead keep right at mile 2.5 and at mile 3.3. You pass an intersection with the Colorado Trail at mile 3.6. Road 365 is rough in spots but regular cars can reach the end of the road at the trailhead.

Comment: I bring good news to the Colorado hiker. There is a Bear Lake more
scenic than the popular one in Rocky Mountain National Park. This hike actually
brings you to three very special destinations. First there is Horn Fork Basin with
three encircling fourteeners. Second there is very high and scenic Bear Lake. And
third there is Mount Harvard, the third highest peak in Colorado.

This hike follows the drainage of the Horn Fork of North Cottonwood Creek
in the Collegiate Peaks Wilderness and requires considerable stamina.

The Hike: Begin to the west from the trailhead sign. You will quickly cross a bridge
and a trail register. After passing through the forest, including some aspen trees
and another creek crossing, you will reach a sign and trail fork at 1.3 miles from
the trailhead. The left fork leads to Kroenke Lake and Browns Pass. You continue
west-northwest up the right fork into Horn Fork Basin. After 2.2 miles through the
trees you will emerge into the lovely basin near timberline. Mount Columbia will
be on your right and Mount Harvard north at the head of the basin. Continue by
trail another 1.5 miles to a bench above some willows and a trail fork. The right fork
leads to Mount Harvard. You continue straight over a small creek and reach Bear
Lake within 0.25 mile. From above, this lake has the contours of a bearskin rug. After relaxing at the lake, return by trail to the last fork and go left (north-northwest)
and ascend the less distinct and at times steep trail to the saddle to the left of the

Mount Harvard

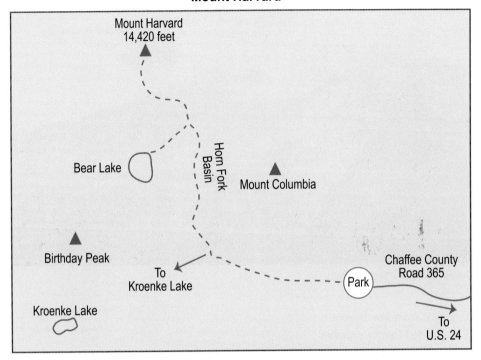

Mount Harvard
14,420 feet

Bear Lake

Horn Fork Basin

Mount Columbia

Birthday Peak

To
Kroenke Lake

Kroenke Lake

Park

Chaffee County
Road 365

To
U.S. 24

nondescript Mount Harvard high point. At the saddle, follow the ridge trail north to the pile of boulders at the top. Sign the register cylinder and enjoy the panorama before retracing your long ascent route back to the trailhead by way of Horn Fork Basin. The ridge between Mount Harvard and Mount Columbia is demanding and requires considerable time and energy. Therefore avoid returning that way unless you really know what you are doing.

Mount Yale

Hike Distance: 6.0 miles each way
Hiking Time: Up in 186 minutes. Down in 123 minutes.
Starting Elevation: 9,900
Highest Elevation: 14,196 feet
Elevation Gain: 4,666 feet (includes 185 extra feet each way)
Trail: All the way
Difficulty: More difficult
Relevant Maps: Trails Illustrated Number 129 or 148; Mount Yale 7½ minutes; Chaffee County Number Two; San Isabel National Forest

Mount Yale from Birthday Peak

Views from the Summit:
N to Mount Columbia
NNE to West and East Buffalo Peaks
NNW to Missouri Mountain, Mount Belford, Mount Oxford, and
Mount Harvard
NW to Huron Peak
ENE to Pikes Peak and Buena Vista
SSE to Mount Princeton, Mount Antero, Tabeguache Peak, and
Mount Shavano
SW to Hartenstein Lake
WNW to Pyramid Peak and Capitol Peak
WSW to Taylor Park Reservoir

Getting There: From U.S. 24 in central Buena Vista, drive west on Chaffee County Road 306, which is also known as West Main Street and Cottonwood Pass Road. Follow this paved road for 12 miles from U.S. 24 and park on the right at the Denny Creek Trailhead.

Comment: Mount Yale lies west of Buena Vista in the Collegiate Peaks Wilderness. There is a very good trail all the way to the top from the Denny Creek Trailhead. This fourteener is of mid-level difficulty and there are no special dangers. Be sure to carry enough water and protection from rain, cold, and sun for any high country hiking, but especially for the higher peaks.

The Hike: Begin northwest from the parking area. Pass a signboard and then a trail register. Ascend the wide trail and make two creek crossings before reaching a fork and a sign after 1.5 miles from the trailhead. Take the right fork and proceed north up Delaney Gulch. This trail rises and falls through the trees and parallels Delaney Creek before reaching a shoulder of Mount Yale. It is 2.3 miles from the fork up Delaney Gulch to timberline. Continue on the cairn-marked trail as it rises through many switchbacks to reach the northwest ridge after 1.8 miles from timberline. The trail then continues southeast another 0.4 mile along the rocky ridge to the top of Mount Yale. There are two register cylinders at the rocky flat high point. Enjoy the views and try to identify some of the many high peaks in the area. Return by the good trail of your ascent route.

Mount Yale

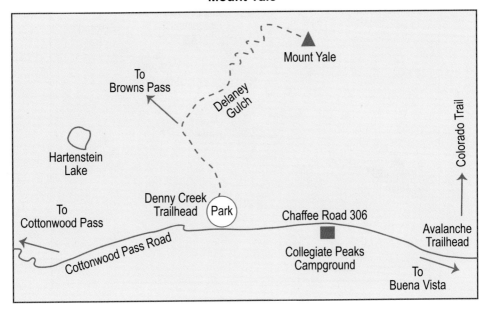

Silver King Lake

Hike Distance: 11.9 miles each way
Hiking Time: Up in 295 minutes. Down in 245 minutes.
Starting Elevation: 8,960 feet
Highest Elevation: 12,634 feet
Elevation Gain: 3,924 feet (includes an extra 125 feet each way)
Trail: All the way
Difficulty: Most difficult

Relevant Maps: Trails Illustrated 129 or 148; Harvard Lakes 7½ minute; Mount Harvard 7½ minutes; Chaffee County Number One; San Isabel National Forest

Silver King Lake

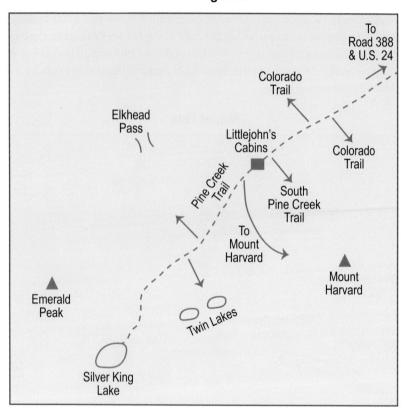

Getting There: On U.S. 24 either drive 6.4 miles south from the intersection with Colorado 82 or 13.3 miles north from the intersection with Main Street in Buena Vista. Then leave U.S. 24 and take Chaffee County Road 388 leading southwest. Keep left after 0.3 mile and fork to the right after another 0.3 mile. Park here since the road becomes too rough beyond. Regular cars can reach this final fork.

Comment: The trail to Silver King Lake follows Pine Creek up into a lovely valley in the Collegiate Peaks Wilderness. Four fourteeners and several other high peaks and lakes can be reached from this valley. The abundant flowing water, Littlejohn's Cabins at mile 6.6, and Bedrock Falls at mile 8.2 combine to make this an especially beautiful route.

The Hike: From the trail sign and a closure gate at the trailhead, proceed south on a good trail for 1.6 miles to a trail register. The trail then steepens. Keep right at a fork with Pine Creek below on your right. There are some narrow trail segments with abrupt drop-offs in this area. Be careful. Pass a Wilderness sign. At mile 4.7 from the trailhead cross Pine Creek on a bridge as the Colorado Trail angles off to your left. Continue west up the valley and soon pass the other leg of the Colorado Trail on the right. Avoid the South Pine Creek Trail on the left. After 1.9 miles from the bridge crossing you will reach the abandoned Littlejohn's Cabins in a semi-open area. These were built around 1881 and are listed in the National Registry of Historic Landmarks. A trail up Mount Harvard leads southeast from this complex.

Continue to ascend southwest past Bedrock Falls on the left and enter beautiful Missouri Basin. Avoid the right fork that leads to Elkhead Pass and ascend 2.5 more miles southwest along Pine Creek and past timberline to Silver King Lake amid alpine tundra. About 0.5 mile before Silver King the Twin Lakes lie a few hundred yards off the trail to the southeast. The magnificent vista from Silver King Lake includes Emerald Peak to the west-southwest; Iowa Peak northwest; Missouri Mountain north-northwest; Mount Belford to the north; Mount Oxford and Waverly Mountain to the north-northeast, and Mount Harvard to the northeast. Relax and enjoy before your very long trek back to the trailhead.

Emerald Peak from Silver King Lake

Neighboring towns: Estes Park, Gould, Walden
Size: 66,791 acres
Elevation: 8,000 to 12,702 feet
Miles of trails: 70

Mild tundra slopes of the Mummy Range, flanked by dense lodgepole pine forests, represent much of the Comanche Peak Wilderness. The crest of the Mummy Range denotes the northern boundary of Rocky Mountain National Park, and Comanche Peak Wilderness is north of this ridge.

The Big South Fork of the Cache la Poudre River is mostly responsible for draining Comanche Peak, and it joins with the Little South Fork to form Colorado's only Wild and Scenic River drainage. There is good trout fishing on the rivers as well as in several lakes and streams.

Common game animals inhabit the wilderness, including a large elk herd around Signal Mountain, and several moose have migrated from nearby Laramie River Valley along the Rawah Range.

Comanche Lake

Hike Distance: 5.0 miles each way
Hiking Time: Up in 140 minutes. Down in 125 minutes.
Starting Elevation: 9,355 feet
Highest Elevation: 9,990 feet
Elevation Gain: 1,975 feet (includes 670 extra feet each way)
Trail: All the way
Difficulty: Moderate
Relevant Maps: Trails Illustrated 112; Pingree Park 7½ minute; Comanche Peak 7½ minute; Larimer County Number Three; Roosevelt National Forest

Getting There: From the junction with U.S. 287 northwest of Fort Collins drive west on Colorado 14 for 26.5 miles up Poudre Canyon. Then take the left fork on the Pingree Park Road (Larimer County 63E). Follow this good, dirt road that becomes Road 44E past several side roads and through a burn area for 5.6 miles. Then turn right into Tom Bennet Campground. Take two right forks after mile 0.1 and mile 0.2 and continue past Sky Ranch after 1.5 miles from the Pingree Park Road. Continue another mile until the road ends at the Beaver Creek Trailhead. (If the gate is closed at Sky Ranch, the path on the right leads to the Beaver Creek Trailhead.)

Comanche Lake and Comanche Peak

Comment: This is a very good water hike as you pass Hourglass and Comanche Reservoirs en route to Comanche Lake. A June hike will bring you lots of flowing water.

The Hike: Begin to the north-northwest from the signboard. A mile brings you past the Hourglass Reservoir on the left, and 1.25 miles farther Comanche Reservoir is on the left. Continue straight at a junction and after another 1.5 miles reach a fork. Go left and enter the Wilderness. Soon cross Beaver Creek, ascend a steep section and finally reach Comanche Lake encircled by trees.

Comanche Lake

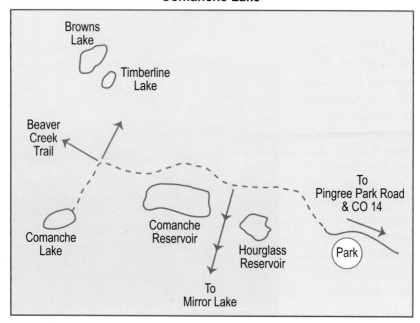

Signal Mountain

Hike Distance: 6.0 miles each way
Hiking Time: Up in 195 minutes. Down in 140 minutes.
Starting Elevation: 7,920 feet
Highest Elevation: 11,262 feet
Elevation Gain: 4,032 feet (includes 345 extra feet each way)
Trail: All but the final 50 yards
Difficulty: More difficult

Relevant Maps: Trails Illustrated Number 200 and 101; Pingree Park 7½
minutes; Crystal Mountain 7½ minutes; Glen Haven 7½ minutes; Larimer
County Number Four; Roosevelt National Forest
Views from the Summit:
NE to Lookout Mountain
SSE to Twin Sisters Peaks
SSW to Mount Meeker, Longs Peak, and South Signal Mountain
SW to Mount Dickenson and Mount Dunraven
W to Comanche Peak
WSW to Storm Peaks

Getting There: From Drake, which is west of Loveland on U.S. 34, take a right
fork on Larimer County 43. After 6 miles on this paved road turn right onto Dunraven Glade, which is Larimer County 51B. Keep left on this good dirt road after
0.1 mile and follow the main road for 2.1 more miles until it ends at the Dunraven
Trailhead. Park here.

Comment: The hike to Signal Mountain ascends Bulwark Ridge and enters the
Comanche Peak Wilderness. The trail is long and steep. The hiker's special reward
comes at the highest elevations when Signal Mountain becomes visible and there
are great views in all directions, especially toward the peaks of nearby Rocky Mountain National Park. This little unused trail will usually be free of significant snow
from mid-June until late October.

Signal Mountain

The Hike: From the parking area begin hiking west up a blocked road. After 0.3 mile turn right past a trail register. Then steeply enter the trees and follow the good trail west up Bulwark Ridge. After 1.25 miles from the trailhead take a left (west) fork at a sign and enter the Comanche Wilderness 1.4 miles farther on. The trail continues upward through a thick forest until it reaches a ridge from which Signal Mountain and South Signal Mountain become visible. Signal Mountain lies to the north (right).

The trail now descends and is marked by a series of cairns as it passes northward before ascending the eastern flank of Signal Mountain. Leave the trail and ascend west the last 50 yards to a small rock shelter and a register cylinder at the high point. Enjoy the scenery and if you have the time and energy, walk 0.75 mile south-southwest over tundra to the easy rocky summit of South Signal Mountain. Then proceed east and southeast, skirt some rocky cliffs and rejoin the trail for your lengthy descent. This side trip will add about half an hour to your return.

Signal Mountain

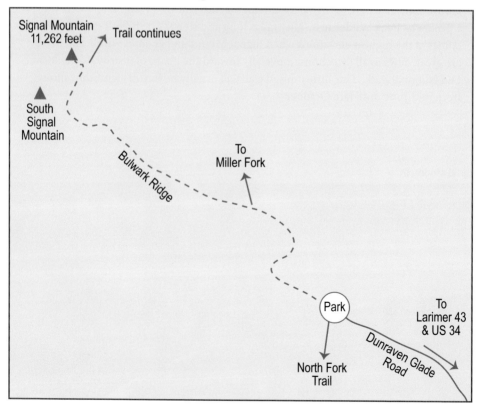

Neighboring towns: Dillon, Frisco, Vail
Size: 132,906 acres
Elevation: 7,850 to 13,534 feet
Miles of trails: 180

Eagles Nest wasn't designated Wilderness without heated controversy. Denver wanted the water and timber industries wanted the spruce forest that covers the lower elevations. Thankfully these interests did not prevail, and the jagged peaks, valleys, forests, and waterfalls of the Gore Range have been preserved. The Gore Range's highest peak is 13,534-foot Mount Powell, named after John Wesley Powell, who made the first recorded ascent in 1868.

Heavy snow accumulates on the heights of Eagles Nest Wilderness, providing a major contribution to the waters of the Colorado River. Melting snow in spring plunges from the heights to create marshy meadows and sloughs, as well as turbulent thundering creeks when temperatures soar abruptly. This is an area more vertical than horizontal, with sheer rock faces, keen-edged ridges, deep valleys, jagged peaks, and dense forests lower down, so foot travel can be strenuous. Most of the trails dead-end at pristine alpine lakes. Off-trail hiking can be difficult, but several informal routes climb the steep passes of the area's craggy core.

Eagles Nest Wilderness Area

Bighorn Cabin

Bighorn Cabin

Hike Distance: 4.1 miles each way
Hiking Time: Up in 118 minutes. Down in 100 minutes.
Starting Elevation: 8,595 feet
Highest Elevation: 10,780 feet
Elevation Gain: 2,485 feet (includes an extra 150 feet each way)
Trail: All the way
Difficulty: Moderate
Relevant Maps: Trails Illustrated Number 108 or 149; Vail East 7½ minute;
Eagle County Number Two; White River National Forest

Getting There: Drive on Interstate 70 to Exit 180 at East Vail. Then drive east on the Frontage Road to the south of Interstate 70. After 0.7 mile on this road turn left on Columbine Drive. Follow this road north (and under the highway) for 0.2 mile and park near the trailhead on your left. Regular cars should have no difficulty reaching the trailhead.

Bighorn Cabin

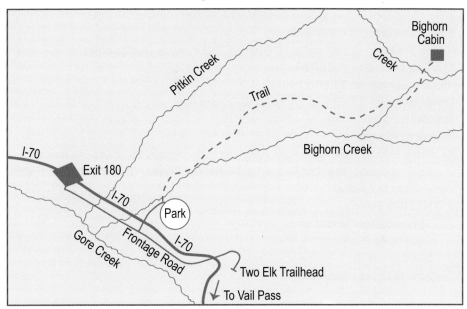

Comment: Here is a hike up one of the lush valleys north of Interstate 70 around Vail. Some of these valleys lead to high mountain lakes. This trail ends instead above an old abandoned cabin with unnamed, jagged peaks looming above in three directions. Hiking traffic is not heavy in this drainage. Bicycles are forbidden and dogs must be on leash. The season for this hike is July through early October. The best times are in the latter half of July when the wildflowers are abundant and in bloom and in the middle of September when the thick stands of aspen are turning gold.

The Hike: Start on the steep trail to the north. Quickly pass a trail register and later an Eagles Nest Wilderness sign. At times the trail becomes more gradual but there are many steep areas as you ascend the valley, with Bighorn Creek always on your right. About halfway up there are waterfalls on your right and in the second half of July a large bank of columbines are blooming to the left of the trail. Shortly before reaching the cabin a side creek is crossed. At the cabin, which has many old artifacts, the trail forks. The right fork descends a short way to Bighorn Creek. The left fork leads a bit farther up the valley before ending. There are many lovely flat areas for camping or picnics in the vicinity of the cabin. On your return, the views back into the Vail Valley compensate for the long steep descent.

Eccles Pass

Hike Distance: 5.2 miles each way
Hiking Time: Up in 190 minutes. Down in 136 minutes (senior time).
Starting Elevation: 9,157 feet
Highest Elevation: 11,900 feet
Elevation Gain: 3,043 feet (includes 150 extra each way)
Trail: All the way
Difficulty: Moderate
Relevant Maps: Trails Illustrated 108; Frisco 7½ minute; Vail Pass 7½ minute;
    Summit County Number Two; Arapaho National Forest (Dillon Ranger District)
Views from the Pass:
    N to Red Peak
    ENE to Buffalo Mountain
    S to Pacific Peak
    SSE to Peak 1
    SSW to Copper Mountain

Eccles Pass

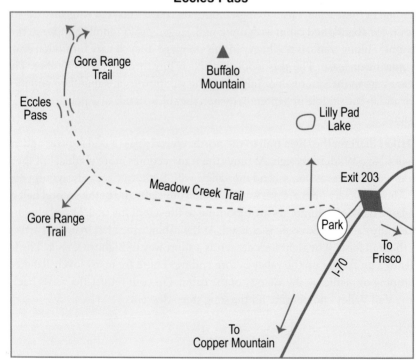

From Eccles Pass to the north

Eccles Pass

Getting There: Take Exit 203 from Interstate 70 between Silverthorne and Frisco. From the roundabout north of I-70 drive west on the frontage road for 0.6 mile and park at the Meadow Creek Trailhead and the end of the road.

Comment: This very good trail takes you over three crossings of Meadow Creek to a lovely high meadow beneath high peaks. The vistas from Eccles Pass are special.

The Hike: Ascend steeply north and pass an unmarked trail on the right and soon a signed trail on the right to Lily Pad Lake. Continue straight and at 1.4 miles from the trailhead cross Meadow Creek on a log. It is another 1.9 miles through aspen and lodgepole pine forest to another Meadow Creek crossing. Soon emerge into a scenic basin, make another creek crossing, and arrive at a junction with the Gore Range Trail on the left. Continue straight up the basin to switchbacks and unmarked Eccles Pass at a four-way intersection and great views. The Gore Range Trail continues down into the South Willow Creek Drainage.

Gore Lake

Hike Distance: 6.5 miles each way
Hiking Time: Up in 178 minutes. Down in 144 minutes.
Starting Elevation: 8,640 feet
Highest Elevation: 11,400 feet
Elevation Gain: 4,160 feet (includes an extra 700 feet each way)
Trail: All the way
Difficulty: More difficult
Relevant Maps: Trails Illustrated Number 108 or 148; Vail East 7½ minute; Willow Lakes 7½ minutes; Eagle County Numbers Two and Four; White River National Forest

Getting There: Drive on Interstate 70 to Exit 180 at East Vail. From the south side of Interstate 70 drive west on the Frontage or Bighorn Road for 2.2 miles and park on the left at the trailhead.

Comment: This demanding hike to Gore Lake in the Eagles Nest Wilderness uses a well-defined and scenic trail. Reaching the lake, which empties into Gore Creek,

Gore Lake

View from Gore Lake

Gore Lake

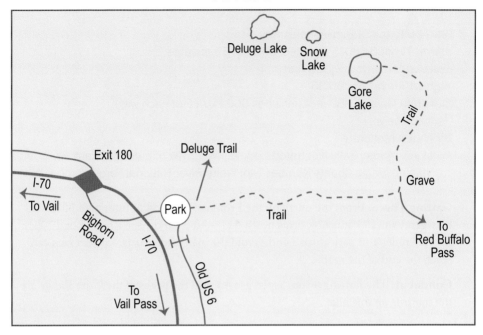

requires over 4,000 feet of elevation gain as the trail rises and falls, often requiring extra effort from the hiker.

The Hike: Begin northeast up the trail from the trailhead register and signboard. Within 100 yards reach a junction and continue straight. (The left fork leads to Deluge Lake.) Every fork after this one will be to the left. Ascend steeply through the lovely forest with Gore Creek always on your right. After 2.2 miles from the trailhead cross Deluge Creek on a wooden bridge, as Deluge Creek rushes into Gore Creek. In 2.6 miles reach a fork and a sign. The left fork leads to Gore Lake and the right fork to Red Buffalo Pass. A few yards above this fork to the northwest lies the marked grave of the Recen brothers from Sweden, who were successful in silver mining until the country adopted a gold standard. For many hikers this will be an adequate destination.

Continue left (north) and ascend more steeply through the trees for the final 1.7 miles to Gore Lake. At about 0.8 mile, pass through some lovely meadows before the final ascent to the southwest to reach Gore Lake just below timberline. Most of the adjacent mountains, although quite impressive, are unnamed. Future generations can name them after their heroes. Be sure to give yourself enough time for the 6.5-mile descent back to your vehicle.

Piney River Falls

Hike Distance: 2.8 miles each way
Hiking Time: Up in 75 minutes. Down in 65 minutes.
Starting Elevation: 9,355 feet
Highest Elevation: 9,735
Elevation Gain: 1,380 feet (includes 500 extra feet each way)
Trail: All the way
Difficulty: Moderate
Relevant Maps: Trails Illustrated 108; Vail West 7½ minute; Vail East 7½
    minute; Eagle County Number Two; White River National Forest

Getting There: From the north on the Frontage Road off of Interstate 70 in Vail between Exits 173 and 176, drive north on the Red Sandstone Road (Road 700) for 11.3 miles and park at road end. Avoid the many side roads. Regular cars can reach the end of the road.

Comment: The flowing water, aspen groves, and the peaks of the Gore Range are the rewards on this hike.

Piney River Valley

Piney River Falls

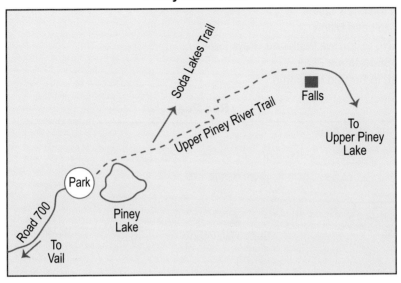

The Hike: Begin east-northeast on the trail with a ranch on the right. Pass along the left side of Piney Lake. After 0.5 mile reach the Upper Piney River Trailhead. Continue up the open valley, and take a right at a fork. (The left fork goes to the Soda Lakes.) At 0.75 mile past the Wilderness sign go left at a fork. The trail becomes rougher, rises and dips. Creeks descend from the left and cross the trail. Pass a rocky overlook of a small meadow on the right. Avoid side trails and stay on the main trail. Pass a large boulder on the right. A hundred yards farther brings you to the falls rushing between rocky walls. The trail continues up to Upper Piney Lake.

Red Peak

Hike Distance: Up in 8.6 miles. Down in 8.1 miles. Total 16.7 miles.
Hiking Time: Up in 257 minutes. Down in 209 minutes
Starting Elevation: 9,157 feet
Highest Elevation: 13,189 feet
Elevation Gain: 5,342 feet (includes an extra 760 feet)
Trail: Initial 6.7 miles
Difficulty: More difficult
Relevant Maps: Trails Illustrated Number 108; Willow Lakes 7½ minute; Vail Pass 7½ minute; Frisco 7½ minute; Summit County Number Two; Arapaho National Forest

Views from the Summit:
   N to Willow Lakes
   E to Lake Dillon
   ENE to Torreys Peak and Grays Peak
   SSE to Jaque Peak
   SE to Buffalo Mountain

Red Peak

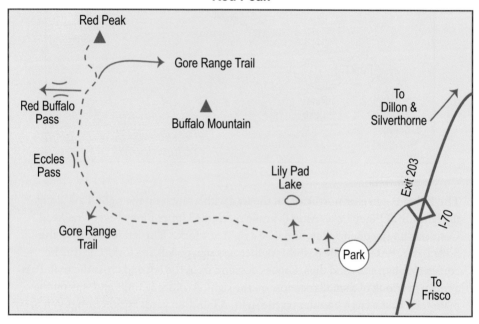

Getting There: Drive to Exit 203 from Interstate 70 between Silverthorne and Frisco. From the roundabout north of I-70 drive west on the Frontage Road for 0.6 mile and park at the Meadow Creek Trailhead and the end of the road.

Comment: This hike traverses Eccles Pass above treeline and soon leaves the trail up to the striking Red Peak. Colorado is full of Red Mountains and Red Peaks. This is one of the highest of these.

The Hike: Ascend north from the trailhead sign. In two minutes take the left fork. After another 0.5 mile take another left fork at a sign. (The right fork leads to Lily Pad Lake.) After hiking 1.4 miles from the trailhead, you will make the first of three crossings of Meadow Creek. The second occurs 1.9 miles after the first, and the third, with no bridge, occurs 0.9 mile from the second. In 0.4 mile past the third creek crossing, the Gore Range Trail joins the trail from the left. From here it is 0.5 mile with several switchbacks to Eccles Pass. Continue down from the pass to the northwest. In 0.5 mile you will pass an unnamed lake on your left. Follow the trail

0.4 mile farther and then leave the trail and ascend up to the left (northwest) to reach the ridge. You may encounter a faint partial trail at times between here and the summit but don't count on it.

Upon reaching the ridge work your way up over the rocks to the north. Eventually Red Peak will come into view as you continue up the ridge. The final approach is straightforward and involves no special risk. At the summit there is a cairn and an embedded wooden plank. The best return is to the south down the drainage to regain the trail that you left on your ascent. Then continue over Eccles Pass and back to the trailhead along the Meadow Creek Trail.

Surprise Lake and Tipperary Lake

Hike Distance: 4.7 miles each way

Hiking Time: Up in 87 minutes to Surprise Lake. 61 minutes more to Tipperary Lake. Back down in 144 minutes.

Starting Elevation: 8,590 feet

Highest Elevation: 10,405 feet

Elevation Gain: 2,894 feet (includes 1,079 extra feet)

Trail: All the way

Difficulty: Moderate

Relevant Maps: Trails Illustrated Number 107; Mount Powell 7½ minute; Summit County Number One; Arapaho National Forest—Dillon Ranger District

Tipperary Lake

Surprise & Tipperary Lakes

Getting There: From Interstate 70 at Silverthorne take Exit 205 and drive north on Colorado 9 for 16.7 miles. Then turn left onto Road 30. Follow this paved road, with Green Mountain Reservoir on the right, for 5.3 miles. Then make a sharp left turn and ascend Road 1725, the Cataract Road, which is unpaved and bumpy, for 2.3 miles and park at the Surprise Lake Trailhead on the left.

Comment: This hike features great foliage and two lovely lakes in the Eagles Nest Wilderness. Other nearby and connecting trails make this area, west of Green Mountain Reservoir, quite popular with hikers, backpackers, and people who like to catch fish.

The Hike: From the trailhead signboard and register, begin to the south and quickly cross a bridge over Cataract Creek. Then ascend steeply into the forest with many aspen. The good, clear trail soon passes a Wilderness sign as it rises steadily to reach a junction with the Gore Range Trail at mile 2.5. Continue west up the right fork and reach Surprise Lake on the left after another 0.2 mile. Water lilies usually decorate this modest lake beneath Dora Mountain to the south.

Continue on the Gore Range Trail to the south-southwest and reach a signed fork at mile 3.4. The left fork rises to Upper Cataract Lake but you descend to the right (north) from this intersection, which is the highest point of this hike. Your spirits will groan as you descend 500 feet over the next mile to another sign at a fork. Leave the Gore Range Trail here and descend another 155 feet to picturesque Tipperary Lake, named after an Irish town. Water lilies may line some of the shore. Rest up and refresh before ascending back to the high point and returning as you ascended.

Uneva Pass

Hike Distance: 6.5 miles each way
Hiking Time: Up in 169 minutes. Down in 150 minutes.
Starting Elevation: 9,680 feet
Highest Elevation: 11,900 feet
Elevation Gain: 2,950 feet (includes 730 extra feet)
Trail: All the way (Gore Range Trail)
Difficulty: Moderate
Relevant Maps: Trails Illustrated Number 108; Vail Pass 7½ minute; Summit County Number Two; White River National Forest

Getting There: On Interstate 70, drive west of Frisco and 0.6 mile before Exit 195 at Copper Mountain, park in the designated, paved area on the right from the westbound lane. This is the Gore Range Trailhead.

View north from Uneva Pass

Comment: Uneva Pass is one of the four hiking destinations that can be readily reached from the southern Gore Range Trailhead. The other three are the Wheeler Lakes, Lost Lake, and Uneva Peak.

The new southern trailhead adds 0.6 mile each way but provides a more ample and safer starting point.

The Hike: Start out to the south-southwest, cross a pond on a bridge, and turn left on the clear trail. With Interstate 70 and the Curtain Ponds on your left, continue as the trail curves to the right

Uneva Pass

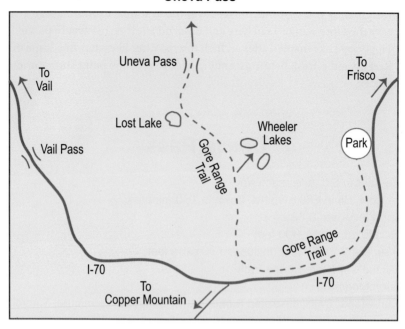

as you remain parallel to the Interstate. As the highway noise fades away, you enjoy periodic views on your left of Copper Mountain. At mile 1.5, the trail takes you past an Eagles Nest Wilderness sign. Your ascent reaches a signed fork at mile 2.9 of this hike. The Wheeler Lakes lie to the right. You take the left fork and continue on the Gore Range Trail. Pass by two tarns on the left, some nice meadows, and a rock field before reaching Lost Lake on the left at mile 5.4. It is another 1.1 miles through open terrain to Uneva Pass, which is marked only by two cairns, before the trail begins a descent to the west. Uneva Peak lies to the northwest. Relish the scenery at this turnaround point before your long trek back to the trailhead through the lovely Eagles Nest Wilderness.

Willow Creeks Loop

Hike Distance: 4.7 miles (total loop)
Hiking Time: 147 minutes (senior time)
Starting Elevation: 8,845 feet
Highest Elevation: 9,650 feet
Elevation Gain: 1,097 feet (includes 292 extra feet)
Trail: All the way

Buffalo Mountain from Willow Creeks Loop

Difficulty: Easy
Relevant Maps: Trails Illustrated 108; Dillon 7½ minute; Willow Lakes 7½
minute; Summit County Number One; Arapaho National Forest

Getting There: From I-70 at the Dillon Silverthorne exit, drive north on Colorado
9 for 1.8 miles. Then turn left into the Willowbrook Community and follow the
main ascending road for 1.1 miles to the Willow Creek Open Space Trailhead on
the left. Take the left fork 0.3 mile before the trailhead.

Comment: This trail follows North and South Willow Creeks and connects with
the Gore Range Trail and the Mesa Cortina Trail. There are many creek crossings
and lots of fallen trees alongside the clear trail.

The Hike: Follow the trail to the west and quickly pass a trail on your left. This is
the trail on which you complete the loop. Continue straight with occasional steep
upward trail segments. After 0.7 mile reach a signed fork and ascend left on the
North Willow Creek Trail. Soon reach another fork and go left as the Three Peaks
Trail goes to the right. Pass a Wilderness sign and reach the Gore Range Trail. Go
left and cross North Willow Creek. Rise to the high point of this loop and a good
view of Buffalo Mountain to the southwest. Descend to a junction with Mesa Cortina Trail and South Willow Creek nearby. Continue left, cross the creek, and reach

another signed fork after 0.5 mile. Turn left on the South Willowbook Trail and descend with South Willow Creek on the left. Reach a creek crossing and reach the fork that you passed as you began the loop. The trailhead will be on the right.

Willow Creeks Loop

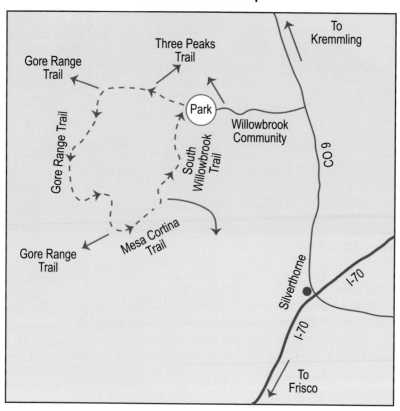

Neighboring towns: Meeker, Yampa, Steamboat Springs, Glenwood Springs
Size: 235,035 acres
Elevation: 7,600 to 12,994 feet
Miles of trails: 160

Arthur Carhart's 1919 visit to Trappers Lake in the verdant embrace of the Flat Tops prompted him to be the first U.S. Forest Service official to initiate a plea for wilderness preservation. No wonder he found the area so enticing: behind Trappers Lake loom majestic volcanic cliffs, and beyond them a vast subalpine terrain yields to alpine tundra (part of the White River Plateau with an average elevation of about 10,000 feet). Approximately 110 lakes and ponds, often unnamed, dot the country above and below numerous flat-topped cliffs. Roughly 100 miles of fishable streams are in this Wilderness.

The hiking is inviting and limitless. Elk, deer, and moose can be found in the area in the summer. A skeletal forest of dead spruce and fir stretches across the higher slopes below the tundra, the legacy of a 1940s bark beetle epidemic. In 2002, more than 17,000 acres burned around Trappers Lake and over 5,500 acres in the vicinity of Lost Lakes, amounting to almost 10 percent of the area of the Wilderness. The Flat Tops is Colorado's second largest Wilderness, a precious expanse of breathtakingly beautiful open land.

Flat Tops Wilderness Area

Big Fish Lake

Hike Distance: 3.4 miles each way
Hiking Time: Up in 90 minutes. Down in 88 minutes (senior time).
Starting Elevation: 8,780 feet
Lowest Elevation: 8,736 feet
Highest Elevation: 9,423 feet
Elevation Gain: 996 feet (includes 309 extra feet)
Trail: All the way
Difficulty: Easy
Relevant Maps: Trails Illustrated 122; Ripple Creek 7½ minute; Big Marvine
　　Peak 7½ minute; Garfield County; White River National Forest

Big Fish Lake

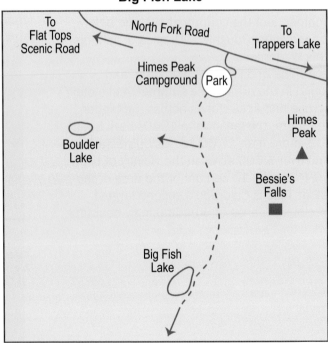

Getting There: From Yampa take the scenic Flat Tops Road 42 miles west to the
North Fork Road (Garfield 8A). Turn left on this road and go 5 miles to the Himes
Peak Campgound sign on the right. Follow the road to the campground 0.3 mile
and park near the trailhead.

Comment: The Flat Tops Wilderness contains many lakes accessible by trail. Big
Fish Lake, with a modest elevation gain, is easily reached with connections to other

lakes. Due to creek crossings, the best time for this hike is in the later hiking season. Remnants of the Big Fish Fire of 2002 are much in evidence.

The Hike: Descend south from the sign and register and quickly cross the north fork of the White River on a bridge. Then gradually rise up the valley with Big Fish Creek always on the right. Patches of burn areas from the Big Fish fire are abundant. After 1.25 miles, a trail to Boulder Lake is passed on the right. Cross a few creeks and notice Bessie's Falls above on the left. Reach a high point and descend to Big Fish Lake. The trail continues along the left side of the lake.

Black Mandall Lake

Hike Distance: 4.5 miles each way
Hiking Time: Up in 124 minutes. Down in 115 minutes.
Starting Elevation: 9,765 feet
Highest Elevation: 10,840 feet
Elevation Gain: 1,699 feet (includes 624 extra feet)
Trail: All the way
Difficulty: Moderate
Relevant Maps: Trails Illustrated Number 122; Orno Peak 7½ minute;
　　　Garfield County; Routt National Forest

Black Mandall Lake

Black Mandall Lake

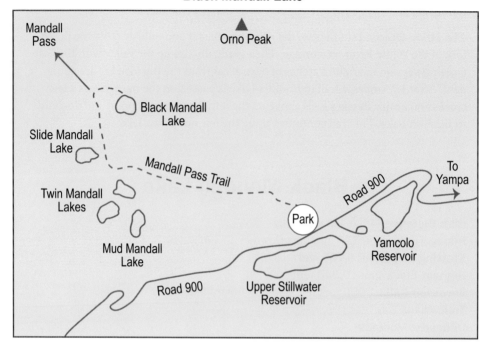

Getting There: From Yampa off of Colorado 131, drive west on County Road 7, which becomes Forest Road 900, for 13.2 miles to the Mandall Pass Trail on the right, just past a campground on the left. Park off the road.

Comment: the Flat Tops Wilderness contains many lakes including several Mandall Lakes. The many connecting trails in the Flat Tops make this a hikers paradise. You may encounter sheep dogs and grazing sheep on this hike.

The Hike: The Mandall Creek Trail leads to Mandall Pass and also to Black Mandall Lake via a short spur trail. The clear trail winds up through an aspen forest, over a ridge to a large high meadow, and then up through lush forest past Slide Mandall Lake on the left, a mile before a signed junction is reached. The left trail leads north to Mandall Pass. Straight ahead leads quickly to Black Mandall Lake after a modest descent. Water crossings, flies, and mosquitoes can be problems on this hike through lovely forest and meadow. Orno Peak hovers over Black Mandall Lake to the north-northeast.

Devils Causeway

Hike Distance: 3.5 miles each way
Hiking Time: Up in 104 minutes. Down in 78 minutes.
Starting Elevation: 10,275 feet
Highest Elevation: 11,800 feet
Elevation Gain: 1,755 feet (includes 115 extra feet each way)
Trail: All the way
Difficulty: Moderate
Relevant Maps: Trails Illustrated Number 122; Devils Causeway 7½ minute;
    Orno Peak 7½ minute; Garfield County Number One; Routt National Forest
Views from the Summit:
    NW to Causeway Lake
    ESE to Flat Top Mountain and Little Causeway Lake
    S to Rainbow Lake
    SE to Stillwater Reservoir
    SW to Chinese Wall

Devils Causeway

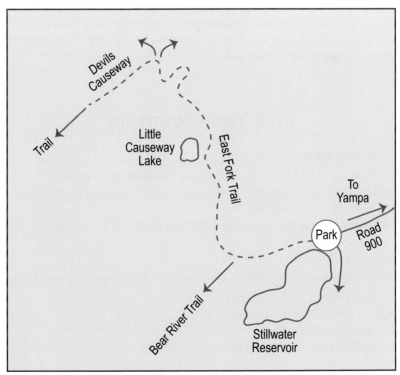

Getting There: From Yampa on Colorado 131, drive from the south end of Main Street on Routt County Road 7, which becomes Forest Road 900, for 16.7 miles to road end at the Stillwater Reservoir. There is a large parking area. Regular cars can easily reach this point.

Comment: The hike to the Devils Causeway in the Flat Tops Wilderness is a great introduction to this interesting geologic area. (A causeway is a raised highway.) The approach from the southeast is relatively short, well marked, and takes the hiker past Stillwater Reservoir and Little Causeway Lake. The Devils Causeway is a narrow, rocky ledge about 150 feet long with steep drop-offs on either side. If you are fearful of heights, think twice about crossing it. You may choose to stop just short of it on the trail and make that the terminus of this hike.

The Hike: Begin to the southwest from the parking area at a signboard. Follow this Bear River Trail for 0.2 mile, with the Stillwater Reservoir on your left, to a trail register and fork. Continue on the trail to your right and ascend southwest on the East Fork Trail (Number 1119). Pass through thin forest, with Little Causeway Lake on the left after 1 mile from the fork. Continue up to the north-northwest on the good, rocky trail to a grassy basin below a saddle. The trail then rises with switchbacks to the saddle and a trail sign. Proceed to the left (south) at the saddle and follow a good, clear trail 0.5 mile up to the mesa and the Devils Causeway. The mesa trail continues over the rocky crossing and deeper into the Flat Tops Wilderness. The views are gorgeous and extensive. Return as you ascended. Little Causeway Lake is worth a brief side trip on the way down.

Flat Top Mountain

Hike Distance: 4.8 miles each way
Hiking Time: Up in 163 minutes. Down in 144 minutes (senior time).
Starting Elevation: 10,300 feet
Highest Elevation: 12,354 feet
Elevation Gain: 2,494 feet (includes 440 extra feet)
Trail: Initial 60 percent
Difficulty: Moderate
Relevant Maps: Trails Illustrated 122; Orno Peak 7½ minute; Garfield County Number 1; Routt National Forest
Views from the Summit:
    N to Yamcelo Reservoir
    NW to Orno Peak and Upper Stillwater Reservoir

Getting There: From Yampa, off Colorado 131 south of Steamboat Springs, drive west on Routt County 7, which becomes Road 900, for 16.7 miles and park at road end and Stillwater Reservoir.

Comment: Flat Top Mountain is the highest in the Flat Tops Wilderness. With the summit in view, a long walk over tundra brings you to a vast talus field at the top.

The Hike: Begin south-southwest and quickly fork left on Trail 1122, the North Derby Trail, with Stillwater Reservoir on the right. Follow the North Derby Trail down past some ponds and then up through forest on a rocky, occasionally steep trail to a saddle at 11,600 feet. The main trail will descend to some lakes but you take the trail leading east and rise to an overlook as the trail ends. Flat Top Mountain is now visible. Hike directly to it over tundra past two saddles and reach a large cairn with a register cylinder on the left side of the flat, talus-covered summit.

Flat Top Mountain

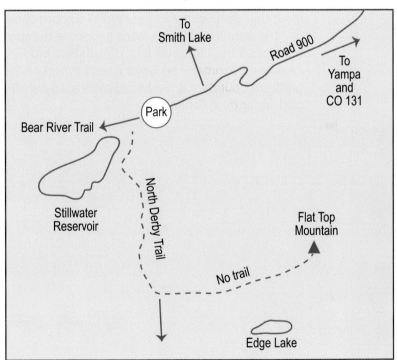

Neighboring towns: Gunnison, Salida, Crested Butte
Size: 32,179 acres
Elevation: 9,000 to 13,254 feet
Miles of trails: 26

The Wilderness is made up of raw granite that overlooks several shallow high mountain lakes and long valleys carved by ancient glaciers. Pine, spruce, fir, and aspen are found here. The limestone ridge rises above 13,000 feet, climbing well beyond treeline, and contains the fossilized remains of numerous prehistoric sea creatures.

Searching for gold, miners dug at several sites that are still scarred by their efforts, but this bit of history somehow enhances the area's overall attractiveness. Elk and deer thrive in the area along with a small group of mountain goats and a larger herd of bighorn sheep.

The area's half-dozen lakes support a number of introduced trout species, including brown, brook, and Yellowstone cutthroat. The Taylor River Canyon on the area's northern boundary is renowned among anglers for its cold-water trout fishery.

Henry Lake

Hike Distance: 7.5 miles each way
Hiking Time: Up in 205 minutes. Down in 158 minutes.
Starting Elevation: 9,200 feet
Highest Elevation: 11,704 feet
Elevation Gain: 3,048 feet (includes 272 extra feet each way)
Trail: All the way
Difficulty: More difficult
Relevant Maps: Trails Illustrated Numbers 131 and 132; Taylor Park Reservoir
7½ minute; Fairview Peak 7½ minute; Gunnison County Number Three;
Gunnison National Forest

Getting There: From Buena Vista on Main Street (U.S. 24) drive west at the stoplight on County Road 306 over Cottonwood Pass on the good road to Taylor Park Reservoir. Go left on Road 742 at the end of the Cottonwood Pass Road and drive around the left side of Taylor Park Reservoir on Road 742, which is called the Taylor River Road. At 3.7 miles west of the Taylor Park Dam turn left onto the Lottis Creek Campground road. Continue straight another 0.5 mile and park at the South Lottis Creek Trailhead.

Comment: This remote and lengthy hike rewards with a beautiful lake just below treeline, abundant aspen in the initial third of the hike, and an excellent, sometimes rocky trail in the Fossil Ridge Wilderness. This is a popular horse trail.

Henry Lake and Henry Mountain

The Hike: Start out to the south-southeast through an unlocked gate. After 0.2 mile go right and leave the road at a sign. Cross Lottis Creek on logs and continue gradually up the valley with South Lottis Creek on your right. After about 5 miles take a right fork (south) and continue up into a basin with a boulder field on the left. The gradual trail becomes very steep for the final 0.3 mile before Henry Lake, with Henry Mountain above to the south-southwest.

Henry Lake

Neighboring towns: Redcliff, Minturn, Vail, Leadville, Aspen, Basalt
Size: 122,797 acres
Elevation: 8,000 to 14,003 feet
Miles of trails: 164

The Holy Cross Wilderness lies immediately west of the Continental Divide, just over the ridge from the Arkansas River Valley. There are innumerable pools and cascades of the area's many streams, dozens of alpine lakes, and wide expanses of valleys inundated by spring snowmelt. The Wilderness is named after 14,005-foot Mount of the Holy Cross. Photographer William H. Jackson embellished the peak's reputation by doctoring his nineteenth-century photographs of the perpendicular snow-filled gullies that are on the mountain's east face. More than twenty-five peaks over 13,000 feet in elevation dot this Wilderness.

Holy Cross has ridges and peaks made of 1.7 billion-year-old schist and gneiss that tower over U-shaped, glacial-carved valleys whose headwaters contain tranquil emerald lakes. The streams are great for fishing, and the area's remote valleys are home to deer, elk, black bear, bobcat, and lynx. Fall hiking is special due to all the aspen groves.

Galena Mountain

Hike Distance: 5.1 miles each way
Hiking Time: Up in 160 minutes. Down in 82 minutes.
Starting Elevation: 9,960 feet
Highest Elevation: 12,893
Elevation Gain: 3,073 feet (includes 70 extra feet each way)
Trail: Initial 2.6 miles
Difficulty: Moderate
Relevant Maps: Trails Illustrated Number 126; Homestake Reservoir 7½ minute;
   Lake County; Colorado Trail Number Eight; San Isabel National Forest
Views from the Summit:
   NNE to Homestake Peak
   NNW to Mount of the Holy Cross
   S to Mount Elbert
   SSE to Buffalo Peaks
   SSW to Mount Massive
   SE to Mount Sherman, Leadville, and Turquoise Lake

Getting There: Drive to the west end of Turquoise Lake, which lies west of Leadville. At 0.3 mile northwest of the side road to May Queen Campground take an unpaved side road to the west and park at the trailhead which is within 200 yards.

Comment: Galena Mountain overlooks Leadville and Turquoise Lake and can be reached by way of the Colorado Trail and some off-trail hiking over tundra and rocks. Located in the Holy Cross Wilderness, the summit of Galena Mountain can be a great platform to view the surrounding peaks. Galena is a metal, the principal ore of lead.

The Hike: Start out to the north-northeast from the parking area on the Colorado Trail. Pass a trail register and after 0.7 mile, there is a Wilderness sign. Continue to ascend and reach a saddle as the trail begins to descend at mile 2.6 of this hike. Here you leave the trail and ascend to the left (north-northwest). Hike to the left around the subpeak on your right and then angel north to the ridge. The Galena Mountain summit will now come into view. It's another 0.7 mile clockwise up the grassy slope to the summit rock and register jar. Take advantage of your high vantage point before you descend back to the Colorado Trail at the saddle.

Galena Mountain

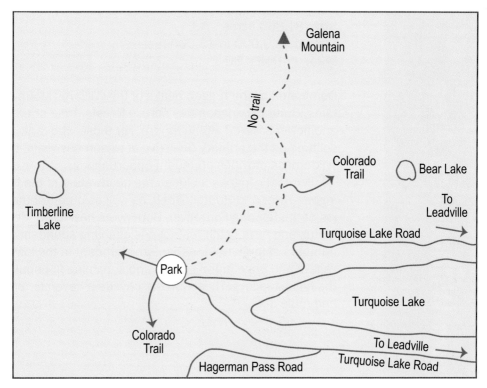

Galena Mountain

Neighboring towns: Aspen, Woody Creek, Leadville
Size: 81,866 acres
Elevation: 9,000 to 13,000 feet
Miles of trails: 50

Dominated by the rugged peaks of the Williams Mountains, Hunter-Fryingpan has spruce forests, trout streams, and flower-covered alpine tundra. For those who rank solitude as the primary objective of wilderness visits, this Wilderness provides abundant opportunities.

Hunter-Fryingpan includes the headwaters of the Fryingpan River and Hunter Creek, as well as other tributaries of the Roaring Fork River. Both rivers have Gold Medal status and have catch restrictions enabling abundant numbers of large trout. Aspen are abundant in the lower valleys and Engelmann spruce and subalpine fir populate the higher valleys. These forests provide a haven for elk and mule deer.

Deer Mountain (Pitkin County)

Hike Distance: 4.5 miles each way

Hiking Time: Up in 185 minutes. Down in 128 minutes.

Starting Elevation: 10,794 feet

Highest Elevation: 13,761 feet

Elevation Gain: 3,117 feet (includes 75 extra feet each way)

Trail: All the way to the west ridge with some faint trail on the ridge to the summit.

Difficulty: Moderate

Relevant Maps: Trails Illustrated 127 or 148; Mount Champion 7½ minute; Independence Pass 7½ minute; Pitkin County Number One; San Isabel National Forest

Views from the Summit:

NNE to Mount Oklahoma

NE to Mount Elbert

SSE to Mount Champion

SSW to Grizzly Peak

SE to French Mountain and
    La Plata Peak

SW to Twining Peak, Pyramid Peak, the
Maroon Bells, Snowmass Mountain,
and Capitol Peak

W to Mount Sopris

Deer Mountain

Deer Mountain from Indendence Pass

Deer Mountain

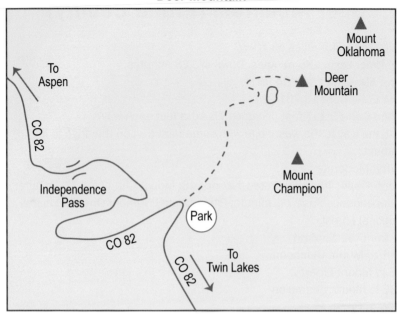

Getting There: From U.S. 24 between Leadville on the north and Buena Vista on the south, drive west on Colorado 82 for 19.5 miles toward Independence Pass. Cut off the paved road to the right onto a dirt road just before a "10 miles per hour" sign and just before a big bend in the road as it rises toward Independence Pass. Park around here off the road.

Comment: Deer is a name given to many mountains. This one lies on the Continental Divide and forms part of the boundary between Pitkin and Lake County, the White River and San Isabel National Forests, and the Mount Massive and Hunter-Frying Pan Wilderness Areas. There are a surprising number of impressive looking peaks, some named but others unnamed, visible from this basin.

The Hike: Follow the dirt road to the northeast. In 0.6 mile the road ends and a trail leads off to the left (northwest). Proceed on this trail and soon pass a Wilderness boundary sign. There are some undulations in the trail as you ascend the valley. You will cross a creek at least twice. In the upper basin the trail disappears at times. With or without the trail continue north from the upper basin and keep the main creek of this drainage on your right. Now above timberline you follow the trail as it winds up to an unnamed high lake and to a saddle with prominent Deer Mountain on your right. Scramble up east from this saddle to gain the west ridge and continue over mostly tundra and talus with occasional scree to the top. A small cairn and a register cylinder mark the high point. On your descent, head directly west toward the unnamed lake that lies just below the saddle. As you approach the lake, veer to your left and meet the trail again.

Fryingpan Lakes

Hike Distance: 4.5 miles each way
Hiking Time: Up in 125 minutes. Down in 115 minutes.
Starting Elevation: 9,960 feet
Highest Elevation: 11,030 feet
Elevation Gain: 2,190 feet (includes 560 extra feet each way)
Trail: All the way
Difficulty: Moderate
Relevant Maps: Trails Illustrated number 127 or 148; Mount Champion 7½
    minute; Pitkin County Number; White River National Forest

Getting There: From Hagerman Pass near Leadville drive west for 14.3 miles and turn left onto the Fryingpan Lakes Road. After 5.8 miles on this good main road, park at road end at the trailhead and water diversion facilities. The Fryingpan Lakes Road can also be reached from Basalt and driving east past the Ruedi Reservoir. Regular cars with good clearance can reach this trailhead.

Comment: These lovely, remote lakes are reached on a good, gradual trail up a scenic valley with two "centennial" peaks at the head of the valley—Mount Oklahoma and Deer Mountain. The long drive to the trailhead is the most difficult aspect of this outing.

The Hike: Start out to the south and pass the trail to Lily Pad Lake on the left before crossing a bridge and plunging into the forest. The Fryingpan River will be on

Upper Fryingpan Lakes from Deer Mountain

your left until a log crossing at the approximate halfway point. The trail rises and falls through lush forest until the two adjacent lakes are reached after passing a pool on the right. Mount Oklahoma looms above to the southeast and Deer Mountain can be seen at the head of the valley to the south-southeast. Your return time will be close to the ascent time due to trail undulations.

Fryingpan Lakes

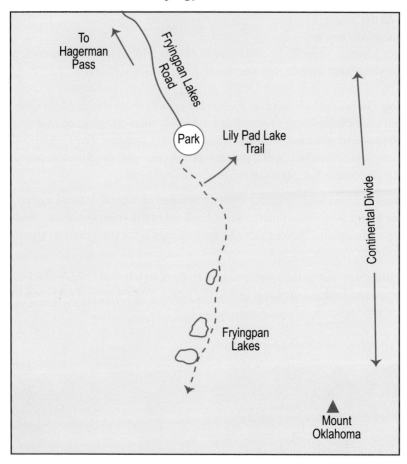

Lost Man Loop

Hike Distance: 8.8 miles (total loop)
Hiking Time: 223 minutes (total loop) (senior time)
Starting Elevation: 11,506 feet
Highest Elevation: 12,500 feet (Lost Man Pass)

Lost Man Lake

Elevation Gain: 1,494 feet (includes 500 extra feet)

Trail: All the way

Difficulty: More difficult

Relevant Maps: Trails Illustrated Number 127 or 148; Independence Pass 7½ minute; Mount Champion 7½ minute; Pitkin County Number Two; White River National Forest

Getting There: to higher trailhead: 1.8 miles west of Independence Pass on Colorado 82 and park on the right (north).

Lower trailhead: 11.4 miles west of Independence Pass on Colorado 82 and park on the right (north)

Comment: Counterclockwise is the best route for this scenic loop hike. A car at each trailhead is required. The far point of the loop elicits a feeling of being deep in the wilderness.

The Hike: Start out north-northwest on the clear trail. Go right at a signed fork after 0.25 mile. There are several creek crossings as you ascend open terrain and reach Independence Lake. At mile 2 of this hike follow the trail along the left side of the lake up to Lost Man Pass. Continue down to the north and pass Lost Man Lake on its right side. A long descent takes you into a lovely basin as the trail curves left. At a signed fork descend left. (The right fork ascends to South Fork Pass.) The good trail takes you down the valley to the south, past Lost Man Reservoir to the lower trailhead and hopefully an awaiting vehicle.

Lost Man Loop Trail

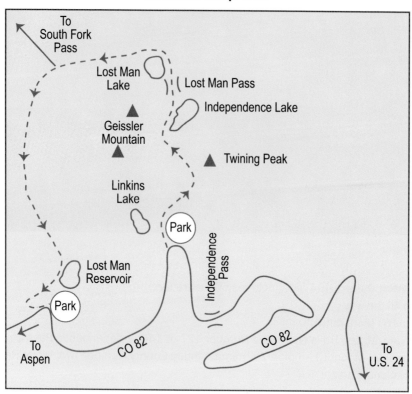

Midway Pass

Hike Distance: 4.0 miles each way
Hiking Time: Out in 125 minutes. Back in 90 minutes.
Starting Elevation: 9,290 feet
Highest Elevation: 12,120 feet
Elevation Gain: 3,355 feet (includes 525 extra feet)
Trail: All the way
Difficulty: Moderate

Midway Pass Trail going northeast

Relevant Maps: Trails Illustrated Number 127 or 148; Thimble Rock 7½ minute; Independence Pass 7½ minute; Mount Champion 7½ minute; Pitkin County Number Two; White River National Forest

Getting There: On Colorado 82 between Aspen and Independence Pass, either drive northwest 5.8 miles from Independence Pass or 13.8 miles southeast from the intersection of Mill Street and Main Street (which is Colorado 82) in Aspen. Then park in the lot by the trailhead sign off the north side of the highway.

Comment: The shorter access to little-used Midway Pass, east of Aspen, begins at the Lost Man Trailhead, off of Colorado 82. The route climbs through pine forest to the Hunter-Fryingpan Wilderness to a high meadow above timberline and then descends a mile from the highest elevation to the actual pass.

To access Midway Pass from the west, one follows the Hunter Creek Road northeast of Aspen.

The Hike: Start west from the Lost Man Trailhead signboard on a clear trail. In about 100 yards, cross a bridge and soon keep left at an unmarked fork. About 60 yards farther, reach a trail sign and intersection. The right trail leads to Lost Man Reservoir and up the valley to South Fork Pass. You go left (southwest) and follow a series of switchbacks up through the forest to reach a high grassy plain above timberline. The views to the south and west are great. Continue past a small pond on the left before reaching the highest point of this hike. This is not the pass. With the Williams Mountains above on your right, continue gradually down to Midway Pass at 11,841 feet. The trail continues downward to the northwest along Midway Creek. The pass is your turnaround point. Enjoy the solitude and the high country grandeur before your return.

Midway Pass

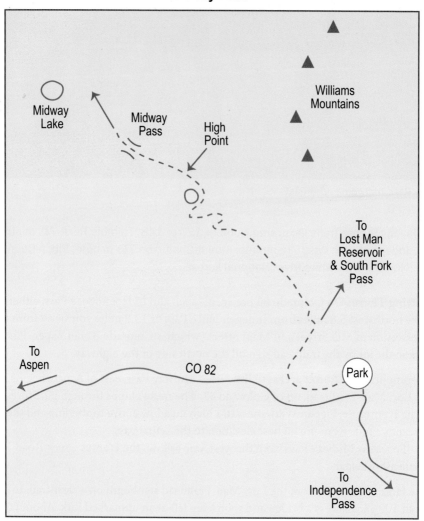

Sawyer Lake

Hike Distance: 4.5 miles each way
Hiking Time: Up in 130 minutes. Down in 100 minutes.
Starting Elevation: 9,500 feet
Highest Elevation: 11,020 feet
Elevation Gain: 1,814 feet (includes 147 extra feet each way)
Trail: All the way
Difficulty: More difficult
Relevant Maps: Trails Illustrated Number 126 and 127 or 149; Meredith 7½
minute; Pitkin County Number Two; White River National Forest

Getting There: From Colorado 82 at Basalt drive east on the Fryingpan Road past Ruedi Reservoir for 38.2 miles and turn right at a sign for Norrie Colony. Set your odometer to zero. Continue on the good dirt road and take a left fork at mile 0.2. At mile 3.1 a sign directs you onto a right fork. Follow the road into a vast meadow and park at road end at the trailhead at mile 3.5.

Comment: Located in the Hunter-Fryingpan Wilderness, the hike to serene Sawyer Lake has a few interesting features in addition to lovely meadows and forest. The clear trail makes several creek crossings, passes a cabin ruin, and passes an unnamed pool.

Sawyer Lake

The Hike: The trail begins to the south-southeast across an open meadow before crossing several small creeks. Pass a Wilderness sign after 0.3 mile. The initial two-thirds of your route traverses lovely countryside as you gradually gain elevation. The final third rises more steeply through shaded pine forest before reaching a meadow on the right just before Sawyer Lake, with its horseshoe shape and a large protruding rock at its northeastern edge. The peak to the southeast is unnamed.

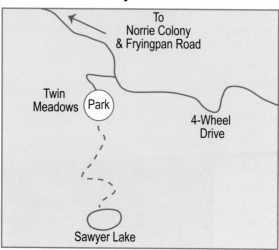

Sawyer Lake

Neighboring towns: Nederland, Granby, Grand Lake, Allenspark, Ward, Fraser, Winter Park, Eldora
Size: 76,486 acres
Elevation: 8,300 to 13,502 feet
Miles of trails: 133

Overall, the Wilderness stretches approximately 18 miles north-south and 15 miles east-west at its widest point. There are seven peaks over 13,000 feet, and approximately 35 percent of the land area is above treeline. There are 28 maintained trails and over 50 lakes, many just a short distance from readily accessible trailheads. The icy remains of the last glacial period sculpted out the rugged terrain of the Indian Peaks. Chill winds off perpetual snowfields have created an environment near treeline of stunted trees and alpine plants unusual for this part of the state.

Indian Peaks is one of the most popular and heavily used Wilderness Areas in the country due to its close proximity to the Denver/Boulder metro area. Because of its popularity and its fragile alpine landscape, Indian Peaks has more restrictions than other Wilderness Areas.

Indian Peaks from the trail to Niwot Mountain

Isabelle Glacier

Hike Distance: 3.8 miles each way
Hiking Time: Up in 138 minutes. Down in 125 minutes.
Starting Elevation: 10,520 feet
Highest Elevation: 12,020 feet
Elevation Gain: 2,000 feet (includes 250 extra feet)
Trail: All the way
Difficulty: Moderate
Relevant Maps: Trails Illustrated Number 102; Ward 7½ minute; Monarch Lake 7½ minute; Boulder County; Roosevelt National Forest

Getting There: From the roundabout in the town of Nederland, drive northwest on Colorado 72 for 12 miles and turn left onto the Brainard Lake Road. Continue on this good, paved road for 5.7 miles and park at the Long Lake Trailhead lot, which is often full.

Comment: Here is a hike along South Saint Vrain Creek past a series of lakes to the Isabelle Glacier, lying just below the Continental Divide and some of the glorious Indian Peaks. This glacier constantly feeds the lakes below and South Saint Vrain Creek.

Apache Peak and Isabelle Glacier

Isabelle Glacier

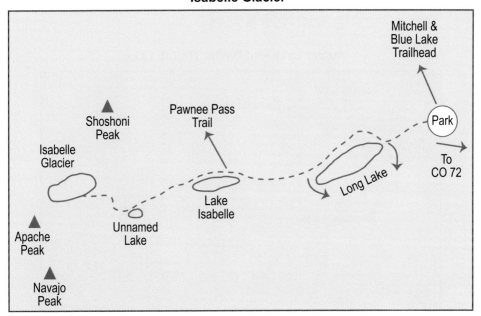

The Hike: Start southwest from the trailhead sign. Keep right after a few hundred yards as the Jean Lunning Nature Trail begins to the left. Continue through the trees with Long Lake on your left. After 1 mile from the trailhead take the right fork at a trail sign. After another 0.8 mile keep straight at a junction and trail sign. (The right fork leads up to Pawnee Pass.) Pass lovely Lake Isabelle on the left. The trail becomes a little faint around here but continues up into the basin to a smaller, unnamed lake. At the far (west) end of this lake follow the trail as it ascends west-northwest (right) past a series of cairns to reach the lip of the Isabelle Glacier. There is a small pond in the middle of the glacier. Apache Peak looms above to the southwest, Navajo Peak impresses to the south, as does Shoshoni Peak to the north-northeast. Enjoy!

Jasper Lake and Devils Thumb Lake

Hike Distance: 4.9 miles to Jasper Lake. 1.1 mile farther to Devils Thumb Lake
Hiking Time: Up in 214 minutes. Down in 134 minutes.
Starting Elevation: 9,000 feet
Highest Elevation: 11,150 feet
Elevation Gain: 2,774 feet (includes 312 extra feet each way)
Trail: All the way
Difficulty: More difficult

Relevant Maps: Trails Illustrated Number 102; East Portal 7½ minute; Boulder County; Roosevelt National Forest

Jasper Lake and Devils Thumb Lake

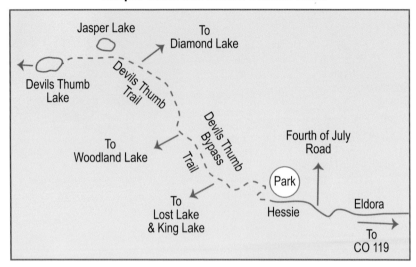

Getting There: From the junction of Colorado 119 and Colorado 72 in Nederland (west of Boulder) drive south on Colorado 119 for 0.6 mile and turn right toward the town of Eldora. Keep right after 1.5 miles and continue through Eldora. Ascend the dirt road to a junction and signs 4.9 miles from Colorado 119. Some cars park here, but with good clearance you can descend the left fork, and after 0.4 mile park at the Hessie Trailhead.

Jasper Lake

Comment: There are three wonderful routes to the Devils Thumb Lake in the Indian Peaks Wilderness. One begins at Rollins Pass. Another starts out from Road 128 east of Winter Park and Fraser. This hike originates from west of Nederland and Eldora and is the most demanding of the three. The rocky pinnacle northwest above the lake gives it its name.

The Hike: Cross the north fork of Boulder Creek on a bridge and continue west past a road barrier. After 1 mile take the right fork at a trail sign just before a bridge. Ascend steeply before the clear trail becomes more gradual and pass Indian Peaks Wilderness signs at mile 1.6 of this hike. Another mile brings you to a signed fork. Left leads to Woodland Lake. You ascend right (north) on the Devils Thumb Trail

Devils Thumb Lake from the Continental Divide

for 1.5 more miles to the Diamond Lake Trail on the right. Continue straight ahead 0.7 mile to a trail rising to the right from the main trail. This leads to Jasper Lake within 100 yards. Then return to the Devils Thumb Trail and quickly pass a cabin ruin and then the outflow from Jaspser Lake as you continue west past some campsites for another 1.2 miles to reach the clear waters of Devils Thumb Lake. The trail continues up to Devils Thumb Pass and a junction with the Continental Divide Trail, which has merged with the High Lonesome Trail.

Lake Gibraltar

Hike Distance: 8.2 miles each way
Hiking Time: Up in 234 minutes. Down in 178 minutes.
Starting Elevation: 8,670 feet
Highest Elevation: 11,190 feet
Elevation Gain: 3,640 feet (includes 560 extra feet each way)
Trail: All the way until 200 yards from the lake
Difficulty: More difficult
Relevant Maps: Trails Illustrated Number 102; Allens Park 7½ minute; Isolation Peak 7½ minute; Boulder County; Roosevelt National Forest

Lake Gibraltar

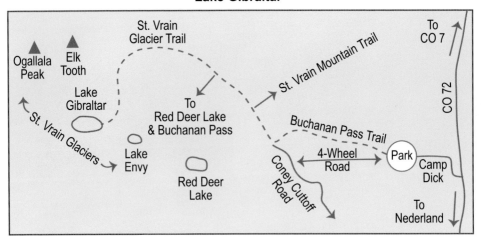

Getting There: Drive north on Colorado 72 from Nederland for 17.5 miles and turn left into Camp Dick. Avoid the campsites and drive 1.2 miles from Colorado 72 to a parking area where the road to the west becomes rocky and rough.

Comment: The long hike to Lake Gilbralter leads to a lovely basin beneath the Saint Vrain Glacier in the Indian Peaks Wilderness. The length of the hike and lack of other destinations in the area explain the relatively light use of this beautiful trail. There are three crossings of Middle Saint Vrain Creek in the upper third of this hike. I would, therefore, recommend this outing after mid-July when the water level is lower.

The Hike: The hike begins west on the rough road leading from the parking area. Within 100 yards, take a right fork and descend northwest on the Buchanan Pass Trail. Cross Middle Saint Vrain Creek by bridge and ascend west up the valley on a good trail for 4 miles to a signed junction with a wide, rocky road (at one unmarked fork keep right). At the road, continue to the right (southeast). After another 0.5 mile pass the Indian Peaks Wilderness boundary and the Saint Vrain Mountain Trail on the right.

Continue northwest up the gradual road. You are now on the Saint Vrain Glacier Trail. This is a very scenic valley with several of the Indian Peaks on the horizon.

After 0.9 mile from the Wilderness boundary, take the right fork at a sign. (The left fork leads to Red Deer Lake and Buchanan Pass.) Rise higher in the valley and pass some wooden remnants on your left. You soon will make a series of creek crossings. Three of these cross Middle Saint Vrain Creek on logs. Follow the good trail. The terrain becomes more open and full of flowers as you ascend. When the trail becomes less distinct, cairns guide you. Eventually you reach the outflow of Lake Gibraltar. Follow the trail with this creek always on your right. Ascend a grassy basin and pass the final cairn. It is clockwise another 200 yards southeast and south and over a final boulder field before you reach somber Lake Gibraltar beneath some of the Saint Vrain Glacier. Elk Tooth is the peak to the northwest and Ogallala Peak lies to the west-northwest. Enjoy this striking destination in this remote cul-de-sac before the long walk back.

Meadow Mountain

Hike Distance: 4.0 miles each way
Hiking Time: Up in 130 minutes. Down in 92 minutes.
Starting Elevation: 8,800 feet
Highest Elevation: 11,632 feet
Elevation Gain: 3,052 feet (includes 110 extra feet each way)
Trail: All the way until the final 0.3 mile
Difficulty: Moderate
Relevant Maps: Trails Illustrated Number 200; Allens Park 7½ minute; Boulder
    County; Roosevelt National Forest
Views from the Summit:
    N to Twin Sisters Peaks
    NW to Longs Peak
    S to Mount Audubon
    SSW to Saint Vrain Mountain
    WSW to Copeland Mountain

Approaching Meadow Mountain

Getting There: From the western edge of Lyons, drive southwest and west on Colorado 7 for 18.6 miles, turn left into Allenspark for 0.1 mile on the paved road. Then turn right onto Ski Road 107. Follow this good dirt road as it passes several homes to the south for 1.6 miles to a sign and fork. Ascend to the right another 0.5 mile and park at the Saint Vrain Mountain Trailhead. Regular cars can reach this trailhead.

Comment: From Meadow Mountain, southwest of Allenspark, the mountain vistas into Rock Rocky Mountain National Park are magnificent. The abundant waters of Rock Creek accompany the good trail with many switchbacks. Lying within the Indian Peaks Wilderness and just below the southern boundary of Rocky Mountain National Park, the route is forbidden to bicycles and dogs must be leashed. The season for this hike will usually be from July through October.

The Hike: From the parking area, begin west from the signboard. The trail passes through a lovely aspen forest and reaches a Wilderness sign after 0.75 mile. Continue up the basin and reach the Rocky Mountain National Park boundary at mile 3.7, near a saddle with Saint Vrain Mountain visible ahead. Leave the trail here and ascend tundra and rocks to the north for 0.3 mile with 400-foot elevation gain. A rock shelter marks the flat summit. Take some pictures before retracing your route back to the trailhead.

Meadow Mountain

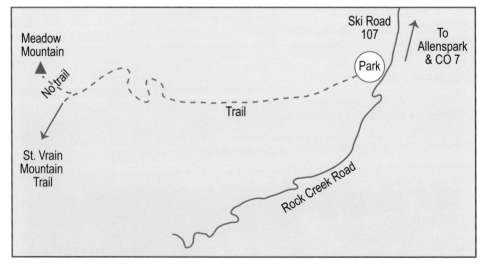

Navajo Peak

Navajo Peak in the center

Hike Distance: 6.3 miles each way
Hiking Time: Up in 229 minutes. Down in 198 minutes.
Starting Elevation: 10,520 feet
Highest Elevation: 13,409 feet
Elevation Gain: 4,389 feet (includes 750 extra feet each way)
Trail: To just below Isabelle Glacier and on the Niwot Ridge to the summit.
Difficulty: More difficult
Relevant Maps: Trails Illustrated Number 102; Ward 7½ minute; Monarch Lake
    7½ minute; Boulder County; Roosevelt National Forest
Views from the Summit:
    NNE to Shoshoni Peak
    NNW to Paiute Peak
    NE to Lake Isabelle
    NW to Apache Peak
    ESE to Arikaree Peak
    SSE to North Arapaho Peak

Navajo Peak

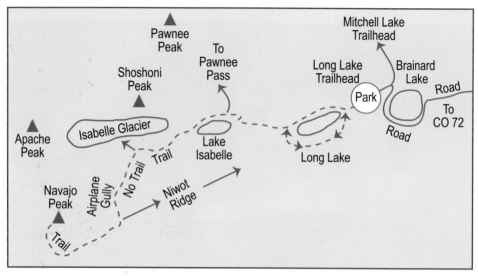

Getting There: From the roundabout in Nederland, west of Boulder, drive northwest on Colorado 72 for 12 miles and turn left onto the Brainard Lake Road. Continue on this paved road for 5.7 miles from Colorado 72 and park at the Long Lake Trailhead, which is often full.

Comment: Navajo Peak is the most striking mountain in the beautiful and popular Indian Peaks Wilderness. Navajo's conical summit looks daunting but the route to the top is, although lengthy, clear and requires only a little, easy rock work. A side feature is the wreck of a plane crash from the late 1940s in the upper reaches of the so-called "Airplane Gully," which provides hiking access to the Niwot Ridge and then to the summit.

The Hike: Begin west from the trailhead signs and quickly pass Long Lake on the left. After a mile, take the trail on the right at a sign. The good trail passes scenic Lake Isabelle on the left and a trail on the right to Pawnee Pass at the 2-mile mark. Continue up the valley with Navajo Peak in full view. South Saint Vrain Creek on your left provides cascading water, which adds to the beauty of this hike. At mile 3.5 pass an unnamed tarn on the left and either continue on the trail or angle up to the south-southwest. Your destination by either route is Airplane Gully, the second couloir to the left at the base of Navajo Peak. If you continue on the trail, leave it just below Isabelle Glacier and without losing too much elevation go directly toward the peak.

At Airplane Gully note the airplane fragments that are widely spread. Ascend the left side of the gully where the rock is more firm. Avoid knocking rocks down on any climbers below. Near the top, angle to the right up a side gully and pass the main airplane wreckage. Continue up to tundra on Niwot Ridge and good views down to the Boulder watershed on the left (no public access). Follow cairns and a trail along the ridge and then veer left to ascend the Navajo Cone in a clockwise direction. Generally proceed west in a series of switchbacks and arrive at the summit ridge and the Continental Divide. Here you ascend the white boulders on your right and carefully negotiate the last 200 feet north to the summit. Some easy rock climbing and route finding are necessary. A small cairn and rock wind shelter mark the high point. If you are blessed with good visibility, take in the magnificent scenery before retracing your lengthy ascent route.

Niwot Mountain

Hike Distance: 4.0 miles each way
Hiking Time: Up in 98 minutes. Down in 96 minutes.
Starting Elevation: 10,345 feet
Highest Elevation: 11,472 feet
Elevation Gain: 1,426 feet (includes an extra 300 feet)
Trail: All the way until the last 0.7 mile

Niwot Mountain summit

Difficulty: Moderate

Relevant Maps: Trails Illustrated Number 102; Ward 7½ minute; Boulder
County; Roosevelt National Forest

Views from the Summit:

N to Twin Sisters Peak

NNW to Longs Peak and Mount Meeker

NW to Mount Audubon

SSE to Mount Evans

SE to Pikes Peak

SW to South Arapaho Peak and North Arapaho Peak

W to Apache Peak and Shoshoni Peak

WNW to Pawnee Peak, Little Pawnee Peak, Paiute Peak, and Mount Toll

WSW to Arikaree Peak and Navajo Peak

Niwot Mountain

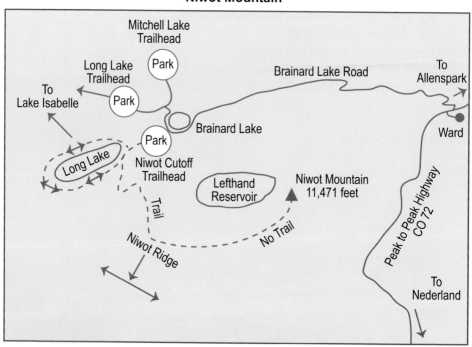

Getting There: From the roundabout in Nederland, drive north on Colorado 72
for 12 miles and turn left onto the Brainard Lake Road. Pay the fee at mile 2.6 and
follow the good road around the left side of Brainard Lake and park at mile 5.4
from Colorado 72 at the Niwot Cutoff Trail parking area on the far side of Brainard
Lake. If you park elsewhere, walk to this trailhead.

Comment: The Indian Peaks area is scenic and very popular. Beautiful lakes and dramatic peaks abound. This hike passes by Long Lake and ascends to a grassy ridge that leads to the smallest-named Indian Peak, Niwot Mountain. There are splendid views back to the Indian Peaks from the large, rocky wind shelter at its summit. You traverse a small segment of the trail en route to Niwot Mountain that is outside the Wilderness area. Niwot was a well-known Native American of the Arapaho Tribe who was called "Chief Left Hand." Bikes are forbidden and pets must be leashed.

The Hike: Cross the road and proceed west-northwest from the trailhead sign. It is 0.5 mile to Long Lake and a trail fork. Go left on the Jean Lunning Trail at this intersection and cross several boardwalk segments. Within 75 yards from the fork take the narrow trail on the left and ascend south. (The trail continuing to the right circles Long Lake.)

Follow the occasionally overgrown trail through the trees to reach the open Niwot Ridge. A series of cairns now marks the trail. Continue to a saddle where the trail begins a descent into the next valley. From the highest cairn at this saddle leave the trail and proceed east without a trail over tundra for the last 0.7 mile to Niwot Mountain, which has a rock shelter and a nearby cairn on its top. Left Hand Reservoir lies below to the left.

Enjoy the scenery as you return by your ascent route.

Pawnee Lake

Hike Distance: 8 miles each way
Hiking Time: Up in 200 minutes. Down in 168 minutes.
Starting Elevation: 8,330 feet
Highest Elevation: 10,880 feet
Elevation Gain: 2,750 feet (includes 100 extra feet each way)
Trail: All the way
Difficulty: More difficult
Relevant Maps: Trails Illustrated Number 102; Monarch Lake 7½ minute;
Grand County Number Two; Arapaho National Forest

Getting There: From U.S. 40 at the western edge of Granby, drive north on U.S. 34 for 5.4 miles. Turn right on the Arapaho Bay Road (Grand County Number 6) and drive another 9.5 miles on the good, wide, main road to a road barrier at Monarch Lake. Park nearby.

Pawnee Lake

Pawnee Lake

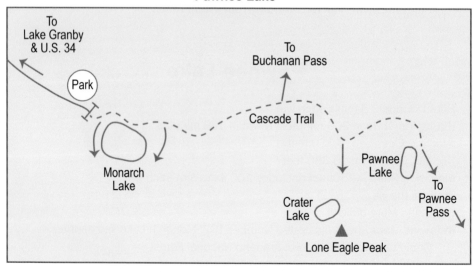

Comment: The long trek to Pawnee Lake takes you through beautiful terrain and alongside the rushing waters of Cascade Creek within the popular Indian Peaks Wilderness. The trail continues east above and beyond Pawnee Lake over Pawnee Pass and down to Lake Isabelle and Long Lake. A vehicle at both the Monarch Lake and Long Lake trailheads would enable a great one-way hike in either direction.

The Hike: Begin to the left of Monarch Lake at the trail sign on the Cascade Trail and proceed east-southeast. Pass the Wilderness boundary and enter the forest with the creek on your right. At a signed fork, go left as the Southside Trail leads to the right. Continue up the valley and pass the trail to Buchanan Pass on the left at mile 2.8 of this hike. Another 3.75 miles brings you to a trail on the right that leads to Crater Lake, which lies beneath striking Lone Eagle Peak. Continue up the left fork another 1.5 miles as the trail curves to the right to reach the shores of Pawnee Lake, nestled in a rocky bowl. The route continues steeply up and southeast to Pawnee Pass on the Continental Divide but the lake is your destination. Enjoy the grandeur before the long return on the Cascade Trail.

Pawnee Peak

Hike Distance: 4.7 miles each way
Hiking Time: Up in 157 minutes. Down in 140 minutes.
Starting Elevation: 10,520 feet
Highest Elevation: 12,943 feet
Elevation Gain: 2,543 (includes 60 extra feet each way)
Trail: All the way to Pawnee Pass (12,541 feet)
Difficulty: Moderate
Relevant Maps: Trails Illustrated Number 102; Ward 7½ minute; Monarch Lake
    7½ minute; Boulder County; Roosevelt National Forest
Views from the Summit:
    NNW to Mount Toll, Paiute Peak, Longs Peak, and Mount Meeker
    NE to Mount Audubon
    E to Lefthand Reservoir
    S to South Arapaho Peak and North Arapaho Peak
    SSW to Shoshoni Peak, Navajo Peak, and Apache Peak
    SE to Kiowa Peak
    WNW to Lake Granby

Getting There: From the roundabout in Nederland (west of Boulder), drive northwest and then north on Colorado 72 for 12 miles and turn left onto the good, paved road to Brainard Lake. Follow the road for 5.7 miles to the Long Lake Trailhead parking area, which fills early.

Comment: Pawnee Pass forms part of the Continental Divide and the boundary between Boulder and Grand Counties and the Roosevelt and Arapaho National Forests. Weekday hiking in this area is recommended if you dislike lots of people on your hikes.

The Hike: Begin from the trailhead signs and proceed southwest. In less than five minutes, keep right past Long Lake on your left. In 0.8 mile take the right fork at a sign and continue the gradual ascent to the west. At mile 2 from the trailhead, lovely Lake Isabelle, surrounded by beautiful peaks, will appear to your left. Take the right fork at a sign and ascend a series of switchbacks above Lake Isabelle and at mile 4.1 reach a large sign at Pawnee Pass. Stay on the trail for a few minutes before leaving it and traversing the tundra to the north and ascend the modest slope of Pawnee Peak. Keep to the right of the ridge. A faint trail is intermittently present and leads over talus to a rock shelter at the summit. From the pass to the top of Pawnee Peak is 0.6 mile. Return by your ascent route. (The Pawnee Pass trail continues west and down to Pawnee Lake and eventually to Monarch Lake.)

Pawnee Peak

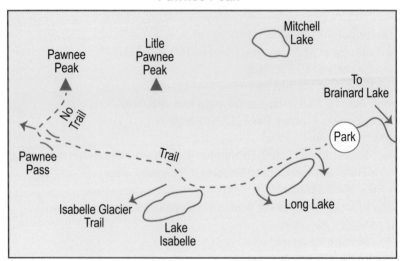

Red Deer Lake

Hike Distance: Up in 7.3 miles. Down in 7.4 miles (clockwise loop)
Hiking Time: Up in 160 minutes. Down in 180 minutes (loop).
Starting Elevation: 9,190 feet
Highest Elevation: 10,485 feet
Elevation Gain: 2,532 feet (includes 1,237 extra feet)
Trail: All the way
Difficulty: Moderate
Relevant Maps: Trails Illustrated Number 102; Ward 7½ minute; Allens Park 7½ minute; Boulder County; Roosevelt National Park

Red Deer Lake

Getting There: From the roundabout in Nederland (west of Boulder), drive northwest then north on Colorado 72 for 14.2 miles and turn left on the good dirt Road 96 that takes you 2.7 miles to Beaver Reservoir and the four-wheel drive Road 507 on the right. Park here without blocking the road.

Comment: This loop to Red Deer Lake allows one to experience a large northern segment of the beautiful Indian Peaks Wilderness. The initial part of the hike traverses a rough four-wheel drive road for 3.7 miles to reach the Coney Flats Trailhead. The Indian Peak vistas open up around this point and flowing water is abundant.

The Hike: Begin on foot up Road 507 to the northwest. Follow this rocky, narrow road as it rises and falls to finally emerge at Coney Flats. Cross Coney Creek on a bridge and reach the Coney Flats Trailhead signboard.

    Continue southwest by trail, pass a trail to Coney Lake on the left and ascend the basin 2 miles from the Coney Flats Trailhead to a signed fork. The left fork proceeds west to Buchanan Pass. To reach Red Deer Lake descend to the north for 1 more mile and reach a sign and trail on the left. Ascend west up this side trail the final 0.5 mile to lovely Red Deer Lake, nestled into rocky slopes to the west. The distinctive summit of Elk Tooth can be seen to the west-northwest.

    Return by the final spur trail and fork down to the left (northwest) to continue the loop for another mile. Cross a bridge over Middle Saint Vrain Creek and take the right (east) trail down the valley for 1.4 miles to the Middle Saint Vrain Four-wheel Trailhead. Continue east on the wide road for 100 yards and ascend a right fork to the east. After 0.5 mile on this rocky four-wheel drive road, you will reach the familiar Coney Flats Trailhead. From here retrace your route over the creeks and back up the rough road to Beaver Reservoir.

Red Deer Lake

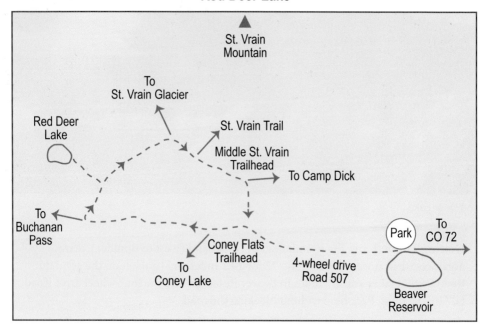

Satanta Peak

Hike Distance: 3.7 miles each way
Hiking Time: Up in 113 minutes. Down in 77 minutes (senior time).
Starting Elevation: 10,046 feet
Highest Elevation: 11,979 feet
Elevation Gain: 2,249 feet (includes 150 extra feet each way)
Trail: All the way to Caribou Pass
Difficulty: Moderate
Relevant Maps: Trails Illustrated Number 102; Monarch Lake 7½ minute; Grand County Number Four; Arapaho National Forest
Views from the Summit:
  NE to North and South Arapaho Peaks
  E to Caribou Lake
  SSE to Mount Neva
  W to Meadow Creek Reservoir
  WNW to Strawberry Lake

View from Satanta Peak toward North Arapaho Peak and the Continental Divide

Getting There: Between Fraser and Tabernash on U.S.40 turn east on the road to Devils Thumb Ranch. After 0.4 mile turn left on Road 84. After another 1.1 miles take the left fork and follow the main, good, dirt road up toward Meadow Creek Reservoir. At mile 6.3 from U.S. 40 encounter a fee station on the left. At 0.6 mile farther take the right fork. Follow signs to the Junco Trailhead and park at the trailhead 11.2 miles from U.S. 40.

Comment: The trail through forest passes many lovely meadows en route to great vistas from the top of Satanta Peak.

The Hike: Begin east on the wide rocky trail. After 0.1 mile pass the High Lonesome Trail on the right. After passing an Indian Peaks Wilderness sign it is 275 yards farther to a junction. Straight leads to Columbine Lake. Ascend the left fork as the trail gets steeper and passes through some meadows before reaching Caribou Pass. Go left here and ascend grassy slopes to a large cairn atop Satanta Peak. An option to return is to descend grassy terrain to the south-southeast to reach the ascent trail.

Satanta Peak

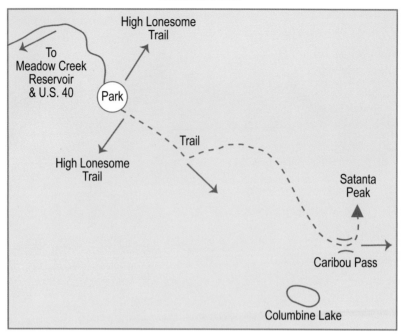

Shoshoni Peak

Hike Distance: 4.9 miles to the Shoshoni Peak summit. Back in 4.3 miles (loop)
Hiking Time: Up to 170 minutes. Down in 130 minutes.
Starting Elevation: 10,370 feet
Highest Elevation: 12,967 feet
Elevation Gain: 2,957 feet (includes 180 extra feet each way)
Trail: Initial 3.8 miles
Difficulty: Moderate
Relevant Maps: Trails Illustrated Number 102; Ward 7½ minute; Monarch Lake
7½ minute; Boulder County; Roosevelt National Forest
Views from the Summit:
N to Longs Peak
NNE to Pawnee Peak
NNW to Chiefs Head Peak and Pagoda Mountain
NE to Mount Audubon
ENE to Lake Isabelle, Long Lake, Brainard Lake, and Left Hand Reservoir
S to South Arapaho Peak and North Arapaho Peak
SSW to Navajo Peak, Apache Peak, and Isabelle Glacier
SE to Kiowa Peak
WNW to Lake Granby

Shoshoni Peak

Getting There: From the roundabout in Nederland (west of Boulder), drive northwest on Colorado 72 for 12 miles and turn left onto the paved road to Brainard Lake. Continue on this road for 5.7 miles to the Long Lake parking area, which is often full.

Comment: Shoshoni, one of the more neglected of the Indian Peaks, lies on the Continental Divide and offers a grand view of the many nearby peaks and lakes. The Brainard Lake area is often crowded. You may therefore wish to hike there during the week and avoid weekends.

The Hike: Begin southwest from the Long Lake Trailhead and very quickly arrive at a fork at the northeastern edge of Long Lake. Go to the right and proceed west-southwest through the trees, parallel to the lake. In 1 mile go right at the trail fork and sign. (The trail to the left circles Long Lake.) In 1.8 miles from the trailhead arrive at a trail sign and a fork on the north side of scenic Lake Isabelle. Take the right fork and ascend toward Pawnee Pass. Follow this trail as it generally ascends northwest. As you reach a large flat area above timberline, the tilted summit of Shoshoni Peak will come into view to the southwest.

Continue on the trail until the last switchback to the right at 12,120 feet. Leave the trail at this point and head southwest over talus and boulders to the northwest ridge of Shoshoni Peak. The ascent to the ridge is very gradual. Be sure to keep well left and below the two unnamed high points along the ridge to your right. When you reach Shoshoni's northwest ridge, turn left (southeast) up the tundra to a subpeak. Then descend some to your left and approach the final summit block in a clockwise direction. Some easy handwork is necessary just below the small rock pile on the top. There are sheer drop-offs in every direction but the summit is large enough for comfort.

After taking in the wonderful views in all directions, return to the base of the summit block and then loop downward to the north-northeast over talus and boulders. Pick your way down to the grassy floor of the basin and proceed directly back to the Pawnee Pass Trail and the trailhead. This more direct descent from summit to trail will save you some time and 0.6 mile.

Shoshoni Peak

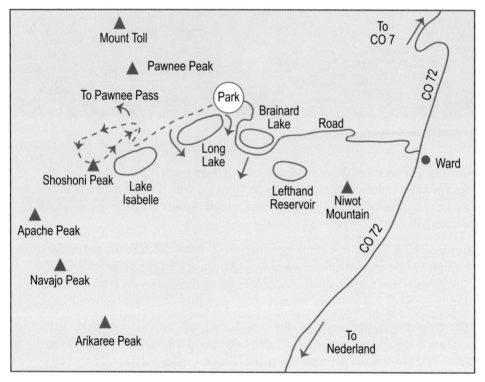

South Arapaho Peak

Hike Distance: 4.8 miles each way
Hiking Time: Up in 172 minutes. Down in 110 minutes.
Starting Elevation: 10,180 feet
Highest Elevation: 13,397 feet
Elevation Gain: 3,287 feet (includes 35 extra feet each way)
Trail: All the way

South Arapaho Peak

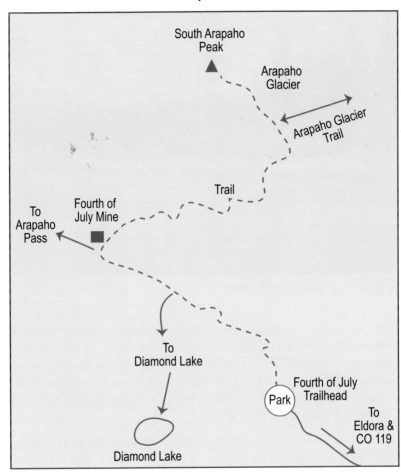

South Arapaho
Peak

Arapaho
Glacier

Arapaho Glacier
Trail

Trail

Fourth of
July Mine

To
Arapaho
Pass

To
Diamond Lake

Fourth of July
Park   Trailhead

To
Eldora &
CO 119

Diamond Lake

Difficulty: Moderate

Relevant Maps: Trails Illustrated Number 102; East Portal 7½ minute; Monarch
Lake 7½ minute; Boulder County; Roosevelt National Forest

Views from the Summit:

N to Longs Peak and Mount Meeker

NNW to North Arapaho Peak

NE to Niwot Mountain

E to Caribou Peak

S to Grays Peak and Torreys Peak

SSE to Diamond Lake

SE to Pikes Peak and Eldora Ski Area

SW to Mount Neva

WSW to Lake Dorothy

Diamond Lake and South Arapaho Peak

Getting There: From the roundabout in Nederland, drive south on Colorado 119 for 0.6 mile and turn right (west) off of Colorado 119. Drive 9.1 miles on this side road through the town of Eldora to trailhead parking near the Fourth of July Campground. En route to this trailhead, keep right at mile 1.5 and again at mile 4.9 from Colorado 119. Keep left at 7.7 and stay on the main road as it winds up the valley. Regular cars can reach the parking area.

Comment: South Arapaho Peak looms impressively above the access trail from the southeast. On a clear day the very top of the peak can be seen from the trailhead area. Dogs must be kept on a leash and bikes are forbidden in this very popular area west of Nederland.

The Hike: From the Fourth of July Trailhead and signboard begin north on the excellent trail into the trees. At mile 1.3 take the right fork at a sign. (The left fork descends to Diamond Lake.) Soon emerge from the forest and continue up the scenic, right side of the valley and reach a fork at the remnants of the Fourth of July Mine at mile 2.3 from the trailhead. South Arapaho Peak is dramatic from this area.

Continue on the right fork to the north-northeast. (The left fork ascends to Arapaho Pass and beyond.) Proceed upward another mile to timberline. Pass several large cairns for the next mile as the trail turns to the left and joins the Arapaho Glacier Trail descending from grassy slopes on the right. Several yards farther is the Arapaho Saddle and a gorgeous overlook of the Arapaho Glacier beneath the dual towers of South and North Arapaho Peaks.

A good ridge trail with several side trails now leads steeply up the final 0.5 mile over rock to the summit of South Arapaho Peak. A benchmark, a few rocky wind shelters, and a metal disc pointing out various distant mountains lie at the summit. The ridge continues around to the more challenging North Arapaho Peak, which should be left to the very experienced hiker.

Enjoy the fabulous panorama before returning by the ascent route.

Strawberry Lake

Hike Distance: 10.8 miles (total loop)
Hiking Time: Up in 166 minutes. Down in 98 minutes (senior time).
Starting Elevation: 8,330 feet
Highest Elevation: 9,370 feet
Elevation Gain: 1,450 feet (include 410 extra feet—estimated)
Trail: All the way
Difficulty: Moderate
Relevant Maps: Trails Illustrated Number 102; Monarch Lake 7½ minute;
Strawberry Lake 7½ minute; Grand County; Arapaho National Forest

Strawberry Lake

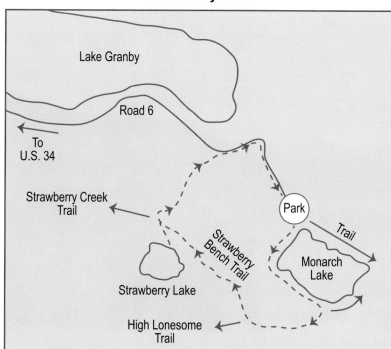

Getting There: From U.S. 34 between Granby and Grand Lake, turn east onto Grand County Road 6 and continue on the good, wide, dirt road for 9.5 miles and park at a road barrier just before Monarch Lake.

Comment: Beautiful Strawberry Lake can be reached by several trails. This loop access uses the Continental Divide Trail, the High Lonesome Trail, the Strawberry Bench Trail, and the Strawberry Creek Trail. A middle section traverses the Indian Peaks Wilderness.

The Hike: Start out on the trail along the right side of Monarch Lake. After 1.7 miles leave the Continental Divide Trail and ascend the High Lonesome Trail at a sign on the right. After 1.6 miles of steep ascent reach a signed fork and take the Strawberry Bench Trail on the right. This trail rises and falls as you leave the Indian Peaks Wilderness and cross over the highest point of this loop. At 4.2 miles on this trail you reach a signed fork and proceed sharply left 0.1 mile to a cabin ruin, a sign, and a metal walkway to a metal platform at the edge of Strawberry Lake in a vast treeless meadow. Santana Peak can be seen to the east-southeast and Mount Neva to the southeast. To continue the loop, return to the Strawberry Bench Trail and go left to quickly cross Strawberry Creek at some signs. Take the unmarked trail on the right, which descends alongside Strawberry Creek, 1.1 miles to the road that leads to Monarch Lake. Go right on this road 2 more miles to your starting point just below Monarch Lake.

Jessica Pearson, David Berman, and Alicia and Jim Steimel at Strawberry Lake

Neighboring towns: Nederland, Rollinsville, Winter Park
Size: 17,015 acres
Elevation: 9,200 to 13,294 feet
Miles of trails: 20

The area is named after its most prominent peak, 13,294-foot "James Peak," in honor of Dr. Edwin James, an early explorer, historian, and botanist who was a member of the famous Stephen H. Long expedition to Colorado in 1820.

The Wilderness consists of high altitude peaks, alpine tundra, and over a dozen small alpine lakes and tarns nestled on the eastern edge of the Continental Divide above treeline. The Wilderness contains lodgepole pine and spruce-fir forests, mainly on the northern end, and in drainages on the eastern perimeter. The western portion of the Wilderness tops out at the top of a line of treeless peaks that march north-south, forming the Continental Divide. Many of the trails in the Wilderness begin below treeline and end at small alpine lakes beneath cliffs or granite peaks that reach the top of the Continental Divide.

The James Peak Wilderness isn't nearly as big or as rugged as its northern neighbor, Indian Peaks Wilderness, but it isn't as visited either even though it is only a short distance from Denver, so if you are looking for solitude this is a good place to visit.

James Peak Wilderness Area

Bill Moore Lake

Hike Distance: 4.2 miles each way

Hiking Time: Up in 127 minutes. Down in 110 minutes (senior time).

Starting Elevation: 10,400 feet

Highest Elevation: 11,520 feet

Elevation Gain: 1,810 feet (includes 690 extra feet)

Trail: All the way

Difficulty: Moderate

Relevant Maps: Trails Illustrated Number 103; Empire 7½ minute; Clear Creek County; Arapaho National Forest

Getting There: From Interstate 70 west of Idaho Springs take Exit 238 and drive north on the Fall River Road for 6.8 miles. Then take the dirt road on the left at a large house as the road curves sharply right. Follow this rough road for 1.8 miles and park at a junction with mine ruins on the right. Most regular cars can reach this point.

Comment: This segment of the Continental Divide Trail was completed in 2008 and offers a more pleasing route to Bill Moore Lake than the older four-wheel drive road. The lake lies just within the James Peak Wilderness.

The Hike: From the 5-way road intersection ascend the road to the east-southeast and within 20 yards take the signed trail on the right leading south-southwest. With many switchbacks ascend out of the valley on a shelf trail. Keep straight at a road crossing and soon break out of the trees into scenic vistas. The trail curves left and

Bill Moore Lake

descends about 300 feet with Witter Peak above on the right. The trail reaches a road. Turn right (west) and quickly pass a barrier and a James Peak Wilderness sign just before Bill Moore Lake. The Continental Divide Trail continues southwest from the barrier to Breckenridge Peak above on the left. Return by retracing your route.

Bill Moore Lake

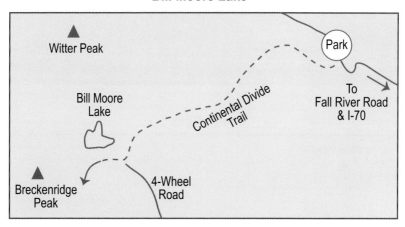

James Peak (southern approach)

Hike Distance: 4.8 miles each way
Hiking Time: Up in 138 minutes. Down in 118 minutes.
Starting Elevation: 10,130 feet
Highest Elevation: 13,294 feet
Elevation Gain: 3,434 feet (includes 135 extra feet each way)
Trail: All the way
Difficulty: More difficult
Relevant Maps: Trails Illustrated Number 103; Empire 7½ minute; Clear Creek County; Arapaho National Forest
Views from the Summit:
   N to Longs Peak
   ESE to Squaw Mountain and Chief Mountain
   S to Grays Peak, Torreys Peak, and Mount Bancroft
   SSE to Mount Evans and Mount Bierstadt
   SE to Pikes Peak
   SW to Parry Peak
   WSW to Byers Peak

James Peak

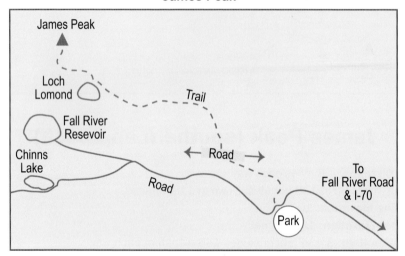

Getting There: From Interstate 70 just west of Idaho Springs take Exit 238 and within 0.2 mile access the Fall River Road north of the highway. Set your odometer to zero. Drive up Fall River Road for 6.7 miles. Then turn left onto a dirt road as the paved road curves sharply to the right. Follow this rocky road for 1.6 miles and park on the left with the trailhead sign on the right. En route avoid side roads and a road on the right at mile 1. A high clearance vehicle can reach this trailhead.

Comment: The Continental Divide Trail provides access to the summit of James Peak from the north and the south. This description is the southern approach. The second half of this hike lies within James Peak Wilderness.

The Hike: Start out by trail to the north-northwest. Ascend through the forest for 1 mile to a dirt road. Cross the road and rise to the left through more forest. The good trail soon breaks out of the trees with Loch Lemond below and great mountain vistas. Enter the James Peak Wilderness after crossing an old road. Follow the trail up to the left, pass a trail entering from the left, and ascend by switchbacks into the Wilderness area and beyond to a rock wind shelter and great scenery at the summit. The Continental Divide Trail continues northward but your return retraces the ascent route.

Mount Flora and Breckinridge Peak

Hike Distance: 4.6 miles each way
Hiking Time: Up in 155 minutes. Down in 133 minutes.
Starting Elevation: 11,315 feet (Berthoud Pass)
Highest Elevation: 13,132 feet (Mount Flora)
Elevation Gain: 2,411 feet (includes 594 extra feet)
Trail: All the way (Continental Divide Trail) except 80 yards to Breckinridge Peak
Difficulty: Moderate
Relevant Maps: Trails Illustrated Number 103; Berthoud Pass 7½ minute; Empire 7½ minute; Clear Creek County; Grand County Number Four; Arapaho National Forest

Right: Mount Flora from Breckinridge Peak.
Below: View from Mount Flora toward Colorado Mines Peak

Getting There: Drive on U.S. 40 to Berthoud Pass and park in the lot to the east. The pass lies between Empire to the south and Winter Park to the north.

Comment: This scenic hike uses the Continental Divide Trail, which enters the James Peak Wilderness. Mostly above treeline, the trail affords great views.

The Hike: Begin south up the wide road. After 0.2 mile, take the trail to the left at a sign. The Continental Divide Trail then rises to a saddle between Colorado Mines Peak and Mount Flora. The trail then rises past several false summits to reach the flat summit of Mount Flora and some large cairns. Follow the trail as it descends east-southeast toward Breckinridge Peak. For almost a mile leave the trail and ascend to the right and reach the flat summit of Breckinridge Peak. Enjoy the scenery and some refreshments before retracing the route back to Berthoud Pass.

Mount Flora and Breckinridge Peak

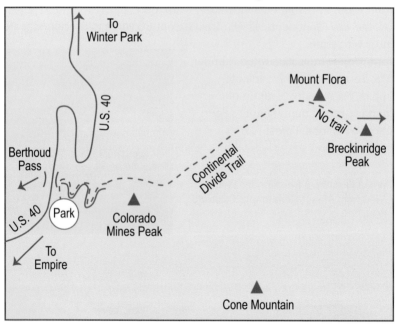

Upper Forest Lake

Hike Distance: 0.4 mile each way
Hiking Time: Down in 9 minutes. Up in 14 minutes.
Starting Elevation: 11,060 feet
Highest Elevation: 11,060 feet
Lowest Elevation: 10,820 feet
Elevation Gain: 240 feet
Trail: All the way
Difficulty: Easy
Relevant Maps: Trails Illustrated Number 103; East Portal 7½ minute; Gilpin
    County; Roosevelt National Forest

Getting There: From Rollinsville on Colorado 119 drive west on Road 149 for
7.3 miles to a fork. Continue up right on Road 149, the rocky Rollins Pass Road, for
11 miles and park at the Forest Lake Trailhead on the left. Regular cars with good
clearance can reach this trailhead. A four-wheel drive vehicle can negotiate this
road more quickly.

Upper Forest Lake

Upper Forest Lake

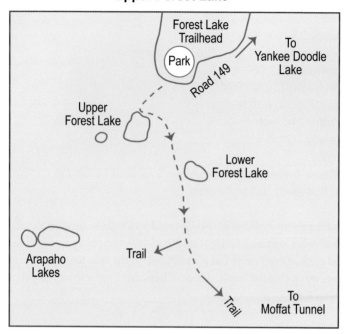

Comment: This outing demands more of the vehicle in reaching the trailhead than it does of the hiker. A route to Upper Forest Lake from a lower, more accessible trailhead begins near the Moffat Tunnel. This upper lake is much larger than the other forest lakes.

The Hike: Begin down to the west and pass a signboard on the rocky trail. At a signed fork go to the right and a trail down to lovely Upper Forest Lake below the Continental Divide. The main trail descends to a trail to the Arapaho Lakes and a lower connection to the South Boulder Creek Trail.

Witter Peak

Hike Distance: 4.5 miles each way
Hiking Time: Up in 163 minutes. Down in 124 minutes.
Starting Elevation: 10,225 feet
Highest Elevation: 12,884 feet
Elevation Gain: 2,799 feet (includes 70 extra feet each way)
Trail: Initial third

Witter Peak from the Continential Divide Trail

Difficulty: More difficult

Relevant Maps: Trails Illustrated Number 103; Empire 7½ minute; Clear Creek
County; Arapaho National Forest

Views from the Summit:
N to Mount Bancroft
NNW to Mount Eva and Parry Peak
S to Grays Peak and Torreys Peak
SSE to Mount Evans and Mount Bierstadt
SE to Pikes Peak
SW to Breckinridge Peak and Mount Flora

Getting There: From Interstate 70 just west of Idaho Springs take Exit 238 and
within 0.2 mile access the Fall River Road, north of the highway, and set your
odometer to zero. Drive up Fall River Road for 6.7 miles and turn left onto a dirt
road as the main road curves sharply right. Follow this main rocky road for 1.9
miles and park as three side roads descend from the left to join the main road.

Comment: Although a "twelver," Witter Peak offers some challenges over this approach from the east. Talus slopes and boulder fields must be traversed without a trail and some use of hands is needed approaching the summit.

The Hike: Begin by ascending the third road on the left to the southeast. Within 20 yards reach the trailhead sign and follow the trail on the right. Rise steeply on a series of switchbacks to a James Peak Wilderness sign and a 4-way intersection 1 mile from the trailhead. Continue straight (southwest) and soon reach open terrain and great vistas. At the high point of the trail with Witter Peak visible ahead, leave the trail and ascend right (north-northwest) to treeline and beyond toward Witter Peak. Stay right of the ridge and cross many rocks to reach a saddle on the ridge before the final summit block. Continue up to the left around a corner and curve right over talus and tundra. The grade levels as you pass a subpeak on the left and reach a summit rock pile. Drink in the views before returning by your ascent route.

Witter Peak

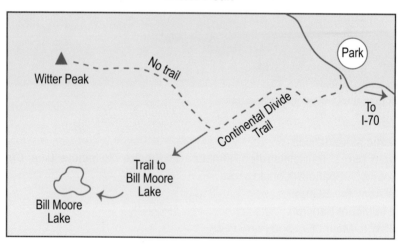

Neighboring towns: Lake City, Creede, South Fork, Saguache, Powderhorn, Gunnison
Size: 128,858 acres
Elevation: 9,000 to 14,014 feet
Miles of trails: 175

This is one of Colorado's lesser-known Wilderness areas and one of the state's original five. Lagarita means "the lookout" in Spanish, and this Wilderness deserves the name. From the summit of its single fourteener (14,014-foot San Luis Peak), climbers can see across the upper Rio Grande Valley and down the long stretch of the San Luis Valley.

La Garita's gentle alpine terrain offers refuge to thriving herds of elk, mule deer, and bighorn sheep. Hikers are likely to encounter elk in the open alpine bowls along the Divide. Many trailheads open onto approximately 175 miles of pathways, almost all especially well suited for horseback riding.

On the southern slopes in Wason Park and Silver Park you'll find a surprising ancient forest of towering spruce and fir. This is a land of rushing streams, broad and gentle alpine meadows, fascinating beaver ponds, long talus slopes, and tremendous mountain beauty.

The Wheeler Geologic Area hides in the southeast corner of the Wilderness. It once claimed to be Colorado's most visited site and is probably the state's most unusual geological formation: fine, light-gray volcanic ash compressed into rock and wildly eroded into a striking series of domes, spires, caves, ledges, pinnacles, ravines, and balanced rocks. The bumpy old road leading to the edge of Wheeler was left out of Wilderness designation, allowing motorized access deep into the area.

La Garita Wilderness Area

San Luis Peak

Hike Distance: 6.1 miles each way

Hiking Time: Up in 212 minutes. Down in 150 minutes.

Starting Elevation: 10,500 feet

Highest Elevation: 14,014 feet

Elevation Gain: 4,224 feet (includes 355 extra feet each way)

Trail: All the way

Difficulty: More difficult

Relevant Maps: Trails Illustrated Number 139; Elk Park 7½ minute; Stewart Peak 7½ minute; San Luis Peak 7½ minute; Saguache County Number Three; Gunnison Basin

Views from the Summit:
N to Stewart Peak and Baldy Alto
NNE to Spanish Peaks
ENE to Organ Mountain
W to Uncompahgre Peak

San Luis Peak

San Luis Peak

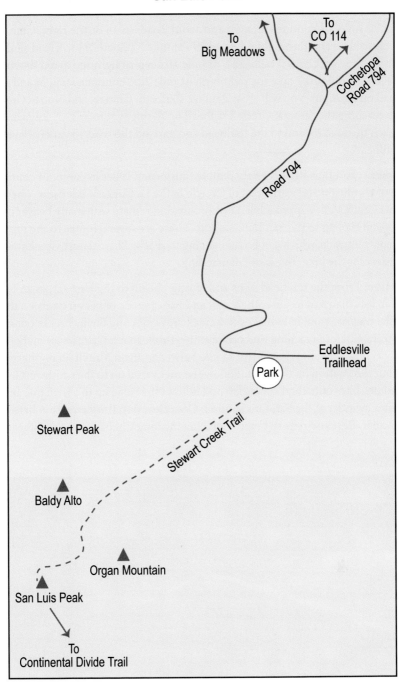

Getting There: From U.S. 50, 8 miles east of Main Street in Gunnison, drive south on Colorado 114 for 20 miles. Turn right on Road NN14 and set your odometer to zero. At mile 3.4 continue straight and avoid Road KK14 on the right. Continue past Dome Lake and turn right on Road 794 at mile 7 (Road 794 will lead all the way to the Stewart Creek Trailhead). At mile 16 keep straight and avoid the road on the left. At mile 20.7 take the right fork. At mile 22.8 continue straight and avoid the road on the right. You will cross Pauline, Perfecto, Chavez, and Nutras Creeks before reaching the Stewart Creek Trailhead on the right at mile 27.2. Regular cars can reach the final turnoff to the trailhead and park off the road 30 yards above the trailhead.

Comment: San Luis Peak is a very remote fourteener. It lies in gorgeous country south of Gunnison and northwest of Creede in the La Garita Wilderness. The Stewart Creek Valley approach is a lovely corridor, replete with many beaver dams and a good trail up to the San Luis summit. There are several routes to the top from different trailheads, which can be challenging to reach. This Stewart Creek route is the easiest for the hiker but is still demanding.

The Hike: From the trailhead signs and register, begin to the west across an open plain. In less than a mile, enter the forest and pass a series of beaver dams on the left. The trail rises and falls, makes two creek crossings, and finally breaks out into open terrain before reaching timberline at the 4-mile mark. Cairns now mark the steeper trail as it ascends south to a saddle between Organ Mountain on the left and your destination on the right. Follow the rocky trail up to the southwest from the saddle. The route then curves left and follows the ridge up to a rock pile and a register cylinder at the San Luis summit. On a clear day, the views from here are spectacular. Rest and refresh before retracing the long trip back to the trailhead.

San Luis Peak

Neighboring towns: Telluride, Ophir, Silverton, Ouray, Ridgway, Dolores
Size: 41,193 acres
Elevation: 9,000 to 14,246 feet
Miles of trails: 37

Lizard Head Wilderness is a land of rugged mountain splendor with lovely cirque lakes, fish in swift mountain streams that often plunge over dramatic waterfalls, and a spruce-fir forest opened by expanses of alpine vegetation. Golden aspen blanket the lower slopes in vast unbroken reaches every fall. Human use is light on about 37 miles of strenuous trails.

Named for a prominent spire near Lizard Head Pass, this area contains the westernmost 14,000-foot peaks in Colorado. Located in the San Juan Mountain, these four-teeners provide much of the recreational allure of the area, but they are not for the fainthearted. Mount Wilson and El Diente are two of the most difficult climbs in the state. Visitors are drawn to the magnificent unbroken expanses of aspen covering the area's lower slopes.

The summit of Lizard Head Peak, a 400-foot-tall tower of rotten and unsafe rock, has been voted as one of Colorado's most dangerous and difficult climbs. Dolores Peak (13,290 feet) stands in the most western portion of the Wilderness. On a clear day you can stand in snow on any of the area's high peaks and see the red rock canyon lands of southern Utah to the west.

Lizard Head

Black Face Mountain

Hike Distance: 4.2 miles each way
Hiking Time: Up in 140 minutes. Down in 105 minutes.
Starting Elevation: 10,220 feet
Highest Elevation: 12,147 feet
Elevation Gain: 2,517 feet (includes 295 extra feet each way)
Trail: All the way
Difficulty: Moderate
Relevant Maps: Trails Illustrated Number141; Mount Wilson 7½ minute;
    San Miguel County Number Three; Uncompahgre National Forest
Views from the Summit:
    NNE to San Bernardo Mountain and Mount Sneffels
    NNW to Sunshine Mountain
    NW to Lizard Head
    ESE to Trout Lake
    SSE to Sheep Mountain
    SE to Vermillion Peak
    WNW to Cross Mountain, Mount Wilson, and Gladstone Peak

Trail to Black Face Mountain

Black Face Mountain

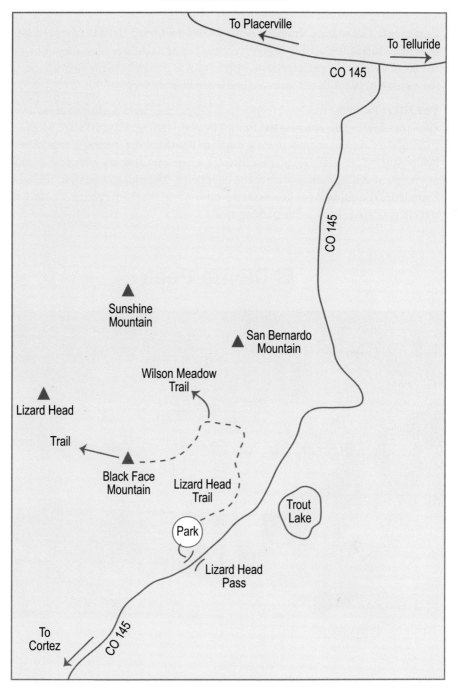

Getting There: From the entrance road into Telluride, drive south on Colorado 145 for 11.8 miles and park in the Lizard Head Trailhead parking area on the right at Lizard Head Pass.

Comment: The soaring, dramatic peaks within the Lizard Head Wilderness, southwest of Telluride, are on full display from the top of Back Face Mountain. The Lizard Head Trail to the peak traverses lush terrain as it rises by many switchbacks to the summit of Black Face Mountain and incredible scenery.

The Hike: From the trailhead register and signboard, begin north and cross an open meadow before entering the trees. The good trail winds northward before curving west. As you ascend, there are intermittent views of inviting Trout Lake below. Just below treeline, you pass through a high meadow and over a false summit before reaching a small cairn at the high point. The trail continues to the west. Experience the euphoria of this exalted platform and take some pictures before retracing your route back to the parking area.

El Diente Peak

El Diente Peak and waterfall

El Diente Peak

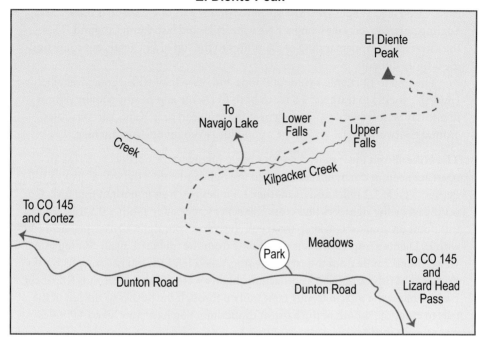

Hike Distance: 7.3 miles each way
Hiking Time: Up in 305 minutes. Down in 285 minutes.
Starting Elevation: 10,085 feet
Highest Elevation: 14,159 feet
Elevation Gain: 5,924 feet (includes an extra 925 feet each way)
Trail: All the way but faint at times
Difficulty: Most difficult
Relevant Maps: Trails Illustrated Number 141; Dolores Peak 7½ minute;
    Delores County Number Three; San Juan National Forest
Views from the Summit:
    N to Wilson Peak
    NNE to Mount Sneffels, Wetterhorn Peak, and Uncompahgre Peak
    NE to Mount Wilson
    S to Dunton Meadows Trailhead
    SW to Dolores Peak

Getting There: From Lizard Head Pass on Colorado 145 (southwest of Telluride), drive south for 5.5 miles and turn right onto the good, dirt Dunton Road. Follow this road for 5.1 miles and turn off onto a rougher road on the right and park after another 0.15 mile near the trailhead and barrier to vehicular traffic. Regular cars can reach this parking area. (There are good campsites in the trailhead area.)

Comment: The Dunton Meadows Trailhead lies almost 400 miles from Denver in the Lizard Head Wilderness. The splendor of this part of Colorado is breathtaking. Soaring peaks, lovely lakes, impressive waterfalls, and lush forests abound. This is the safest and least demanding of the routes to the top of El Diente, but route finding is more difficult.

The trail to El Diente's summit is long and often faint with a great deal of talus (mid-size rocks) to traverse. To reach both El Diente and nearby Mount Wilson in one day is truly heroic. Camping near the trailhead or in Kilpacker Meadows around the two waterfalls might be a good idea even for one summit hike.

The Hike: From the trailhead register begin hiking to the northwest. Cross an open area before the trailhead curves to the right and enters the woods. Pass a Wilderness sign at 1.2 miles and in another 1.5 miles reach an important trail fork. Go northeast by the right fork and cross Kilpacker Creek after another 0.5 mile. From this point on your ascent, keep the creek always on your right. Cross open fields with El Diente's impressive summit, visible from the trailhead, again coming into view. After 0.7 mile from the creek crossing, take a left fork and rise steeply to pass the lower of two waterfalls. Approach the higher waterfall and cavernous Kilpacker Basin. Follow the intermittently faint trail up through the bushes to the left of the falls to enter the mouth of the basin at timberline. You have now hiked 4.7 miles from the trailhead.

Continue up east-northeast over talus into the upper basin for another 2 miles. El Diente's summit will be a little to the west of you. Hike past a cliff and turn left and north onto a cairn-marked faint trail that leads toward steep rocky cliffs. Ascend west (left) under these cliffs and follow the cairns and trail up to a rocky trail along the south side of the ridge. Ascend left via cairns to reach the ridge then turn left and west by a trail on the north side of the ridge a few hundred yards. Then curve up to the left to reach the small summit with a hiking register. Drink in the views and gather your forces before the long trek back to the trailhead. Be sure to remember your lanes off of the ridge as you return by the ascent route.

Neighboring towns: Lake Gorge, Fairplay, Bailey, Deckers
Size: 119,790 acres
Elevation: 8,000 to 12,400 feet
Miles of trails: 130

Lost Creek was named after a creek of the same name that repeatedly disappears underground only to reappear again farther downstream where it ultimately becomes Goose Creek.

There are nearly 130 miles of trails of medium to heavy usage that traverse tree-lined mountain parks, fascinating rounded granite domes, and rare granite arches. The cross-state Colorado Trail passes through the Wilderness.

Black bears, bighorn sheep, deer, elk, and bobcats share the region. Vegetation includes ponderosa, bristle-cone, and lodgepole pine, aspen, spruce, fir, and alpine tundra.

Lost Creek Wilderness Area

Bison Pass

Hike Distance: 4 miles each way
Hiking Time: Up in 128 minutes. Down in 80 minutes.
Starting Elevation: 8,720 feet
Highest Elevation: 11,310 feet
Elevation Gain: 2,880 feet (includes 145 extra feet each way)
Trail: All the way
Difficulty: Moderate
Relevant Maps: Trails Illustrated Number 105; Farnum Peak 7½ minute;
    Park County Number Two; Pike National Forest

Bison Pass

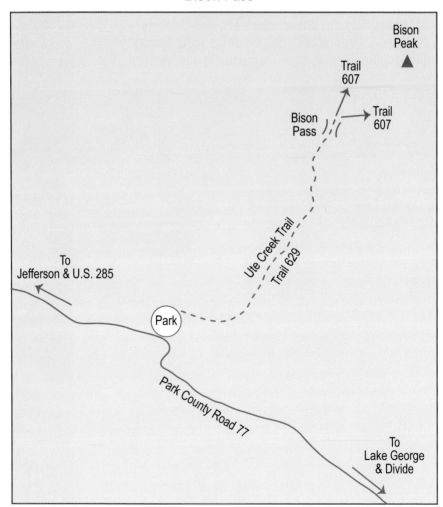

Getting There: From U.S. 285 at Jefferson, southwest of Kenosha Pass, drive southeast on Park County Road 77 for 19.8 miles and park on the left at the Ute Creek Trailhead.

Comment: The Ute Creek Trail (Number 629) enters the Lost Creek Wilderness and connects with the Brookside-McCurdy Trail at Bison Pass. The steep, gravelly trail passes through thick forest with occasional stands of aspen as it parallels Ute Creek. At the unmarked pass and the trail junction, there are good views of the Tarryall Mountains and beyond.

The Hike: Begin east from the trailhead sign and cross Tarryall Creek on a bridge. Follow the trail along the valley floor before it curves left up the Ute Creek drainage and begins to become steeper as it rises to the north. After 4 miles reach Bison Pass at a small rockpile. Thirty yards farther is a sign and a trail junction. The Brookside-McCurdy Trail (Number 607) continues straight (north) down to the Lost Park Road and Trailhead and also east to McCurdy Park. Bison Peak can be seen to the northeast from this trail intersection and can be reached in another 1.5 miles after 1,200 more feet of elevation gain from the trail to the east.

Your descent will be easier and consume less time than your ascent.

Bison Peak and McCurdy Mountain

Hike Distance: Trailhead to Bison Peak summit, 5.9 miles; Bison Peak summit to McCurdy Mountain summit, 3.1 miles; McCurdy Mountain summit back to trailhead, 7.4 miles

Hiking Time: Trailhead to Bison Peak summit, 164 minutes; Bison Peak summit to McCurdy Mountain summit, 80 minutes; McCurdy Mountain summit to trailhead, 168 minutes

Starting Elevation: 8,768 feet

Highest Elevation: 12,431 feet

Elevation Gain: 4,805 feet (includes 1,142 extra feet)

Trail: Initial 90% toward Bison Peak, then the first 75% toward McCurdy Mountain

Difficulty: More difficult

Relevant Maps: Trails Illustrated Number 105; Farnum Peak 7½ minute; McCurdy Mountain 7½ minute; Park County Number Two; Pike National Forest

Views from the Summit:

Bison Peak:

    NNE to Windy Peak

    NW to Mount Evans

W to Bald Mountain and Mount Guyot
S to Mount Silverheels
SE to McCurdy Mountain and Pikes Peak

Bison Peak

McCurdy Mountain:
 NW to Bald Mountain, Mount Guyot, and Bison Peak
 SSW to Mount Silverheels
 SE to Pikes Peak
 SW to Farnum Peak

McCurdy Mountain

Bison Peak & McCurdy Mountain

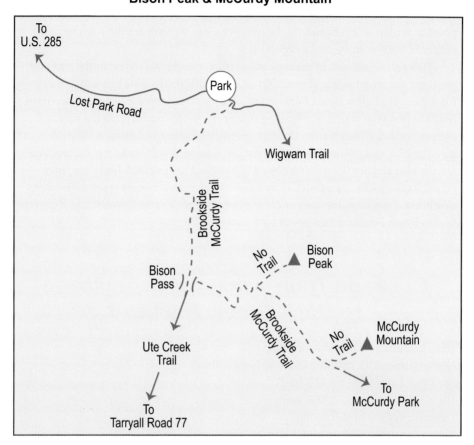

Getting There: From U.S 285 in Jefferson in South Park, drive southeast on a dirt road beginning just north of the gas station. This is Park County Road 77. Follow it for 20.3 miles past the Tarryall Reservoir to a sign and a parking area on the left. One sign denotes that the "Ute Creek Trail Number 629" begins at this point. Park here.

Comment: The rock formations in this Lost Creek Wilderness Area combined with the many upright bare tree trunks (probably from a fire a long time ago) make it unique in my Colorado experience.

The Hike: Begin northeast and cross the bridge over Tarryall Creek. The trail goes east and in 0.6 mile from the trailhead turns north with Ute Creek on your right. Proceed upward past a Lost Creek Wilderness sign, cross the creek, and follow the gravelly trail northeast as it steeply rises to a sign and a three-way intersection at Bison Pass (11,300 feet). Then proceed east toward McCurdy Park. In 1.3 miles from the pass you will reach a ridge above timberline with tundra and many interesting red rock formations. Leave the trail (which is marked by cairns and a pole in this area) and ascend northeast to the Bison Peak summit that is visible as the high point to the left of a subpeak. At the easily reached summit are the ruins of an old platform, a stone stove, and a register jar.

Descend southwest to the trail and continue southeast to regain the trail and continue southeast losing about 300 feet of elevation. In a little more than a mile from the ridge below Bison Peak you reach a junction with a trail coming from the north to join your trail that is leading southeast. At this point, leave the trail and ascend northeast over tundra through sparse, bare tree trunks over a subpeak to gain the McCurdy Mountain high point. This summit is 0.9 mile from where you left the trail and lies 0.3 mile southeast of a slightly lower point. Only a register jar marks the rocky top of McCurdy Mountain, which is readily reached from the northeast. To return, retrace your route over the subpeak to the west and regain the trail to Bison Pass and then south back to the trailhead.

Colorado Trail—Long Gulch Trailhead to Rock Creek Trailhead

Hike Distance: 7.7 miles each way
Hiking Time: 198 minutes one way (senior time)
Starting Elevation: 10,176 feet
Highest Elevation: 10,388 feet
Lowest Elevation: 9,520 feet
Elevation Gain: 637 feet (includes 319 extra feet)
Trail: All the way
Difficulty: Moderate
Relevant Maps: Trails Illustrated Number 105; Observatory Rock 7½ minute; Colorado Trail Map 4; Pike National Forest; Park County Number Two

Getting There: From Kenosha Pass on U.S. 285 drive southwest 3.1 miles and turn left on the Lost Park Road (Number 56). Follow the road 7.3 miles to a fork at a sign to the Rock Creek Trail on the left. Drive one car up the road 1.2 miles to the trailhead parking area. From the turnoff to the Rock Creek Trailhead drive the second vehicle 3.7 miles farther on the Lost Park Road and turn left up Road 817 and park at road end at the Long Gulch Trailhead at a Colorado Trail sign.

Comment: The fifth segment of the Colorado Trail traverses part of the Lost Creek Wilderness and crosses several small streams. The western half has more meadows and vistas.

**Colorado Trail
Long Gulch To Rock Creek**

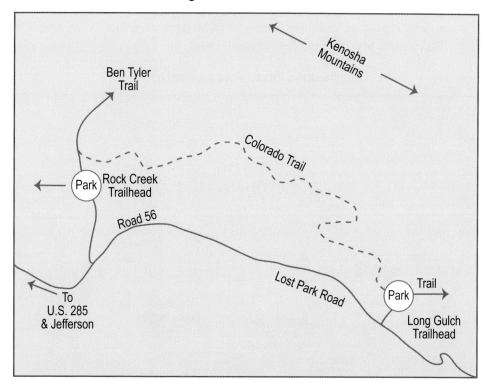

The Hike: At the Long Gulch Trailhead, begin east from the trail sign and ascend left at a fork. After 0.4 mile pass a Wilderness sign. The clear trail meanders up and down with occasional creek crossings. After the highest point of this segment, gradually descend with views of North Tarryall Peak on the left and eventually high peaks to the west. After crossing Rock Creek and a junction with the Ben Tyler Trail on the right, descend 50 yards to a road and follow the Colorado Trail off road to the right. Ascend to a gate and a sharp right turn that leads to the parking area for the Rock Creek Trailhead.

Hankins Pass (west approach)

Hike Distance: 4.8 miles each way
Hiking Time: Up in 122 minutes. Down in 89 minutes.
Starting Elevation: 8,550 feet
Highest Elevation: 10,000 feet

Elevation Gain: 2,070 feet (includes 310 extra feet each way)

Trail: All the way

Difficulty: Moderate

Relevant Maps: Trails Illustrated Number 105; McCurdy Mountain 7½ minute; Park County Number Two; Pike National Forest

Hankins Pass (west approach)

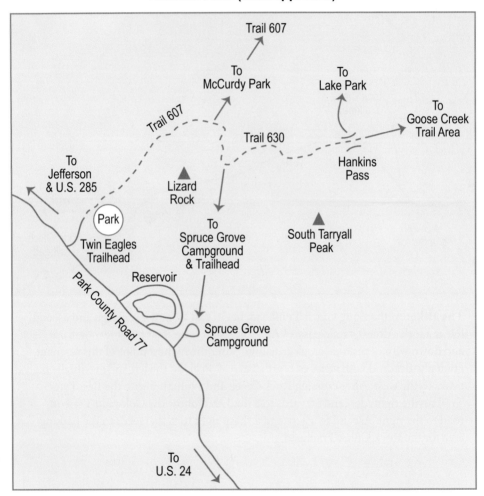

Getting There: From U.S. 285 at Jefferson in South Park drive southeast on Park County Road 77 for 25.8 miles, then turn left and park in another 0.1 mile at the Twin Eagles Trailhead, which is a fee area. Coming from the southeast this trailhead is 16 miles on Park County Road 77 northwest from U.S. 24.

North to McCurdy Mountain from western approach to Hankins Pass

Comment: Hankins Pass lies in the extensive Lost Creek Wilderness Area. This mountain playground is full of connecting trails, sizeable peaks, and gorgeous rock formations. Hankins Pass lies deep within this area and can be reached from several directions. This described route begins at the Twin Eagles Trailhead and ascends the pass from the west. Another popular starting point is the Goose Creek Trailhead from the east. Try this trek from the third week in May until early November.

The Hike: Start to the northeast past a signboard and cross Tarryall Creek on a bridge. Then follow the trail to the left and ascend steeply to an open overlook point. Signs for Trail 607 will keep you on track. The many, lovely large rocks will delight you. After 2 miles on Trail 607 keep right (south-southeast) at a signed fork and enter the Lost Creek Wilderness. Another mile brings you to another fork. Go left and ascend to the south-southwest. You are now on Trail 630, which will lead to Hankins Pass, Lake Park, and the Goose Creek Trailhead. The well-defined trail continues through the forest with occasional views of the Tarryall Mountains and higher peaks to the west. At Hankins Pass there is a trail sign and an intersection. The trail on the left leads to Lake Park and beyond. Straight ahead to the east the trail will descend down to Goose Creek. South Tarryall Peak hovers above to the south. Retrace your ascent route back to the trailhead.

Wigwam Trail to East Lost Park

Hike Distance: 3.2 miles each way
Hiking Time: Out in 82 minutes. Back in 77 minutes (senior time)
Starting Elevation: 9,900 feet
Lowest Elevation: 9,698 feet
Highest Elevation: 9,900 feet
Elevation Gain: 336 feet (includes 67 extra feet each way)
Trail: All the way
Difficulty: Easy
Relevant Maps: Trails Illustrated Number 105; Topaz Mountain 7½ minute;
Windy Peak 7½ minute; Park County Two; Pike National Forest

Getting There: From U.S. 285, 3 miles south of Kenosha Pass, turn east on the Lost Park Road (Number 56) and follow it about 17 miles until it ends at the Lost Park Campground. Follow the left fork to the loop road at the far end of the campground and park.

Comment: This fairly level hike follows Lost Creek to the east and ends at a crossing of an unnamed creek. The Lost Creek Valley presents many striking rock formations. East Lost Park is a large, scenic, open area where two creeks join.

The Hike: Begin to the east and descend through two gates. Cross Lost Creek and always keep it on your left. The trail has several curves as it gently descends along the right margin of the forest. Pass a cabin ruin on the right before reaching an unmarked fork with a rocky outcropping straight ahead. Take the left trail that descends 100 yards to a log crossing of Lost Creek, which turned south. This is the turnaround point of this hike as the Wigwam Trail rises to the left. Take the same trail back to your starting point.

Wigwam Trail to East Lost Park

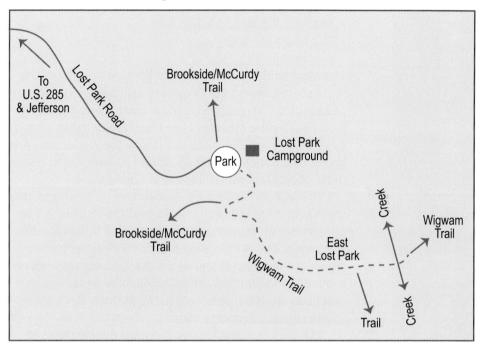

Neighboring towns: Aspen, Snowmass, Basalt, El Jebel, Carbondale, Glenwood Springs
Size: 181,117 acres
Elevation: 7,500 to 14,265 feet
Miles of trails: 100

The Maroon Bells—Snowmass Wilderness captures the most scenic aspects of Colorado: lush aspen forests, lofty peaks lined with perpetual snow, clear flowing streams, blooming alpine meadows, and high alpine lakes ringed by granite peaks. Perhaps this is why the Wilderness Area is one of the most visited spots and considered to be the most photographed landscape in Colorado.

The Maroon Bells area is extremely popular with many tourists and local day hikers. To beat the crowds, arrive early in the morning on a weekday. Avoid holidays and weekends. The area is also popular during the fall. Because of the high volume of visitors, parking may not be available and shuttles are provided for access. You can purchase shuttle bus tickets to the Maroon Bells at the Aspen Highlands sports shop.

Mid summer and fall are the most scenic times to visit. From late July into August the wildflowers are at their peak. The autumn aspen colors are at their peak in late September. Hikers and backpackers willing to hike farther into the Wilderness will experience less crowds and a better wilderness experience.

Castle Peak and Conundrum Peak

Hike Distance: 5.3 miles each way to Castle Peak. An extra 0.25 mile up to
Conundrum Peak

Hiking Time: Up to Castle Peak in 217 minutes. Over to Conundrum Peak in
30 minutes. Down from Conundrum Peak in 125 minutes.

Starting Elevation: 10,180 feet

Highest Elevation: 14,265 feet (Castle Peak)

Elevation Gain: 4,427 feet (includes 342 extra feet)

Trail: All the way

Difficulty: More difficult

Relevant Maps: Trails Illustrated Number 127 or 148; Hayden Peak 7½ minute;
Pitkin County Number Two; Gunnison County Number Three; White River
National Forest

Views from the Summit of Castle Peak:
NNW to Conundrum Peak and Cathedral Peak
NW to Capitol Peak, Pyramid Peak, and Buckskin Peak
E to Taylor Peak
S to Teocalli Mountain
SE to Pearl Pass
WNW to Maroon Peak, North Maroon Peak, and Snowmass Mountain

Castle Peak

Castle and Conundrum Peaks

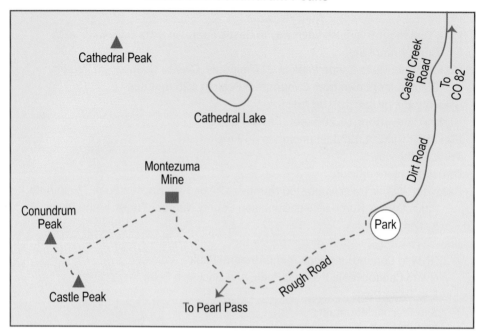

Getting There: From central Aspen at Colorado 82 (Main Street) and Mill Street, drive northwest on Colorado 82 for 1.3 miles and turn left onto the road that leads to Castle Creek Road and Maroon Creek Road. Within 50 yards go left on the Castle Creek Road and follow it for 12.9 miles to a fork. The left fork is a blocked road. Ascend the right fork, which is unpaved and leads to the abandoned Montezuma Mine. After 1.3 miles, park just before the road crosses Castle Creek. Four-wheel drive is needed for the 4 more miles to road end high in the basin. Most regular cars can reach the point before the creek crossing.

Comment: Castle Peak is the highest mountain in the Elk Range and is located in both Pitkin and Gunnison Counties. It lies on the boundary between these two counties. Castle Peak is an official fourteener, while the adjacent Conundrum Peak is located too close for official designation even though it is over 14,000 feet high. Both peaks feed creeks that are named after them.

The Hike: Just before the road crosses Castle Creek, begin hiking south over a footbridge and up the rough road. After 1.8 miles pass the very rough road to Pearl Pass on the left and continue by the right fork. As the basin opens up there are several switchbacks before the final stretch of road past the Montezuma Mine ruins to road end. Continue south-southwest up into the basin, which carries areas of snow throughout the year. An ice axe is recommended for this hike.

Rise to a rocky bench and then decide between a trail on your left that ascends to the ridge or going directly for the saddle between Castle (left) and Conundrum (right). The latter is more direct but will cross snow and ice and some loose rock just beneath the saddle. The left trail leads to Castle Peak's summit and a rock wind shelter in a clockwise direction. The route from the saddle is left (south-southeast) for 0.25 mile on a ridge trail. From Castle descend northwest to the saddle and then up another ridge trail 0.7 mile to a rock pile and register cylinder at Conundrum's high point. To return, go back to the saddle and walk or glissade down into the basin to rejoin the road and follow Castle Creek back to your vehicle.

Cathedral Lake

Hike Distance: 3.5 miles each way
Hiking Time: Up in 90 minutes. Down in 60 minutes.
Starting Elevation: 9,880 feet
Highest Elevation: 11,910 feet
Elevation Gain: 2,470 feet (includes 440 extra feet)
Trail: All the way
Difficulty: Moderate
Relevant Maps: Trails Illustrated Number 127 or 148; Hayden Peak 7½ minute; Pitkin County Number Two; White River National Forest

Cathedral Lake and Cathedral Peak

Cathedral Lake

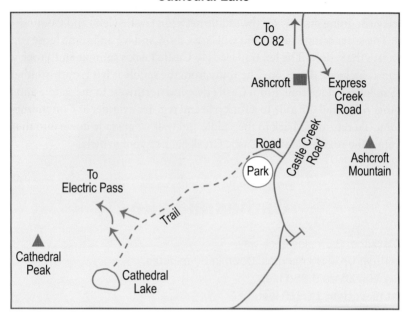

Getting There: From Colorado 82 west of Aspen, go 0.5 mile west of the Castle Creek Bridge and turn south. Within 30 yards go left on the Castle Creek Road. Follow the paved road up this lovely valley through Ashcroft for a total of 11.9 miles from Colorado 82 and turn right onto a dirt road with a sign giving distances to Cathedral Lake and the trailhead parking area. Follow this road for 0.6 mile and park near the trailhead at road end. Regular cars can reach this trailhead.

Comment: The hike to Cathedral Lake in the Maroon Bells—Snowmass Wilderness is one of the grandest in Colorado. Thick groves of aspen, the rushing waters of Pine Creek, and thrilling vistas reward the hiker before reaching this large, gorgeous lake, lying in a rocky bowl beneath two of Colorado's highest peaks.

The Hike: Your trek begins to the south-southwest from the trailhead sign and register. Follow the good trail through a thick aspen grove. Soon the waters of Pine Creek, descending from Cathedral Lake, appear on your left. Pass through several fields of talus and boulders and eventually ascend a series of switchbacks that take you up through a talus slope to enter the forest on a shelf trail. Then quickly reach a signed fork at mile 2.8 from the trailhead and descend the left fork. The trail on the right ascends to Electric Pass. Soon reach another signed fork. Stay to the left again and cross Pine Creek. The right fork again leads to Electric Pass. Then ascend gently to a grassy bench overlooking the lake. Follow either of two trails down to Cathedral Lake and savor the beauty all around you before your return. Cathedral Peak is the rocky behemoth to the west-northwest. Conundrum Peak rises above to the south, and over your shoulder to the northwest is Electric Pass Peak.

Conundrum Creek
(To first Creek Crossing)

Conundrum Creek Trail

Hike Distance: 2.5 miles each way
Hiking Time: Up in 58 minutes. Down in 50 minutes.
Starting Elevation: 8,760 feet
Highest Elevation: 9,360 feet
Elevation Gain: 1,250 feet (includes 325 extra feet each way)
Trail: All the way
Difficulty: Moderate
Relevant Maps: Trails Illustrated Number 127 or 148; Hayden Peak 7½
     minutes; Pitkin County Number One; White River National Forest

Getting There: From Colorado 82 west of Aspen, go 0.5 mile west of the Castle
Creek Bridge and turn south. Within 30 yards go left (south) on the Castle Creek
Road, drive for 4.9 miles and turn right onto the Conundrum Creek Road. Follow
this paved road for 0.2 mile and cross the creek. Then turn left and drive 0.8 mile
on a reasonable, dirt road to the end of the road and park at the trailhead.

Comment: The Conundrum Creek Trail is a popular hike, especially for those wishing to traverse 9 miles to a hot springs and camp nearby. This day hike description takes you up to the first creek crossing after 2.3 miles on the trail. The beautiful Conundrum Creek valley is lush with many aspen, high peaks visible at the head of the valley, and the brisk waters of Conundrum Creek flowing parallel to the trail. If you wish to cross the creek and go higher in the valley, be careful. This creek has claimed human victims.

The Hike: Start south-southwest from the trailhead sign and ascend the tree and flower-filled valley. The trail rises and falls, with frequent views of the creek below. After 1.5 miles there is a cabin ruin on the left in an open meadow. Continue farther and soon cross a small creek before reaching the initial crossing of Conundrum Creek. The trail continues up the valley to the hot springs and to Triangle Pass. Return as you ascended.

Conundrum Creek

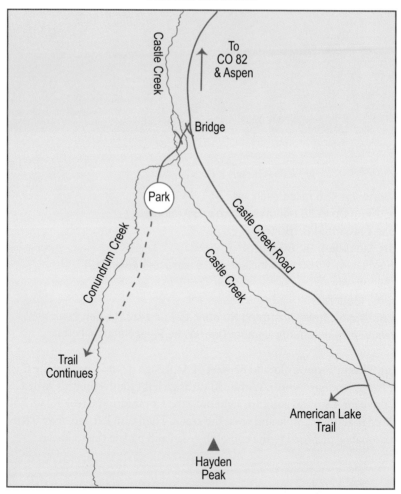

Copper Lake

Hike Distance: 4 miles each way
Hiking Time: Up in 120 minutes. Down in 100 minutes.
Starting Elevation: 9,840 feet
Highest Elevation: 11,363 feet
Elevation Gain: 2,198 feet (includes 675 extra feet)
Trail: All the way
Difficulty: Moderate
Relevant Maps: Trails Illustrated Numbers 128 and 131 or 148; Gothic
7½ minute; Maroon Bells 7½ minute; Gunnison County Number Two;
Gunnison Basin

Copper Lake

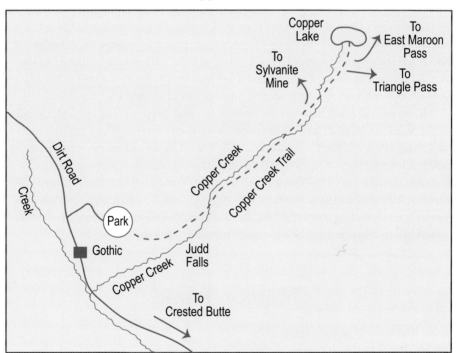

Getting There: From Elk Avenue in Crested Butte, drive north 7.8 miles on Gunnison Road 317 through Mount Crested Butte and on the Gothic Road to the town of Gothic. From the town hall and visitor center in Gothic, continue north on the adequate, dirt road for 0.6 mile and turn right at a fork. Follow this rough dirt road another 0.5 mile to a parking area at the trailhead. The road is blocked at the trailhead. Regular cars can reach this parking area.

Comment: Copper Lake is on my top ten list for beautiful lakes in Colorado. Lying beneath East Maroon Pass and many impressive peaks in the Maroon Bells—Snowmass Wilderness, the kidney-shaped lake is a high mountain jewel.

The route begins north of the town of Gothic and passes by Judd Falls as it continues up the valley parallel to Copper Creek.

There are three crossings of Copper Creek and only one is assisted by a fallen log. If you don't like wading in cold mountain currents, save this hike for late August or September. Due to lingering snow high in the basin, I recommend this hike after the middle of July.

The Hike: From the parking area, hike east up the blocked road. There are good views of Mount Crested Butte and Gothic Mountain during the early part of the hike. Lose some elevation and arrive at a view of Judd Falls and a "T" intersection after 0.6 mile. Ascend to the left past a trail register and signboard and reach the first crossing of Copper Creek at mile 1.8. If you need an assist, a fallen tree trunk provides transit 10 yards above the wide trail. Avoid the narrow trail to the left just before the creek. Continue up the wide road, pass a talus slope on the right and reach the second Copper Creek crossing at mile 3.2 from the trailhead. Wade across here and again over a side creek a few hundred yards up the trail. Then wade across Copper Creek for the final time on your ascent at mile 3.5.

Keep right at a fork just past the creek as the trail steepens. The left fork ascends to the Sylvanite Mine. It is 0.7 mile farther to a signed junction. The right fork leads to Triangle Pass and the Conundrum Creek Trail. You ascend steeply straight ahead and reach a map sign after another 0.25 mile. The sign clarifies camping sites and the East Maroon Pass Trail that leads to the right. You go left (north-northwest) for the final 0.25 mile and walk down to this gorgeous lake. The East Maroon Pass Trail can be seen ascending above the lake. Relax and enjoy this great setting. Maybe you would like to camp and fish before your return down the valley.

Maroon Peak

Hike Distance: 7 miles each way
Hiking Time: Up in 353 minutes. Down in 325 minutes.
Starting Elevation: 9,580 feet
Highest Elevation: 14,156 feet
Elevation Gain: 6,226 feet (includes an extra 825 feet each way)
Trail: Initial 3.3 miles and from mile 4 to the summit.
Difficulty: Most Difficult
Relevant Maps: Trails Illustrated Number 128 or 148; Maroon Bells 7½ minute; Pitkin County Number One; White River National Forest

The Maroon Bells and U.S. Forest Service plaque for the Maroon Bells.
Photo courtesy of Bernie Towne.

Views from the Summit:
  N to North Maroon Peak
  NW to Capitol Peak
  ENE to Pyramid Peak
  ESE to Castle Peak
  WNW to Snowmass Peak

Getting There: Drive west on Colorado 82 from Aspen. Cross the Castle Creek Bridge and take the first left turn after the stoplight. This left turn leads to either the Castle Creek Road (left) or the Maroon Creek Road (right) at a fork within 200 yards from Colorado 82. Follow this right fork up the Maroon Creek Road for 9.9 miles from Colorado 82 and park at the end of the road at the Upper

Maroon Lake parking area. (The Maroon Creek Road is blocked to private vehicles certain hours of each day. Check with Aspen or National Forest officials for this information.)

Comment: The hike to South Maroon Bell, also called South Maroon Peak or Maroon Peak, is more strenuous than most writers report. Due to losses of elevation along the route, the elevation gain is considerable over 7 miles of trail, tundra, and rocky terrain. The key to the hike is the 2.2-mile stretch between the West Maroon Trail and the ridge that goes north and south and leads to the top of Maroon Peak. There is no special danger on this hike if the weather is favorable but considerable stamina is required. The surrounding peaks and valleys are especially lovely. I would recommend from mid-July to mid-August as the best dates for this outing.

The Hike: From the Upper Maroon Lake parking area, begin west on West Maroon-Snowmass Trail that leads 1.5 miles to a fork at a trail sign. Go left and pass Crater Lake on the left. Continue by good clear trail up the West Maroon Creek Valley another 1.8 miles to a group of trees just before the trail crosses West Maroon Creek. From the group of trees ascend west in an open area and angle southwest (240 degrees by compass) toward a mid-point on the grassy side ridge. Be sure to avoid the willows whenever possible. Pass over the first ridge and over yet another before angling more steeply upward to the west. A faint trail will be seen on the left. This leads you to a third side ridge. At this ridge the trail turns northwest and ascends. Follow this trail then upward to gain the north-south ridge around 13,300 feet and then continue north. The top of Maroon Peak will now be visible to the northwest.

Maroon Peak and North Maroon Peak

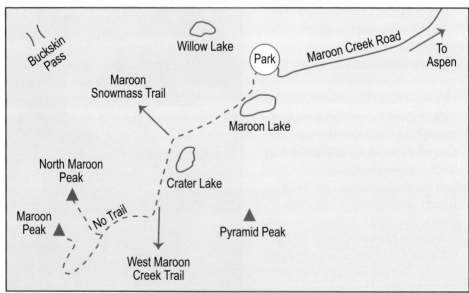

After a segment on the ridge the trail then descends on the west side of the ridge. Follow the cairns that mark this trail and bypass the 13,753-foot subpeak on your right. Ascend Maroon Peak in a clockwise direction with many switchbacks. Be careful with the loose rock and eventually gain the summit, which has a register cylinder and a few rocks. Rest and enjoy the wonderful vistas before gathering your strength for the strenuous, lengthy descent. Some hikers traverse the difficult ridge between the two Maroon Peaks. Unless you have the time, energy, and know this tricky descent route from North Maroon Peak, avoid this option.

North Maroon Peak

Hike Distance: 6.4 miles each way
Hiking Time: Up in 270 minutes. Down in 219 minutes.
Starting Elevation: 9,580 feet
Highest Elevation: 14,014 feet
Elevation Gain: 5,460 feet (includes 500 extra feet each way)
Trail: All the way
Difficulty: Most difficult
Relevant Maps: Trails Illustrated Number 128 or 148; Maroon Bells 7½ minute; Pitkin County Number One; White River National Forest
Views from the Summit:
    NNW to Mount Buckskin
    NE to Crater Lake and Maroon Lake
    NW to Snowmass Mountain
    E to Pyramid Peak
    S to South Maroon Peak

Getting There: Drive west on Colorado 82 from Aspen. Cross the Castle Creek Bridge and take the first left turn after the stoplight. This left turn leads to either the Castle Creek Road (left) or the Maroon Creek Road (right) at a fork within 200 yards from Colorado 82. Follow this right fork up the Maroon Creek Road for 9.9 miles from Colorado 82 and park at the end of the road at the Upper Maroon Lake parking area. (The Maroon Creek Road is blocked to private vehicles certain hours of each day. Check with Aspen or National Forest officials for this information.)

Comment: The standard hiking route from Maroon Lake to the top of North Maroon Peak requires great stamina and some skill in rock climbing. If you are not blessed with good weather, postpone this hike. Bring a helmet for the upper areas. Some hikers attempt to climb both Maroon Peaks in one day. Three reasons against this plan are: the difficult ridge between the two summits, the longer distance, and the primary focus which each mountain deserves.

North Maroon Peak

The Hike: This long trek begins south from the upper parking area above Maroon Lake. Follow the West Maroon—Snowmass Trail parallel to lovely Maroon Lake, enter the Maroon Bells—Snowmass Wilderness and take two right forks that keep you on the Maroon-Snowmass Trail for 1.5 miles to a register and signboard just before Crater Lake.

Ascend the right fork (southwest) for 0.8 mile and take a left fork at a small rock pile and descend to a crossing of Minnehaha Creek. Follow a steep hikers trail to the south and ascend to a grassy bench around timberline. Follow the trail across a large rock glacier to a point at 11,700 fee, just below the lowest cliffs of the northeast ridge of North Maroon Peak. A series of cairns marks the entire route above timberline. Some of these are wrapped with pink ribbons.

Ascend a grassy gully another 1,000 feet to two cairns at a corner of the northeast ridge at 12,800 feet. Turn sharply to the right and ascend a steeper gully by a series of ledges to reach a stone buttress at the head of this gully. A rocky chimney lets you through to gain a ridge between two gullies with the top of North Maroon looming ahead and close. This chimney must be carefully negotiated. Rope here is not essential but is desirable. From the ridge above the chimney keep left of the final summit ridge and follow cairns to a "white chimney" that is filled with loose rock and allows you up the final 50 feet to the summit where a cairn, register cylinder, and incredible vistas greet you. There are several ways to the top over the last 100 feet of elevation gain. On the return carefully follow the cairns and pay special attention to the exit points from each gully.

Pyramid Peak

Hike Distance: 3.8 miles each way

Hiking Time: Up in 294 minutes. Down in 240 minutes.

Starting Elevation: 9,580 feet

Highest Elevation: 14, 018 feet

Elevation Gain: 5,138 feet (includes an extra 350 feet each way)

Trail: First 2.1 miles and last 1.3 miles

Difficulty: Most difficult

Relevant Maps: Trails Illustrated Number 128 or 148; Maroon Bells 7½ minute; Pitkin County Number One; White River National Forest

Views from the Summit:

NW to Capitol Peak, Buckskin Pass, and Mount Sopris

ESE to Cathedral Peak

WNW to North Maroon Bell and Snowmass Mountain

WSW to South Maroon Bell

Pyramid Peak

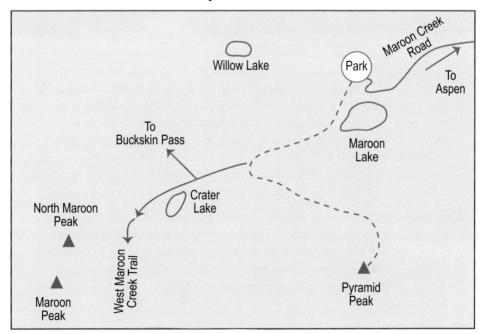

View from Pyramid Peak to The Maroon Bells

Getting There: Drive west on Colorado 82 from Aspen. Cross the Castle Creek Bridge and take the first left turn after the stoplight. This left turn leads to either the Castle Creek Road (left) or the Maroon Creek Road (right) at a fork within 200 yards from Colorado 82. Follow this right fork up the Maroon Creek Road for 9.9 miles from Colorado 82 and park at the end of the road at the Upper Maroon Lake parking area. (The Maroon Creek Road is blocked to private vehicles certain hours of each day. Check with Aspen or National Forest officials for this information.)

Comment: Pyramid Peak is considered one of the most formidable fourteeners in Colorado. No technical climbing is required but the route is quite steep and there are several places on the summit ridge where you must use your hands to ascend and descend. There are also a few exposed areas as you follow a cairn-marked trail for the last 1,000 feet of elevation gain up a series of ledges to the incredible vistas at the summit.

The Hike: Start to the south from the parking area. Descend some stairs to reach the West Maroon—Snowmass Trail that ascends the valley toward Crater Lake and the imposing Maroon Bells. Keep right at two junctions with trail signs. After about a mile you pass through an open rocky area before Crater Lake. Around the middle of this area there will be two cairns separated by about 500 feet on your left.

Each cairn marks a trail ascending to the left. Take either trail since they quickly join and follow a series of cairns that lead to a steep and primitive trail leading for a mile up into a large basin that ends at the foot of Pyramid Peak. Follow the trail for 0.25 mile over snow and talus and then leave the trail and head southeast over the rocks toward the upper left corner of the basin, with Pyramid Peak's summit to your right.

At the last grassy gulch on your right at the top of the basin, a trail leads upward to the east for 0.5 mile to reach a saddle at 12,980 feet. This ascent proceeds clockwise. The counterclockwise route is said to be more difficult. The summit block of Pyramid Peak is intimidating to your right. Do not lose hope and continue southwest up the ridge along a series of cairns and then over some snow to reach more cairns and a trail that initially passes around to the left and then goes to the right of the summit ridge before finishing up on the left (south) side of the summit.

The cairns are frequent and lead you over a few overhanging areas and up some easy rock climbing on a series of ledges to finally emerge about 100 yards north of the high point on an easy ridge. Proceed south to a high pile of rocks, a register cylinder, and a USGS benchmark at the top. The view from here can, of course, be magnificent. Especially striking are the Maroon Bells to the west. The return will be long but more clear because you can see the cairns better from above. Retrace your ascent route and stay on the trail. The ridge between the summit and saddle can be very unforgiving.

View north from Pyramid Peak to Snowmass Peak and Capitol Peak on the right

Neighboring towns: Georgetown, Silver Plume, Idaho Springs, Golden, Highland Park, Evergreen, Conifer
Size: 74,401 acres
Elevation: 8,400 to 14,264 feet
Miles of trails: 77

Mount Evans Wilderness is located approximately 40 miles west of Denver. The Mt. Evans Scenic Byway ascends a non-wilderness corridor into the center of the Wilderness. The road, two 14,000-foot peaks (14,264-foot Mt. Evans and 14,060-foot Mt. Bierstadt), and the close proximity to Denver have contributed to very heavy use. Despite the likelihood of encountering other users, the area offers several unique features worthy of a visit. Evidence of past glaciers can be seen in the steep granite cirques and glacial moraines surrounding the high peaks.

The Wilderness contains small regions of arctic tundra, which is rare south of the Arctic Circle. Unlike typical Colorado alpine tundra, which is dry and brittle once the snow recedes, arctic tundra holds numerous small pools of water. Vegetation ranges from lower spruce-fir and lodgepole forests, through 2,000-year-old bristlecone pines and krummholtz near treeline, to delicate alpine vegetation reaching all the way to the highest peaks. Deer and elk inhabit the subalpine areas, and bighorn sheep and mountain goats are common above treeline.

Mount Evans is accessed by a 105-mile trail network, 77 miles of which are within the Wilderness boundary.

Abyss Lake

Hike Distance: 3.6 miles each way
Hiking Time: Out in 119 minutes. Back in 118 minutes.
Starting Elevation: 13,300 feet
Highest Elevation: 13,523 feet (Epaulet Mountain)
Elevation Gain: 2,346 feet (includes 2,123 extra feet)
Trail: Last 1.5 miles only
Difficulty: Moderate
Relevant Maps: Trails Illustrated Number 104; Mount Evans 7½ minute;
    Clear Creek County; Arapaho National Forest

Getting There: From Interstate 70 in Idaho Springs, drive southeast on Colorado 103 for 13.1 miles to an intersection just above Echo Lake. Turn right onto the Mount Evans Road (Colorado 5) and drive 11.3 miles on the paved Mount Evans Road to the most southern switchback to the right and park off the road at this curve on the left.

Comment: Abyss Lake is tucked into a rocky bowl between two fourteeners—Mount Evans and Mount Bierstadt. The most frequently used route begins from Geneva Park on the south side of Guanella Pass Road and extends 8 miles to reach this very high lake. The route that I describe begins considerably above timberline from the Mount Evans Road, crosses Epaulet Mountain, then descends south in a clockwise direction, then west, and finally northwest into the drainage from Abyss Lake. A trail is then reached that ascends northwest to the lake. There is considerable elevation gain on the return to your high trailhead. This route avoids the dangerous steep rocks on the western flanks of Mount Evans and Epaulet Mountain.

Abyss Lake from Mount Bierstadt with Mount Evans beyond

The Hike: Begin south-southeast with no trail toward the rocky high point. Lose some elevation before crossing over the top of Epaulet Mountain at 13,523 feet. Abyss Lake will be visible to the northwest. Descend south about 0.6 mile over boulders and tundra and gradually curve in a clockwise direction. Then descend a grassy slope with occasional rocks to the northwest. Follow this slope down into the valley and generally persist in a northwesterly direction to finally reach the trail that has just crossed the Lake Fork of Scott Gomer Creek. Stay on the trail 1.5 miles up northwest to austere Abyss Lake surrounded by rocks. The formation called "The Sawtooth" looms above to the northwest. Mount Bierstadt lies to the south and Mount Evans to the north-northeast. I advise that you retrace your route back to your vehicle and avoid any attempts at a short cut. The return route is the more difficult half of this hike.

Abyss Lake

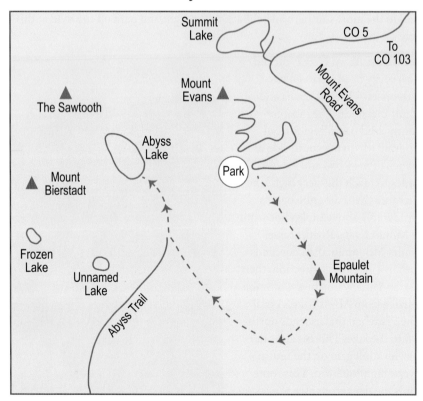

Gray Wolf Mountain

Hike Distance: 3.8 miles each way
Hiking Time: Up in 142 minutes. Down in 105 minutes.
Starting Elevation: 11,669 feet (Guanella Pass)
Highest Elevation: 13,602 feet
Elevation Gain: 2,523 feet (includes 590 extra feet)
Trail: First half
Difficulty: Moderate
Relevant Maps: Trails Illustrated Number 104; Mount Evans 7½ minute;
    Clear Creek County; Pike National Forest
Views from the Summit:
    NW to Rogers Peak
    SSE to Mount Spalding and Mount Bierstadt
    SE to Mount Evans
    SW to Square Top Mountain
    W to Grays Peak and Torreys Peak
    WSW to Pettingell Peak

Gray Wolf Mountain

Getting There: Drive to Guanella
Pass between Georgetown on
the north and Grant to the south.
Park in the lot on the east side of
the road.

Gray Wolf Mountain
from the south ridge

Comment: Gray Wolf Mountain lies within the massive Mount Evans Wilderness but receives far less hiker traffic than its higher neighboring peaks. The higher half of the route to the summit is a long trek over tundra and two false summits.

The Hike: Begin southeast on a trail from the parking area that quickly connects with the Mount Bierstadt Trail. After 1.1 miles at a large boulder on the right, leave the trail and hike to the north-northeast. After 0.25 mile a primitive trail will be encountered. Go right on this trail and follow it up through a grove of trees and to the right of a large rock formation. The trail ends and a few cairns direct you up the tundra. Continue north-northeast over rocks and tundra. Cross two subpeaks before reaching a rock pile atop Gray Wolf Mountain. The views are great from here. To return, retrace your ascent route to the south-southwest. Keep left of Square Top Mountain in the distance.

Gray Wolf Mountain

Hells Hole

Hike Distance: 4.2 miles each way
Hiking Time: Up in 140 minutes. Down in 102 minutes.
Starting Elevation: 9,600 feet
Highest Elevation: 11,200 feet

Hells Hole terminus

Elevation Gain: 2,000 feet (includes 200 extra feet each way)
Trail: All the way
Difficulty: Moderate
Relevant Maps: Trails Illustrated Number 104; Georgetown 7½ minute;
Clear Creek County; Arapaho National Forest

Getting There: From Interstate 70 at Idaho Springs, take Exit 240 and drive south-west on Colorado 103 for 6.7 miles. At a sharp curve to the left, take the West Chicago Creek Road on the right. Follow this good dirt road for 3 miles from Colorado 103 and park at the end of the road near the West Chicago Creek Campground.

Comment: The hike to lovely and misnamed Hells Hole passes through an extensive aspen forest and is an ideal choice around the third week in September, when the fall colors are at their most glorious. This beautiful high basin should carry a better name. The beauty of this area and the proximity to the Front Range make this a popular area for hikers and campers. Dogs must be kept on a leash on this hike.

The Hike: Start south from the trailhead signs and soon pass a trail register. Follow the good trail as it rises steeply in spots to a Mount Evans Wilderness sign at mile 1.2. The trail continues upward, parallel to West Chicago Creek on the left. Eventually break out of the forest with Sugarloaf Peak above on your right and rugged Gray Wolf Mountain ahead on the left.

With beautiful mountains on three sides, the trail begins a gentle descent and finally ends in the midst of the scenic upper basin, with a pond on the left and inviting grassy slopes above.

Hells Hole

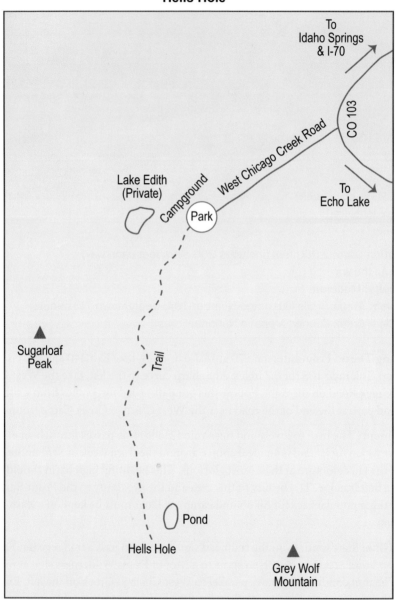

Lincoln Lake

Hike Distance: 5.5 miles each way
Hiking Time: Up in 138 minutes. Down in 126 minutes.
Starting Elevation: 10,650 feet
Highest Elevation: 11,680 feet
Elevation Gain: 2,320 feet (includes 645 extra feet each way)
Trail: All the way
Difficulty: More difficult
Relevant Maps: Trails Illustrated Number 104; Idaho Springs 7½ minute;
Harris Park 7½ minute; Clear Creek County; Arapaho National Forest

Lincoln Lake

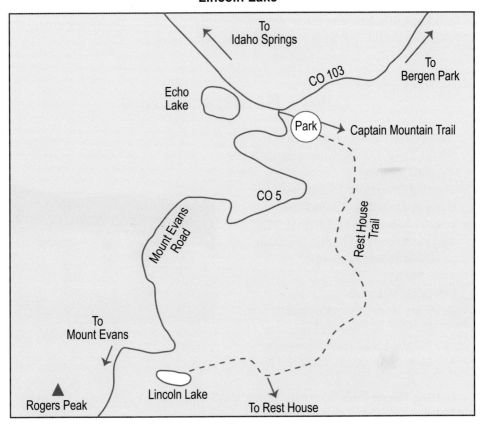

Getting There: From Interstate 70 in Idaho Springs, drive southeast on Colorado 103 for 13.1 miles to an intersection just above Echo Lake. Turn right onto the Mount Evans Road (Colorado 5) and within 100 feet turn left into a parking area.

Comment: The vast Mount Evans Wilderness, south of Idaho Springs, offers many hike destinations. One strenuous option is the trail to Lincoln Lake, which runs parallel to the Mount Evans Road.

The Hike: Begin on the trail to the southeast past campground toilets on your left. Soon pass a signboard and later a trail register along the right side of the clear trail. Ascend gradually for 1.2 miles to a ridge and then descend 0.9 mile to a bridge crossing of Vance Creek. The trail then rises 0.3 mile to an open gravel-covered area with cairns to mark the trail. Reenter the trees and continue another 2 miles to the onset of an extensive burn area. This remnant of an old forest fire extends 0.75 mile along the trail. Before you leave these barren tree trunks, keep straight at a trail junction and a sign. The left fork descends to the so-called Rest House. Continue northwest another 0.8 mile to reach Lincoln Lake below on your left. This small lake is surrounded by rocks, with the Mount Evans Road above to the west and Rogers Peak to the west-southwest. Rest up at the lake for the long return route with considerable elevation gains back to the initial ridge.

Lower Beartrack Lake

Hike Distance: 2.7 miles each way
Hiking Time: Out in 76 minutes. Back in 122 minutes.
Starting Elevation: 13,280 feet
Highest Elevation: 13,280 feet
Lowest Elevation: 11,140 feet
Elevation Gain: 2,180 feet (includes 20 extra feet each way)
Trail: None
Difficulty: Moderate
Relevant Maps: Trails Illustrated Number 104; Mount Evans 7½ minute; Harris Park 7½ minute; Clear Creek County; Arapaho National Forest

Lower Beartrack Lake

Getting There: From Interstate 70 in Idaho Springs, drive southeast on Colorado 103 for 13.1 miles to an intersection just above Echo Lake. Turn right onto the Mount Evans Road (Colorado 5) and go 10.8 miles and park off the road on the left before the road curves sharply to the right on its way up Mount Evans. The Mount Evans road requires a fee.

Beartrack Lakes

Comment: The easiest way to hike to Lower Beartrack Lake is to bushwhack (hiking without a trail) from the Mount Evans Road. The hiking trail route, which begins from near Echo Lake, is much longer.

Starting from above treeline, the hiker is rewarded with great vistas, meadows, canyons, and surrounding high peaks. This is a "Grand Canyon-like hike," with the descent first and the big elevation gain on the return. Mount Evans Wilderness rules apply. Be sure to use a compass or GPS and follow the suggested route. It is easy to become lost in this vast area.

The Hike: Begin hiking down to the east and gradually curve left (southeast) along a ridge that curves to the north. The route follows the ridge and traverses tundra with interspersed rocks. Proceed down to the eastern edge of the ridge at timberline and then descend to the right (south) another 450 feet to Lower Beartrack Lake, which receives few human visitors. There are five Beartrack Lakes and this lower one is the largest. Relax, rest and enjoy this calm, remote lake before the demanding return as you retrace your descent route.

Lower Beartrack Lake

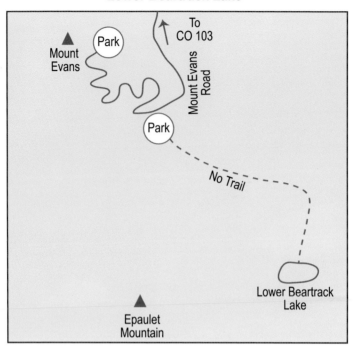

Mount Spalding

Hike Distance: 4 miles each way

Hiking Time: Up in 155 minutes. Down in 115 minutes.

Starting Elevation: 11,669 feet

Highest Elevation: 13,842 feet

Elevation Gain: 2,723 feet (includes 550 extra feet)

Trail: Intermittent for initial two thirds, none thereafter.

Difficulty: Moderate

Relevant Maps: Trails Illustrated Number 104; Mount Evans 7½ minute; Clear Creek County; Arapaho National Forest

Views from the Summit:

E to Summit Lake

SSW to Mount Bierstadt

SE to Mount Evans

WNW to Grays Peak and Torreys Peak

WSW to Squaretop Mountain

Mount Evans from Mount Spalding

Getting There: Drive to Guanella Pass between Grant to the south and George-town to the north and park in the large lot east of the pass. This point is 10.4 miles south from 4th and Rose Street in Georgetown.

Comment: The crowded parking area at Guanella Pass is mainly due to the popular fourteener, Mount Bierstadt. This hike, however, leads to Mount Spalding, one of the centennial peaks (the hundred highest mountains in Colorado), and traverses the lush tundra of the Mount Evans Wilderness. This outing is best in the latter weeks of the hiking season when the terrain is less wet and swampy.

The Hike: Begin by descending on the good, clear trail to Mount Bierstadt. After 0.5 mile, leave the trail and proceed to the east-northeast (left). Head toward the saddle between Gray Wolf Mountain on the left and Mount Spalding on the right. Before long, you are likely to join a trail leading in the desired direction. Follow this primitive trail up to a bench above a small pond and above timberline. From here follow cairns to a creek descending from the aforementioned saddle. The trail ends at this creek. From here ascend east or northeast on the flanks of Mount Spalding. The grade is gradual up to the summit rock and trail register, with great viewing in all directions. Return generally as you ascended and proceed toward the west in a line toward Lower Squaretop Lake across the valley.

Mount Spalding

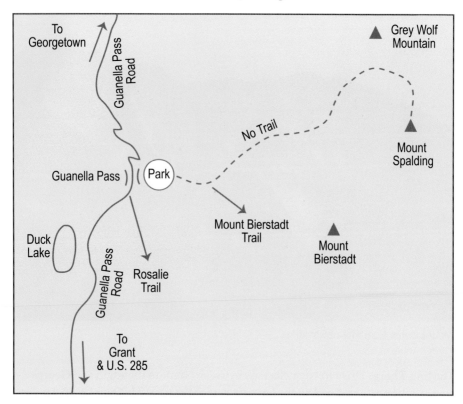

Spearhead Mountain

Hike Distance: 4.2 miles each way
Hiking Time: Up in 163 minutes. Down in 116 minutes (senior time).
Starting Elevation: 9,020 feet
Highest Elevation: 11,244 feet
Elevation Gain: 2,474 feet (includes 125 extra feet each way)
Trail: Initial 80%
Difficulty: Moderate
Relevant Maps: Trails Illustrated Number 104; Mount Logan 7½ minutes;
    Mount Evans 7½ minute; Park County Number Two; Pike National Forest
Views from the Summit:
    NNE to Bandit Peak
    NNW to Kataka Mountain
    S to North Twin Cone Peak

Getting There: From U.S. 285 at Grant ascend the Guanella Pass Road (also called Geneva Creek Road) for 2.8 miles and park on the right at the trailhead.

Comment: The Threemile Trail features many creek crossings and is at its best in mid to late June with rushing water. The final 20 percent is a steep uphill with no trail. The tree-covered summit is unmarked and some distant peaks can be seen.

The Hike: Begin north at a trail register and pass a Mount Evans Wilderness sign within 100 yards. Cross Threemile Creek twice before taking a right fork, with the left trail crossing the creek. The first sixteen creek crossings all have a two-log bridge. Pass a rocky wall on the right and continue up the valley. After the seventeenth creek crossing, reach two cairns alongside the trail and a prominent rock formation on the left. Leave the trail and ascend south steeply without a trail for the final 0.75 mile to the unmarked, tree-covered summit. Peek through the trees for views of adjacent peaks before retracing your route back to the trailhead.

Spearhead Mountain

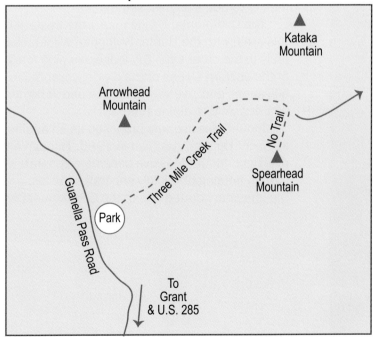

Neighboring towns: Leadville, Twin Lakes, Aspen,
   Glenwood Springs, Basalt
Size: 30,540 acres
Elevation: 10,000 to 14,421 feet
Miles of trails: 20

Mount Massive (14,421 feet), Colorado's second highest peak, and other mountains of the Sawatch Range have two distinctive characteristics: great height and a huge, sloping bulk that makes them relatively easy to climb. Nowhere along the Continental Divide does the ground rise higher than the Sawatch Range, the crest of this continent. Just south of the Wilderness stands Mount Elbert at 14,443 feet, Colorado's highest summit.

The Continental Divide marks the western boundary of this area, with the Hunter-Fryingpan Wilderness immediately to the other side. Dry lodgepole pine forests, typical of the eastern slopes of the divide, cover much of the lower elevations and give way to spruce and fir higher up before all trees yield to alpine tundra.

Mount Massive was proposed as an addition to the adjacent Hunter-Fryingpan in 1980. Through a technical oversight, Mount Massive became a separate Wilderness, though nothing physically separates the two areas except the imaginary dotted line of the Continental Divide.

Bald Eagle Mountain

Hike Distance: 2.2 miles each way

Hiking Time: Up in 76 minutes. Down in 60 minutes.

Starting Elevation: 10,360 feet

Highest Elevation: 11,913 feet

Elevation Gain: 1,573 feet (includes 10 extra feet each way)

Trail: Initial 1.2 miles

Difficulty: Easy

Relevant Maps: Trails Illustrated Numbers 126 and 127 or 149; Homestake
Reservoir 7½ minute; Lake County; San Isabel National Forest; Colorado Trail
Number Nine

Views from the Summit:

N to Homestake Peak

NNE to Jaque Peak

NNW to Mount of the Holy Cross and Galena Mountain

NE to Sugarloaf Mountain, Buckeye Peak, and Turquoise Lake

ENE to Mount Sherman

SSE to Mount Harvard and Mount Elbert

SSW to Mount Massive

SE to East Buffalo Peak and West Buffalo Peak

Bald Eagle Mountain

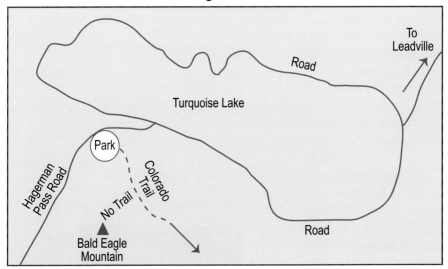

Getting There: From U.S. 24 (Harrison Avenue) in central Leadville, drive west on West 6th Street for 0.8 mile and turn right at the T. Keep left after 0.1 mile farther and go straight in 0.9 more miles. After 1.6 miles farther, take the right fork and stay on the paved road. Keep straight in 0.9 mile more and again at 1.4 miles. In 2 more miles take the left fork and leave the paved road (which will continue around Turquoise Lake). After driving 0.9 mile on this good dirt road, park on the side of the road where two sign poles indicate the Colorado Trail.

Comment: Bald Eagle Mountain lies west of a segment of the Colorado Trail (formerly the Main Range Trail) and provides good views of Mount Elbert and Mount Massive, the two highest peaks in Colorado.

The Hike: From the south side of the road begin southeast on the Colorado Trail and ascend in 1.2 miles to a dirt road running east and west. Leave the trail at this point and bushwhack up to the southwest. Pass under some power lines and in 1 mile from the Colorado Trail pass over the tundra to reach the flat summit area just above timberline. The high point lies on the southwest edge of the summit mesa and consists of several vertical boulders. A wooden tripod and a nearby USGS marker can be found at a lower point on the northeast part of the mesa.

Mount Massive

Hike Distance: 6.8 miles on the ascent. 6 miles on the descent (loop)
Hiking Time: Up in 224 minutes. Down in 149 minutes (loop)
Starting Elevation: 10,070 feet
Highest Elevation: 14,421 feet
Elevation Gain: 4,661 feet (includes 310 extra feet)
Trail: All the way
Difficulty: More difficult
Relevant Maps: Trails Illustrated Number 127 or 148; Mount Massive 7½ minute; Lake County; San Isabelle National Forest; Colorado Trail Nine and Ten
Views from the Summit:
    N to Galena Mountain
    NE to Turquoise Lake and
        Mount Lincoln
    E to Horeshoe Mountain
    ENE to Leadville and
        Mount Sherman
    SSE to La Plata Peak
    SE to Mount Elbert
    SW to North Halfmoon Lakes

Mount Massive

Mount Massive from U.S. 24

Getting There: Drive south on U.S. 24 from the stoplight in Leadville at East 6th Street for 4 miles and turn right (west) onto Colorado 300. After 0.3 mile on Colorado 300 turn left onto Lake County Road 11. After 1.2 miles on this road, turn right and follow this good dirt road past Halfmoon Campground for 5.5 miles and park in an open area on the right at the Mount Massive Trailhead. En route to this point take the left fork at mile 2.5 from Colorado 300. Your parking area is 6.7 miles from Colorado 300.

Comment: Mount Massive is the second highest peak in Colorado and the third highest in the contiguous United States. Although the distance to the top and the elevation gain are considerable, the hike is more pleasant than on many fourteeners due to the excellent gradual trail, the long walk over tundra above timberline before you reach the summit ridge, and the lack of special danger.

The Hike: Start north-northeast past a trail register. The first 3.1 miles of this hike are on the excellent Colorado Trail. During this segment you will cross South Willow Creek and Willow Creek. After 3.1 miles from the trailhead turn left (west) at a sign onto the Mount Massive Trail. Ascend more steeply to reach timberline. Continue west over a grassy area toward a saddle to the left of the summit. Enormous Mount Massive is well named and has several false summits.

Just before the saddle, the trail angles up to the right to reach the ridge. Ascend northwest on the faint trail, cross over a false summit and reach a cairn, pole, and register cylinder at the top. If the weather is clear, the prospect from this privileged position can be awe-inspiring.

To descend you may, of course, return along the ridge. However, I recommend you go down to the northeast and then turn right (east) using an intermittent faint trail over scree. After you get below the boulders to your right, turn farther right (southeast) across tundra past occasional cairns to regain the trail in the basin. This loop will save you time and energy. Be careful to avoid going too far down in the basin to the east. The return to the trailhead will be lengthy but unambiguous by trail.

Mount Massive

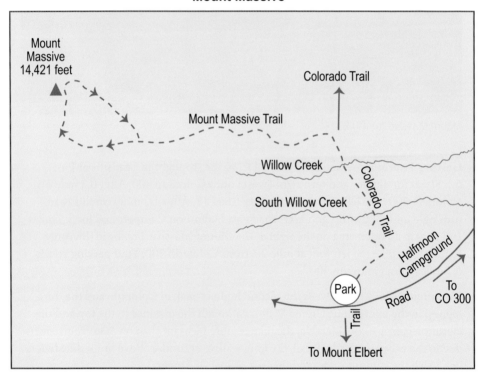

Mount Oklahoma

Hike Distance: 6 miles each way
Hiking Time: Up in 225 minutes. Down in 163 minutes.
Starting Elevation: 10,270 feet
Highest Elevation: 13,845 feet
Elevation Gain: 4,235 feet (includes 330 extra feet each way)
Trail: Initial third
Difficulty: More difficult

Relevant Maps: Trails Illustrated Number 127 or 148; Mount Champion 7½
   minute; Mount Massive 7½ minute; Lake County; San Isabel National Forest
Views from the Summit:
   NNW to Mount of the Holy Cross
   ENE to Mount Massive
   SSW to Mount Champion, Grizzly Peak, and Deer Mountain
   SE to Mount Elbert and French Mountain
   W to Mount Daly
   WNW to Mount Sopris
   WSW to Snowmass Mountain and Capitol Peak

Getting There: From U.S. 24 near the southern edge of Leadville, drive west on
Colorado 300 for 0.8 mile and turn left on Lake County Road 11. Set your odometer to zero. Go south on this road and turn right at mile 1.2 at the sign for Halfmoon Campground. Keep left at a fork at mile 2.6 and continue on the main, dirt
road. Continue past the Mount Elbert and Mount Massive Trailheads at mile 6.3
and 7 respectively. Cross Halfmoon Creek and continue to an intersection at mile
9.5. Road 110 continues another 0.5 mile to the right to reach the trailhead but may
require four-wheel drive. Therefore, park off road near this junction.

Comment: Although it is one of Colorado's 100 highest named peaks and lies on
the Continental Divide, Mount Oklahoma has no trail to its summit. The North
Halfmoon Trail takes the hiker up a splendid valley with Mount Massive on the
right but the way to Mount Oklahoma leaves the trail, reaches a grassy bench, and
then rises across a lengthy talus slope to some great vistas at the top.

Mount Oklahoma from North Halfmoon Lakes

The Hike: Begin hiking up Road 110 and reach the North Halfmoon Trailhead on the right after 0.5 mile. Continue on this good trail to the north through the forest and into the Mount Massive Wilderness. At 1.7 miles from the north Halfmoon Trailhead, pass through a large, open meadow. Your clockwise route up Mount Oklahoma will now be apparent ahead to the northwest. Follow the trail 0.5 mile to another clearing and notice two high, bare tree trunks (called snags) on the left. Continue another 185 yards by trail and just before the trail turns steeply up to the right at a small creek crossing, leave the trail and proceed northwest to reach the high, grassy, flat area below and left of Mount Oklahoma. From the flat, grassy area, ascend a steep green slope and keep south of the rocky buttress on your right. (Cross North Halfmoon Creek and pick a steep ascent route that doesn't lose elevation or pass through heavy willows.) Then you can either go directly up the rocks to the west or angle up to the left to reach the south ridge and high point, where a cairn and register cylinder appear. As you explore the great scenery from the summit area, walk west to a shoulder and look down to the Fryingpan valley and lakes. Return as you ascended.

Mount Oklahoma

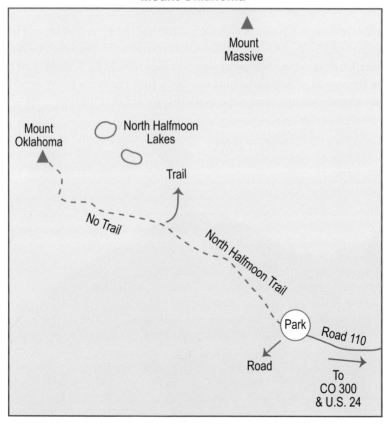

Swamp Lakes

Hike Distance: 3.3 miles each way
Hiking Time: Up in 98 minutes. Down in 80 minutes.
Starting Elevation: 9,629 feet
Highest Elevation: 10,950 feet
Elevation Gain: 1,676 feet (includes 355 extra feet)
Trail: All the way until the last 150 yards
Difficulty: Moderate
Relevant Maps: Trails Illustrated Number 127 or 148; Mount Massive 7½
minute; Lake County; San Isabel National Forest

Swamp Lakes

Getting There: From 6th Street in central Leadville, drive south and west on Harrison Avenue, which is U.S. 24, for 3.9 miles. Then turn west (right) on Colorado 300 and drive 2.3 miles on this road to the Leadville National Fish Hatchery on your left. Continue past, on Colorado 300, for another 0.1 mile and park off the road on the right.

Comment: The Swamp Lakes are seldom visited. The hike uses rough trails through sparse forest in the Mount Massive Wilderness and some route-finding is necessary. The rewards of this outing include a crossing of the Colorado Trail, the beautiful meadow of Kearney Park, and the lakes themselves beneath Mount Massive.

The Hike: The trail begins from a wilderness boundary sign, 50 yards north of your parking area, off of the left side of the road. Ascend to the south-southwest and quickly reach a trail register and signboard. Continue up the rough, old road with some steep sections. Around the 2-mile mark, join the Colorado Trail and continue left (southwest) with Kearney Park on the right. After just 75 yards, leave the Colorado Trail as it bends to the left and take the trail on the right leading west. Occasional cairns will help you stay on the main road. After a mile from the Colorado Trail, reach a fork and Rock Creek. Avoid the dirt road on the right, cross the creek to the west, and pass an old iron stove on the left. The trail ends in another 0.5 mile. At this point, descend east to a meadow and then south a100 yards to the Swamp Lakes in a large clearing with Mount Massive to the south-southwest. Be sure to retrace your identical route back to the trailhead. It is very easy to get lost in the forest.

Swamp Lakes

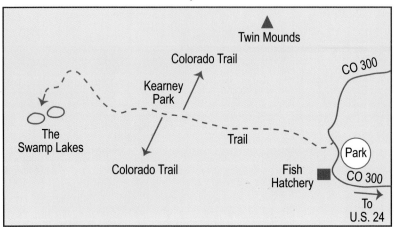

Neighboring towns: Ridgeway, Ouray, Camp Bird, Telluride
Size: 16,565 acres
Elevation: 9,600 to 14,150 feet
Miles of trails: 15

Mount Sneffels, a 14,150-foot intrusion of igneous rock on the eastern verge of this area, stands higher than any other point in the Wilderness. Members of the Hayden Survey purportedly named the peak after the Icelandic mountain in Jules Verne's *Journey to the Center of the Earth.* Sneffels is the Nordic word for snowfield. Westward stretches a sheer vertical world of sharp ridges, icy slopes, and ragged peaks. It makes for dangerous climbing typical of the San Juan Mountains, sometimes called America's Switzerland, a land of unsurpassed mountain drama. Technical climbers are still discovering new routes here, but loose volcanic rock often moves the rating from "dangerous" to "very dangerous."

In early fall, when light dustings of snow highlight the jagged terrain and the aspens have turned gold, you'll encounter an absolutely indescribable world of wonder.

Fifteen miles of trail, in the eastern and western portions, access some of the finest midsummer wildflower spectacles on earth, especially in Yankee Boy Basin just outside the eastern boundary, where you'll find the Blue Lakes Trail leading into the area for about 3.5 miles. The only lakes around, Blue Lakes huddle below the western flank of Mount Sneffels in a deep basin. The forbidding central region of the area is rugged beyond words and relatively seldom explored.

Mount Sneffels Wilderness Area

Blue Lakes

Hike Distance: 4.8 miles each way (Upper Lake)
Hiking Time: Up in 160 minutes. Down in 103 minutes.
Starting Elevation: 9,400 feet
Highest Elevation: 11,710 feet
Elevation Gain: 2,960 feet (includes 325 extra feet each way)
Trail: All the way
Difficulty: Moderate
Relevant Maps: Trails Illustrated Number 141; Telluride 7½ minute;
    Mount Sneffels 7½ minute; Ouray County Number Two; Uncompahgre
    National Forest

Blue Lakes from Mount Sneffels

Upper Blue Lake

Middle Blue Lake

Blue Lakes

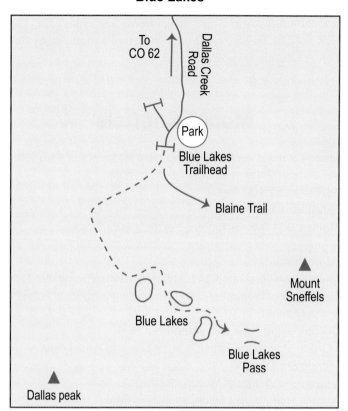

Getting There: From Colorado 62 between Ridgeway to the north and Placerville to the south, drive south on the Dallas Creek Road (Ouray 7) for 8.8 miles to the Blue Lakes Trailhead. En route keep left at mile 0.3 and at mile 1.6. Keep right at mile 2 and at mile 7.1. At mile 8.7, keep straight into the trailhead parking area. Regular cars can reach this trailhead.

Comment: Whenever you are in the Ridgeway, Ouray, or Telluride area, a beautiful lake and flowing water hike is the three Blue Lakes beneath towering Mount Sneffels in the Wilderness Area named after this fourteener. The last half of July and the first half of August should be the best times for flowers and rushing water.

The Hike: Begin hiking to the south and keep right at a signboard and register. The left fork is the Blains Trail. Ascend the clear trail and pass a Mount Sneffels Wilderness sign after 1.3 miles. With many high peaks rimming the basin, continue up to Lower Blue Lake (10,950 feet) at mile 3.3. The bright blue color of the lake will impress you. A trail sign just before the lower lake directs you to the east and over East Dallas Creek to the two higher lakes. The first part of this trail is rough and steep before several switchbacks make the ascent easier. After passing timberline, you will pass Middle Blue Lake (11,540 feet) below on the left before the final, gentle 0.3-mile rise to the Upper Blue Lake (11,690 feet). Mount Sneffels looms above to the north-northeast and the trail continues up to Blue Lakes Pass to the right of Mount Sneffels. Dallas Peak is impressive to the south. Enjoy this lovely high basin before returning as you ascended.

Mount Sneffels

Hike Distance: 1.2 miles each way (if you have a four-wheel drive vehicle)
Hiking Time: Up in 102 minutes. Down in 80 minutes
Starting Elevation: 12,400 feet
Highest Elevation: 14,150 feet
Elevation Gain: 1,924 feet (includes 87 extra feet each way)
Trail: All the way
Difficulty: More difficult
Relevant Maps: Trails Illustrated 141; Mount Sneffels 7½ minute; Telluride 7½ minute; Ouray County Number Two; Uncompahgre National Forest
Views from the Summit:
    NE to Uncompahgre Peak and Wetterhorn Peak
    ENE to Cirque Mountain, Teakettle Mountain and Potosi Peak
    S to Telluride Ski Area
    SSW to Lizard Head, Mount Wilson, and Wilson Peak
    SE to Wrights Lake, Mount Eolus, and Gilpin Peak
    SW to the Blue Lakes and Dallas Peak

Getting There: From Fourth Street in Ouray, drive south on Main Street, which becomes U.S. 550, for 0.4 mile. Then turn right onto Ouray County Road 361, which proceeds up Yankee Boy Basin. A user fee is charged. Regular cars can drive up this main road for 4.7 miles. The road continues up the basin with several intersections and can be driven by a four-wheel drive vehicle to road end at the Blue Lakes Trailhead (12,400 feet), 9.4 miles from U.S. 550. This hike description begins at road end.

Comment: The effort required in climbing Mount Sneffels, at the head of glorious Yankee Boy Basin southwest of Ouray, depends on how high you can drive on the road that becomes progressively rougher as you ascend. This hike description will begin at the Blue Lakes Trailhead, which lies 9.4 miles from U.S. Highway 550. Mount Sneffels is one of Colorado's exalted fourteeners and is mid-level difficulty.

The Hike: From the Blue Lakes Trailhead begin on the trail to the west-northwest. After 0.5 mile over open terrain with Wrights Lake below on your left, take a right fork at a trail sign. Now ascend north-northwest 800 feet over rocks and scree to the ridge. Then follow the faint trail up the rocky couloir on the left (north-north-

Mount Sneffels

west). The rocks are firmer here and snow often lingers until mid summer. After almost 500 feet of ascent, find a crack in the rocks on the left just before reaching the top of the couloir. Continue south through this narrow passage and then up another 100 feet to a register cylinder and rock pile at the summit. Enjoy the superb views before returning by your ascent route.

Mount Sneffels

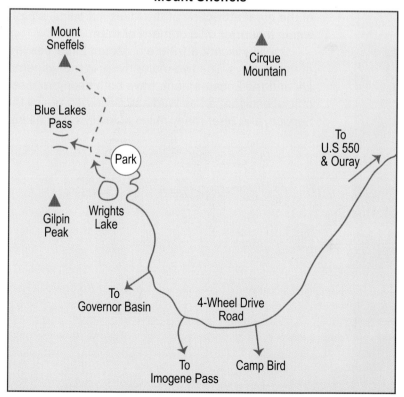

Mount Zirkel Wilderness Area

Neighboring towns: Steamboat Springs, Walden,
   Hahns Peak
Size: 159,935 acres
Elevation: 7,000 to 12,180 feet
Miles of trails: 155

One of the five original Colorado Wilderness Areas, major rivers flow from countless glacial lakes along this north-ernmost stretch of Colorado's Continental Divide. Mount Zirkel and its lakes owe their current shape to Pleistocene glaciation 15,000 years ago. State fish and game manag-ers stock various strains of trout in these lakes, a process that must be repeated on an annual basis. Forest Service managers hope to phase out the stocking of non-native brook and rainbow trout in favor of indigenous cutthroats. Since well over half of all visitors here fish, aerial stocking of these high mountain lakes will likely continue. Because of the great attraction of the lakes, camping is prohibited within a quarter mile of many of them.

One significant attribute of Mount Zirkel lies in its miles of river valleys. The two major rivers in the Wilderness, the Elk and the Encampment, have both been proposed for official designation as Wild and Scenic Rivers by the Forest Service, and offer many miles of lovely valley hiking.

Mount Zirkel

Hike Distance: 8.6 miles each way
Hiking Time: Up in 295 minutes. Down in 216 minutes.
Starting Elevation: 8,460 feet
Highest Elevation: 12,180 feet
Elevation Gain: 5,100 feet (includes 100 extra feet each way)
Trail: All the way to Red Dirt Pass, then an intermittent faint trail on ridge
Difficulty: Most difficult
Relevant Maps: Trails Illustrated Number 116; Mount Zirkel 7½ minute;
     Routt County Number Two; Route National Forest
Views from the Summit:
     SE to Flat Top Mountain
     WSW to Big Agnes Mountain

Mount Zirkel

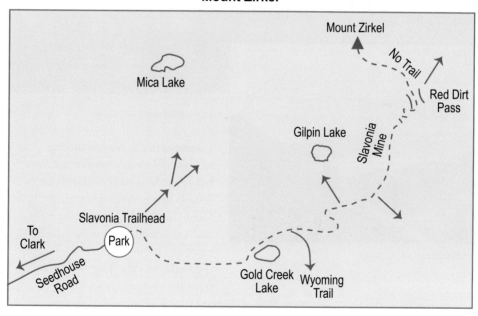

Getting There: From U.S. 40 west of Steamboat Springs, drive northwest on Routt County Road 19 for 17.6 miles (just past Clark). Then turn right onto Seedhouse Road and go 11.6 more miles to road end at the Slavonia Trailhead. En route take the right fork at mile 8.6, go straight at mile 9.2, and left at mile 9.4. Regular cars can reach this trailhead.

Mount Zirkel

Slavonia Work Camp

Comment: The hike to the top of Mount Zirkel requires tenacity but rewards handsomely with lush foliage, lots of rushing water, lovely Gold Creek Lake, connecting trails, and a magnificent basin with some ruins of a mining camp before reaching Red Dirt Pass. Then the views from the summit are special.

The peak and the Wilderness Area are named after Ferdinand Zirkel, a petrologist (student of rocks) of an earlier day. Mount Zirkel lies on the Continental Divide and the border between Routt and Jackson Counties. Although a modest "twelver," Mount Zirkel is more difficult to ascend than some "fourteeners" and is the highest mountain in Routt County. Easier water crossings will be possible in the second half of the hiking season.

The Hike: Begin northeast from the Slavonia Trailhead and within 75 yards reach a fork and a trail register. Avoid the left fork that leads to Gilpin Lake and Mica Lake and go right on the Gold Creek Trail. Soon cross a bridge. Two more creek crossings will be encountered before Gold Creek Lake. One uses two large logs, the other uses rocks. The good trail continues past lovely Gold Creek Lake and soon passes the Wyoming Trail, which leads to Ute Pass, on the right.

After a significant creek crossing, the trail rises above a vast meadow on the right. To reach a signed fork with a trail to Gilpin Lake ascending to the left, continue straight ahead and soon avoid a trail descending on the right. Proceed up in the basin and pass cabin ruins on the left at the former Slavonia work camp at 10,000 feet. In the upper basin a series of switchbacks brings you to Red Dirt Pass, well above treeline. Ascend northwest over rocks and tundra to a bench. Mount Zirkel's rocky summit ridge now comes into view. Cross a vast open plain and find an intermittent ridge trail that leads to the high point on the third hump on the right. The small rocky summit is unmarked. Enjoy the views and gather your strength for the long return to the Slavonia Trailhead.

Rainbow Lake

Hike Distance: 3.5 miles each way
Hiking Time: Up in 97 minutes. Down in 71 minutes.
Starting Elevation: 8,760 feet
Highest Elevation: 10,160 feet
Elevation Gain: 2,126 feet (includes 726 extra feet)
Trail: All the way
Difficulty: Moderate
Relevant Maps: Trails Illustrated Number 117; Pitchpine Mountain 7½ minute; Mount Ethel 7½ minute; Jackson County; Routt National Forest

Rainbow Lake

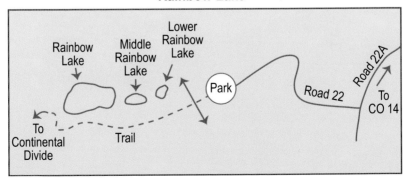

Getting There: From U.S. 40 east of Rabbit Ears Pass, drive north on Colorado 14 at Muddy Pass for 18.2 miles. Then turn left on Jackson County Road 26 and set your odometer to zero. At mile 3.3 on Jackson 26 take the left fork. At mile 7.8 turn right onto Road 5 and go to the right again at mile 8.5. Continue to mile 12.7 and again take the right fork. At mile 15.9 turn left onto Road 22 (which briefly becomes 22A) and at mile 20.2 go to the right. Turn left at mile 22.1. Enter the Routt National Forest and park at road end and the trailhead at mile 23.1. Most regular cars can reach the trailhead.

Comment: Lovely Rainbow Lake at the edge of North Park is the largest in the Mount Zirkel Wilderness. Reaching the trailhead is perhaps the most challenging aspect of this outing. Slide Lake and Roxy Ann Lake lie above Rainbow Lake and are popular backpacking destinations. Of the many Rainbow Lakes in Colorado, this one is special.

The Hike: From the trailhead signboard, follow the trail up to the southwest through dense forest. After a steep grade, the trail levels out as the Grizzly Trail is crossed after 0.75 mile. Continue straight and pass through an aspen forest before reaching the Mount Zirkel Wilderness boundary at mile 1.6. Ascend to a high point of this hike and begin your descent to Rainbow Lake. Shortly before your destination, Middle Rainbow Lake will appear down to the right. Continue over more rocky terrain and be delighted as you reach vast Rainbow Lake, with Mount Ethel, almost 12,000 feet, to the west. The trail continues up the valley to two more lakes before reaching the Continental Divide. Take some pictures before your easy return.

Rainbow Lake and Mount Ethel

Neighboring towns: Estes Park, Granby, Grand Lake
Size: 20,747 acres plus 9,620 acres of proposed
      Wilderness in adjacent Rocky Mountain National Park
Elevation: 8,900 to 12,940 feet
Miles of trails: 20

As its name suggests, Never Summer Wilderness gets hit with large amounts of rain and snow that collect on its storm-wracked peaks, which offer relatively gentle terrain and bear names that hint at their cloud-kissed heights: Cirrus, Cumulus, Stratus, and Nimbus. Seventeen summits rise above 12,000 feet, with Howard Mountain towering over all at 12,810 feet. Never Summer supplies water to three main rivers: the Colorado, the North Platte, and the Cache la Poudre.

In damp gulches above 10,000 feet, trees absorb the abundant moisture and grow old and exceptionally large. Spruce and fir in Bowen Gulch have been measured at four feet in diameter and estimated at 600 years in age. In the northern section, a series of ponds and bogs provide rare habitats for species seldom seen so far from north-country muskegs: wood frogs, bog bean, pygmy shrew, perhaps even a wolverine or two. Moose have been reintroduced and are faring well. Several lakes and streams hold trout.

Never Summer Wilderness Area

Bowen Mountain

Hike Distance: Up in 8.9 miles. Down in 7.2 miles (loop).
Hiking Time: Up in 256 minutes. Down 188 minutes.
Starting Elevation: 8,810 feet
Highest Elevation: 12,524 feet
Elevation Gain: 4,009 feet (includes 295 feet extra)
Trail: All the way to Bowen Pass on the ascent, from Blue Lake on the descent.
Difficulty: More difficult
Relevant Maps: Trails Illustrated Number 200; Grand Lake 7½ minute; Bowen
   Mountain 7½ minute; Grand County Number Two; Arapaho National Forest;
   Rocky Mountain National Park
Views from the Summit:
   NNE to the Never Summer Mountain Range
   NNW to Mount Richthofen and Parika Lake
   ESE to Longs Peak, Pagoda Mountain, Chiefs Head Peak, and
      McHenrys Peak
   SE to Blue Lake
   SW to Ruby Mountain, Parkview Mountain and Ruby Lake
   WNW to Bowen Pass

Getting There: Drive on U.S. 34 north of Granby to the Grand Lake entrance
to Rocky Mountain National Park. A fee is required. Drive north on U.S. 34 from
this entrance for 6.3 miles and turn left into the parking area for the Baker-Bowen
Trailhead.

Comment: Due to its location, the area around Bowen Mountain sees relatively
few hikers. Bowen Pass is on the Continental Divide. The pass, lake, gulch, and
mountain are named after James Bourn, who started the Wolverine Mine at the
base of Bowen Mountain in 1875. The name was incorrectly spelled and became Bowen.

The Hike: Start to the west over a bridge and pass around a barrier to vehicles.
Cross the lovely Kawuneeche Valley and take two successive left forks after 0.2 mile
from the trailhead. Continue southwest and pass a house on the right, cross a creek,
and soon enter the Arapaho National Forest at a sign. After 1.2 miles from this
entry point into the national forest keep right as an old road enters from the left.
In 0.2 mile farther, you will reach a T. Take the right fork that ascends to the west.
Cross the creek in 1 mile from the T, and in 0.2 mile farther cross the creek again at
a Never Summer Wilderness Area sign and a trail register.

Bowen Mountain

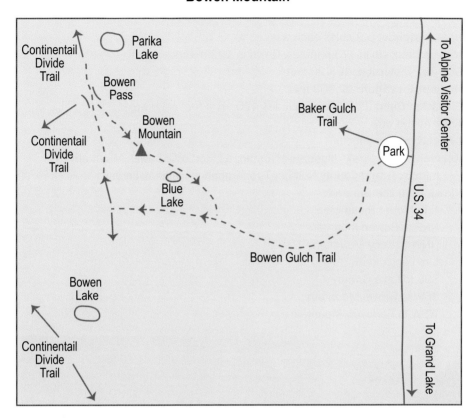

After another mile the trail turns back to the right and reaches a fork. Either fork is acceptable since the trails reconnect quickly. Soon you will pass a Bowen Gulch Trail sign on your right. In 0.8 mile from this sign you will reach a fork and a sign. The left fork goes to Bowen Lake. You go right and ascend more steeply. Pass a large cairn as the trees become sparse and in 1.8 miles from the fork to Bowen Lake you will reach Bowen Pass.

The trail continues west into the Routt National Forest. However, you ascend to your right (east) on a faint trail that soon disappears in the tundra. Continue northeast to the ridge and then continue east along the ridge over several cuts to a pole in a cairn and a USGS marker nearby to mark the summit. There is only one area with some exposure on the ridge and some easy handwork is necessary. Take in the great views, especially of the Never Summer Range to the north. Descend southeast over mostly tundra to Blue Lake. Pass over boulders to the left of the lake and reach a trail that returns you to the Bowen Gulch Trail sign that you encountered on your ascent. The return from here retraces your upward route.

Cascade Mountain

Hike Distance: 5.2 miles each way

Hiking Time: Up in 173 minutes. Down in 123 minutes.

Starting Elevation: 10,420 feet

Highest Elevation: 12,303 feet

Elevation Gain: 2,723 feet (includes 420 extra feet each way)

Trail: All the way

Difficulty: More difficult

Relevant Maps: Trails Illustrated Number 115 or 200; Bowen Mountain 7½ minute; Grand County Number Two; Arapahoe National Forest

Views from the Summit:
N to Mount Richthofen
NNE to Bowen Mountain
NNW to Ruby Mountain
E to Longs Peak
SSE to Lake Granby
SSW to Gravel Mountain
WSW to Parkview Mountain

Cascade Mountain

Getting There: From U.S. 40 west of Granby, drive north on U.S. 34 for 9.8 miles and turn left onto Grand County Road 4. Set your odometer to zero. Follow this good road for 3.2 miles and turn right at a fork onto Road 120, also called the

Cascade Mountain

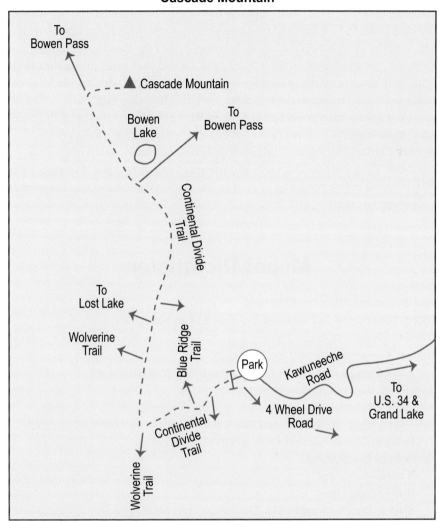

Kawuneeche Road. Follow this road for 9.6 miles from this fork to the road end and parking at the North Supply Trailhead. En route to this point, stay on the main road, follow the signs and go left at mile 8 and again at mile 9. Bear right at mile 9.5. Regular cars can reach this trailhead.

Comment: The Kawuneeche Road west of Grand Lake leads to a variety of outdoor trails. This hike begins at road end from the North Supply Trailhead and follows the Continental Divide Trail to Cascade Mountain in the Never Summer Wilderness. Much of this hike is along the Blue Ridge, with great views. No significant flowing water is encountered above the trailhead creek.

The Hike: Hike around the road barrier and reach signs and a junction at 0.5 mile. Continue up to the right (west) and stay on the Continental Divide Trail. Within 100 yards, take the left fork and continue west up to the Blue Ridge then a right turn onto the Wolverine Trail, which becomes part of the Continental Divide Trail. Continue past a side trail on the left to Lost Lake and later a trail descending to the right. Soon you are on the open ridge with two false summits of Cascade Mountain visible as the trail curves to the left, along the left side of the ridge.

A key intersection is reached at a Never Summer Wilderness sign with Bowen Lake visible below. Continue to the left (west) on the ridge and follow the trail another 2 miles before proceeding directly toward the true summit of Cascade Mountain. Go a few hundred yards and you reach a large rockpile at the top. Enjoy the panorama before returning by your ascent route. Be careful to take the correct trails at intersections.

Mount Richthofen

Hike Distance: 2.3 miles each way
Hiking Time: Up in 147 minutes. Down in 114 minutes.
Starting Elevation: 10,240 feet
Highest Elevation: 12,940 feet
Elevation Gain: 2,854 feet (includes an extra 77 feet each way)
Trail: Initial third and then intermittent
Difficulty: Moderate
Relevant Maps: Trails Illustrated Number 200; Mount Richthofen 7½ minute; Jackson County Number Four; Routt National Forest
Views from the Summit:
    N to Nokhu Crags
    NNE to Static Peak
    NNW to the Diamond Peaks, Clark Peak, and Lake Agnes
    NE to Long Draw Reservoir
    E to Hagues Peak, Mummy Mountain, Mount Fairchild, Ypsilon Mountain, Mount Chiquita, and Mount Chapin
    S to Tepee Mountain
    SE to Twin Sisters Peaks, Estes Cone, Longs Peak, Pagoda Mountain, Chiefs Head Peak, and McHenrys Peak

Getting There: From U.S. 287 northwest of Fort Collins, drive west on Colorado 14 up beautiful Poudre Canyon for 59.2 miles to Cameron Pass. Continue over the pass for 2.4 miles and turn left onto an excellent dirt road. After 0.6 mile farther, turn right, cross a bridge, ascend, and take a right fork that dead ends at a parking area and the Lake Agnes Trailhead. Park here.

Comment: This peak is named after Baron Ferdinand von Richthofen, a German geologist who worked in the western United States between 1862 and 1868. It forms part of the Continental Divide and the boundary of Rocky Mountain National Park with the Never Summer Wilderness. Mount Richthofen is the highest mountain in the Never Summer Range.

The Hike: Begin south at the trail sign (there is a cabin and toilets to your right). Cross a bridge and after a left fork, ascend along the drainage to Lake Agnes with an island in its middle. Continue by trail around the lake to your right to a boulder field at the south end of the lake. Your route now continues upward to the south toward a saddle with Mount Richthofen's summit ridge to the left and an unnamed peak to the right. Rise past timberline over boulders and talus and continue over some scree to the grassy saddle. Then turn left (east) and ascend the ridge. Gain the right edge of the ridge as soon as possible since the rock will be firmer there. Continue over a false summit and follow the broad ridge east up into a final easy couloir that ends at a rock shelter, cairn, and metal trail register at the top. Some easy handwork is needed on some of the scree and on the ridge. Avoid the temptation to try a different route back and retrace your ascent route.

Mount Richthofen

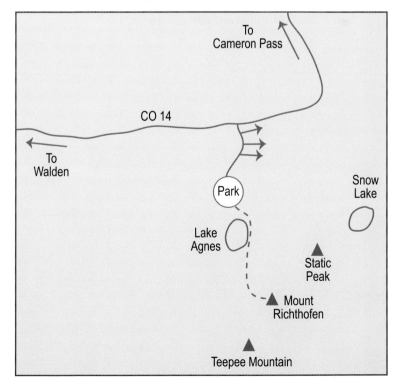

Neighboring towns: Lake City, Gunnison, Creede
Size: 61,510 acres
Elevation: 8,600 to 12,600 feet
Miles of trails: 45

In this Wilderness, the northern verge of the San Juan Mountains reaches out into the Gunnison Basin, a dry land of sagebrush meadows dotted with fish-filled lakes, including Powderhorn Lakes. Scoured by glaciation, the Calf Creek and Cannibal Plateaus are said to be the largest unbroken expanses of alpine tundra in the Lower 48, and the feeling of sheer vastness unparalleled in Colorado.

You'll discover terrain rolling along at around 12,000 feet with views of even higher mountains in the Elk, Sawatch, and San Juan Ranges, broken only by several escarpments that stand especially lovely in the light of the setting sun. Cannibal Plateau was named for Colorado's famous man-eater, Alferd Packer, who supposedly dined on five friends while lost near here during the winter of 1874. Elk and mule deer roam the plateaus and pass through the stands of aspen, pine, spruce, and fir that blanket the lower elevations.

Lower Powderhorn Lake

Hike Distance: 4 miles each way
Hiking Time: Up in 98 minutes. Down in 93 minutes.
Starting Elevation: 11,000 feet
Highest Elevation: 11,670 feet
Elevation Gain: 1,640 feet (includes 485 extra feet each way)
Trail: All the way
Difficulty: Moderate
Relevant Maps: Trails Illustrated Number 245 (partial); Powderhorn Lakes
 7½ minute; Gunnison Country Number Six; Hinsdale County Number One;
 Gunnison Basin Public Lands

Powderhorn Lakes Trail

Getting There: From U.S. 50 west of Gunnison and at the eastern edge of Blue Mesa Reservoir, drive south on Colorado 149 for 20.4 miles. Or drive north from 5th Street and Gunnison Avenue in Lake City for 24.3 miles on Colorado 149. Then turn south on Gunnison County Road 58, which is also called Forest Road 3033 or the Indian Creek Road. Follow this good dirt road for 10.2 miles to the trailhead and the end of the road. Regular cars can reach this point.

Comment: The hike to Lower Powderhorn Lake in the Powderhorn Wilderness takes you through a lovely, vast meadow to a remote high country lake. Located west of the Cannibal Plateau, the two Powderhorn lakes lie between Gunnison to the north and Lake City to the south. The good trail fades away beyond the lower lake, rendering the upper lake more difficult to access.

The Hike: From the signboard at the parking area, begin walking on the good trail into the forest to the south-southwest. Ascend past a trail register and a Wilderness sign to a ridge and descend to cross an open plain. Then reenter the woods. Lose some elevation and pass a pond on the right. Eventually reach a clearing and a signed trail on the left saying "Hidden Lake." Continue straight ahead and pass several ponds on the left before reaching beautiful Lower Powerhorn Lake, which is enclosed by grass and trees on three sides and a rocky ridge on the left. Be sure to have a 7½ minute map if you wish to reach the upper lake before your return.

Lower Powderhorn Lake

Lower Powderhorn Lake

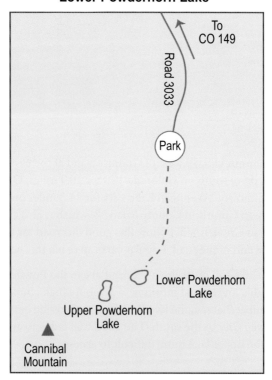

Neighboring towns: Dillon, Breckenridge, Vail
Size: 13,175 acres
Elevation: 9,127 to 12,757 feet
Miles of trails: 41

Most people heading into Summit County on I-70 from the Front Range don't realize that the mountains to their right immediately exiting the Eisenhower Tunnel are the southern boundary of the Ptarmigan Peak Wilderness.

The Wilderness has a very diverse topography ranging from aspen and lodgepole pine forests at the lower elevations, then on to Englemann spruce at the middle elevations, and on up to alpine tundra at the highest elevations. There are only a few trails that enter the Ptarmigan Peak Wilderness, all of which join with the Ute Pass Trail providing access to the spine of the Williams Fork Mountains from Ute Pass in the north to Ptarmigan Pass in the south. Upon reaching the summit of Ptarmigan Pass, elevation 11,777 feet, travelers may continue northeast into the Sulphur Ranger District of the Arapaho National Forest into the Middle and South Fork drainages of the Williams Fork River.

Ptarmigan Peak Wilderness Area

Ptarmigan Pass

Hike Distance: 4.2 miles each way
Hiking Time: Up in 135 minutes. Down in 98 minutes.
Starting Elevation: 9,440 feet
Highest Elevation: 11,777 feet
Elevation Gain: 2,647 feet (includes 155 extra feet each way)
Trail: Initial 2.5 miles (but poorly defined in places)
Difficulty: Moderate
Relevant Maps: Trails Illustrated Number 108; Dillon 7½ minute; Summit
County Number Two; Arapaho National Forest Dillon Ranger District

Ptarmigan Pass

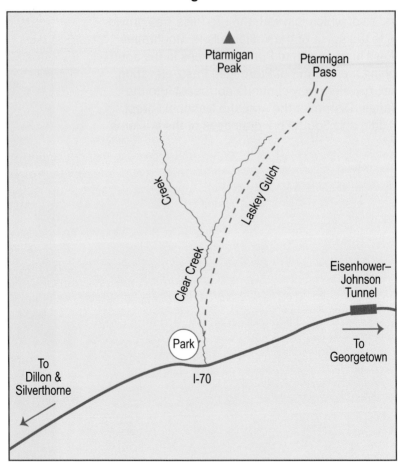

Getting There: Drive west on Interstate 70 from the western end of the Eisenhower-Johnson Tunnel for 5.3 miles and park in the open area off the right side of the highway.

Comment: Could you enjoy hiking on a primitive trail that extends 2.5 miles along a gentle creek, lined by heavy aspen groves, with few other hikers, up to a pass at timberline with great scenery? Then this hike to isolated Ptarmigan Pass, on the Continental Divide in the Ptarmigan Peak Wilderness, is worth a try. The middle of September would be a good time for this outing with the aspen changing color.

The Hike: Begin north on a clear trail that curves down to two creek crossings and then turns left and ascends the valley. This trail will fade away at times and is very primitive in spots but always keep the creek on your left and you won't become lost. Up the valley you will pass a talus and boulder slope on the right and a creek descending from the left to join the creek that you are following. After 2 miles the trail disappears as you continue north along the creek up Laskey Gulch. Cross some easy rocky areas and soon reach an open basin with the pass visible above. A trail then takes you to the pass by way of some switchbacks. At Ptarmigan Pass there is a sign and a junction with the Continental Divide Trail. Ptarmigan Peak lies up the ridge to the west. The views down to Dillon Reservoir to the south-southwest are special. Enjoy the grandeur before following the creek back down to your vehicle.

Ute Peak (via Acorn Creek Trail)

Hike Distance: 5.5 miles each way
Hiking Time: Up in 188 minutes. Down in 125 minutes.
Starting Elevation: 8,600 feet
Highest Elevation: 12,303 feet
Elevation Gain: 4,253 feet (includes 275 extra feet each way)
Trail: All the way until the final 1.25 miles on the ridge
Difficulty: More difficult
Relevant Maps: Trails Illustrated Number 107; Squaw Creek 7½ minute; Ute Peak 7½ minute; Summit County Number One; Arapaho National Forest Dillion Ranger District
Views from the Summit:
NNW to Parkview Mountain
NW to Williams Peak
S to Peak One
SSE to Ptarmigan Peak, Mount Guyot, and Bald Mountain
SSW to Buffalo Mountain

View south from Ute Peak toward Ptarmigan Peak

SE to Torreys Peak and Grays Peak
SW to Mount Powell
WNW to Green Mountain Reservoir

Ute Peak

Getting There: From Interstate 70 take Exit 205 at Dillon and Silverthorne. Drive north on Colorado 9 for 10.9 miles and then turn right onto Road 2400. Follow this road for 1 mile to the Acorn Creek parking area. En route to the parking area keep left at 0.2 mile and right at 0.4 mile from Colorado 9.

Comment: With the lengthening of the Acorn Creek Trail all the way to the ridge at 11,200 feet, a delightful but strenuous alternate route up Ute Peak is now available. Aspen groves and several lush open meadows are encountered on the way. There are some confusing side trails so be sure to bring a compass. This area is little used except in the fall hunting season. En route you traverse the Ptarmigan Peak Wilderness.

Ute Peak is one of the Williams Fork Mountains and lies on the boundary between Summit and Grand Counties.

The Hike: Start hiking at the trailhead sign and register south of the parking area. Proceed east through a gate and within 150 yards take the left trail fork. After 75 yards, take another left fork and soon cross Acorn Creek on a two-log bridge. This creek crossing is 0.5 mile from the trailhead. Continue north through lovely terrain with Ute Peak high above and straight ahead. The trail becomes faint as you pass through two open meadows. At the upper edge of each meadow, however, the trail resumes. At a third meadow, 2.25 miles from the trailhead, a trail resumes up and to the right (southeast) to the top of a grassy bench. Follow this trail up to a ridge and then curve left and up more steeply. An adequate shelf trail then rises steeply in 1.8 miles from the last meadow.

At the ridge, turn left (north) on a faint trail that soon ends. Continue up over tundra past timberline toward the highest peak to your left (north-northwest). The hump on the right is a subpeak of Ute Peak. At the summit there is a sign in a rock pile, two benchmarks, and a register cylinder. Enjoy the views, especially of the Gore Range. Return by your ascent route and be sure to use a compass and take the correct forks. Key turns are (a) where the Acorn Creek Trail ends at the ridge and (b) as you descend the shelf trail from the ridge be sure to take the right fork around the grassy bench back to the third meadow. A trail continues straight at this fork and makes for a more difficult return. If you do get lost on the descent, bear northwest and keep Acorn Creek on your left until you cross it near the trailhead.

Ute Peak

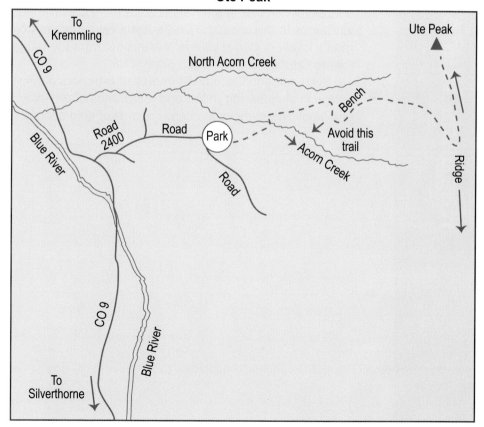

Neighboring towns: Marble, Crested Butte, Aspen
Size: 65,393 acres
Elevation: 7,000 to 13,462 feet
Miles of trails: 49

Prominent rocky slopes striking skyward to a serrated ridge give Raggeds Wilderness its well-deserved name. Ragged Mountain in the northern half rises to 12,094 feet, but other wonderfully scenic peaks crest higher.

Complementing these inaccessible peaks, the Dark Canyon of Anthracite Creek roars below, carving a deep gorge through surrounding benchlands of aspen and spruce. Colorful peaks and prominent intrusive dikes of the Ruby Range angle north through the area's eastern end, perpendicular to the Raggeds. Capping the diversity of landforms in this area, the Oh-Be-Joyful Valley, one of Colorado's loveliest glacial valleys, sweeps out from the range toward Crested Butte and the Slate River.

Every fall, you'll see great unbroken expanses of aspen ablaze in shimmering yellow and rock bands of red, gray, and black rising above a patchwork quilt of gold and green.

Blue Lake (Gunnison County)

Hike Distance: 5.8 miles each way
Hiking Time: Up in 185 minutes. Down in 160 minutes.
Starting Elevation: 8,950 feet
Highest Elevation: 11,055 feet
Elevation Gain: 2,905 feet (includes 400 extra feet each way)
Trail: All the way until the last 200 yards
Difficulty: More difficult
Relevant Maps: Trails Illustrated Number 133; Oh-Be-Joyful 7½ minute;
Gunnison County Number Two; Gunnison Basin

Getting There: From Elk Avenue in Crested Butte, drive north on Gothic Road (Sixth Street) for 0.8 mile and turn left onto Gunnison County Road 734 (Slate River Road). Follow this good, dirt road for 4.5 miles and turn left onto the Oh-Be-Joyful Road. Descend this road for 0.5 mile to the Slate River and park off the road just before it crosses through the waters of the river. Regular cars can reach this point. (Four-wheel drive is needed to continue across the river and ascend 1.5 more miles to road end at the Raggeds Wilderness boundary.)

Comment: This hike along Oh-Be-Joyful Creek takes you into the lush and lovely Raggeds Wilderness. Rushing water and high peaks abound. August and September are the best times for this outing due to the river crossing.

Blue Lake

The Hike: Start your hike with 50 yards of wading across the Slate River and continue on the road as it turns left before steeply ascending to the right. The rough road proceeds northwest and ends at the Wilderness boundary and a register. The trail continues up through the beautiful valley for 2.1 more miles before passing a cabin ruin on the left. A side trail soon leads west (left) toward a prominent rocky subpeak to the west. Ascend steeply to an unmarked fork at 10,500 feet. Go left (south) at this fork and soon enter an open basin ringed by peaks.

At 0.75 mile past this fork, the trail may be obscured by snow even in the latter parts of the summer. Above to the right you will see several waterfalls descending from two grassy benches. Cross the outflow and ascend without trail in a clockwise direction to reach the upper bench and narrow Blue Lake beneath Purple Peak and Afley Peak. From the lake you can see the trail, which you left, continuing east over the ridge to the right of Garfield Peak. Drink in the scenery before the lengthy return by your ascent route.

Blue Lake - Raggeds Wilderness

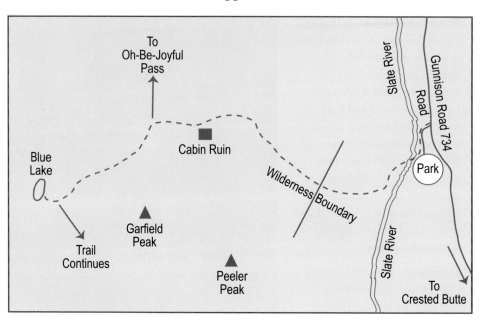

Neighboring towns: Gould, Walden, Cowdery, Glendevey
Size: 73,868 acres
Elevation: 8,400 to 12,951 feet
Miles of trails: 85

Just before the Front Range of the Colorado Rockies fades into Wyoming's Medicine Bow Mountains, the Rawah Wilderness protects a scenic high country of U-shaped glacier-carved valleys and peaks. To the south and west of the area lies an almost roadless Colorado State Forest, an unofficial extension of the Wilderness. Melting snow fills twenty-six lakes within the area. On the upper-forested slopes of the mountains, especially in the southern section, clusters of old-growth spruce and fir abound.

There are twenty-five named lakes, ranging in size from 5 to 39 acres. This high alpine area contains the headwaters of the McIntyre, Rawah, and Fall Creeks, as well as the Laramie River. The Rawahs are host to mammals such as elk, moose, mule deer, black bear, bighorn sheep, marmot, and beaver. There are many species of birds including the red-tailed hawk, white-tailed ptarmigan, golden eagle, raven, Steller's Jay, and a variety of warblers. Lakes and streams are inhabited with lake, cutthroat, rainbow, and brown trout. Graylings are also found in this area.

The Rawah Wilderness is becoming very popular with summer backpackers, hikers, and anglers. It is also popular with hunters in the fall. To encounter the fewest people, plan your trip for mid-week and use the less popular trails.

Rawah Wilderness Area

Blue Lake (Larimer County)

Hike Distance: 5.1 miles each way
Hiking Time: Up in 112 minutes. Down in 88 minutes.
Starting Elevation: 9,482 feet
Lowest Elevation: 9,424 feet
Highest Elevation: 10,805 feet
Elevation Gain: 1,859 feet (includes 478 extra feet)
Trail: All the way
Difficulty: Moderate
Relevant Maps: Trails Illustrated Number 112; Chambers Lake 7½ minute;
Clark Peak 7½ minute; Larimer County Number Three; Roosevelt
National Forest

Blue Lake

Getting There: From the junction with U.S. 287 north of Fort Collins, drive west on Colorado 14 up Poudre Canyon for 53 miles and park at the Blue Lake Trailhead on the right.

Comment: This is one of many Colorado Blue Lakes. It is one of the more accessible destinations in the Rawah Wilderness.

The Hike: Start out to the west and descend to a bridge crossing of Sawmill Creek. Follow the good trail with occasional views of Chambers Lake below on the right. At 2.1 miles from the trailhead cross Fall Creek on a bridge and rise to a Wilderness sign. Continue up 3 more miles from the Fall Creek crossing to an overlook of Blue Lake on the right. Clark Peak is visible above on the left and Cameron Peak on the right.

Blue Lake

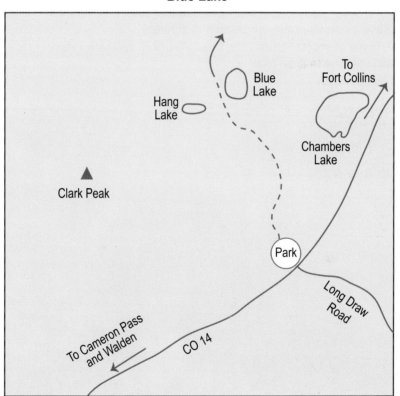

Clark Peak

Hike Distance: 6.5 miles each way
Hiking Time: Up in 215 minutes. Down in 175 minutes.
Starting Elevation: 9,482 feet
Lowest Elevation: 9,424 feet
Highest Elevation: 12,951 feet
Elevation Gain: 4,005 feet (includes 478 extra feet each way)

Trail: All the way to Blue Lake
Difficulty: More difficult
Relevant Maps: Trails Illustrated Number 112; Chambers Lake 7½ minute;
    Clark Peak 7½ minute; Larimer County Number Three; Roosevelt
    National Forest
Views from the Summit:
    N to Timber Lake
    NE to Cameron Peak
    NW to South Rawah Peak and North Rawah Peak
    SSE to the Nokhu Crags and Mount Richthofen
    SE to the Diamond Peaks, Long Draw Reservoir, and Longs Peak
    SW to North Michigan Lake
    N to North Park

Cameron Peak from Clark Peak

Getting There: From its junction with U.S. 287 northwest of Fort Collins, drive west on Colorado 14 up Poudre Canyon for 53 miles and park on the right at the Blue Lake Trailhead.

Comment: Clark Peak is the highest in the Rawah Range, which is a southern projection of the Medicine Bow Mountains. Rawah is an Indian word for wilderness.

The Rawah Wilderness is full of lakes, trails, and 12,000-foot peaks. There are no special problems in reaching the summit over the extensive tundra.

The Hike: Begin to the west-northwest from the trailhead sign. The lower parts of the trail are well marked by blue diamond symbols on the trees. Lose some elevation before quickly crossing Sawmill Creek on a bridge. The trail then will curve toward the northwest with some views of Chambers Lake to your right. After 2.1 miles from the trailhead, you will cross Fall Creek on a bridge and pass a Rawah Wilderness sign. After 3 more miles from the Fall Creek crossing you will arrive at an overlook of Blue Lake to your right.

Leave the trail at this point and ascend the tundra to your left. Proceeding west you will bushwhack past Hang Lake on your right. Work your way to the west and up to a ridge and then go left to the summit with a rock pile, embedded wooden stake, and a trail register. The views are especially impressive to the northwest and the Rawah Wilderness with its numerous lakes. On your descent resist the urge to descend directly to the east to regain the trail below Blue Lake. The easier and equally rapid way is to retrace your ascent route by way of Blue Lake.

Clark Peak

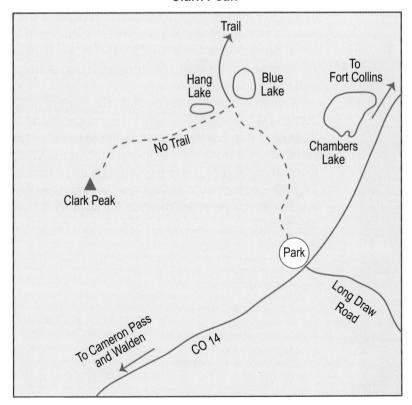

Neighboring towns: Salida, Poncha Springs, Wellsville, Howard, Coaldale, Alamosa, Westcliffe
Size: 226,420 acres
Elevation: 8,000 to 14,294 feet
Miles of trails: 180

Like the famous Teton's of Wyoming, the Sangre de Christo Mountains are fault-block mountains located in south-central Colorado. Sharply uplifted blocks, jagged ridges, and soaring pinnacles characterize the Sangre de Cristos and create one of the most stunning landscapes of the southern Rocky Mountains. The third largest Wilderness in the state, the Sangre de Cristo Wilderness is named after the mountain range of which the northern most portion it contains.

Surrounded on either side by broad valleys, the Sangre de Cristo range forms the eastern perimeter of the San Luis Valley and the western edge of the Wet Mountain Valley. Great Sand Dunes National Park and Preserve abuts the Wilderness on the west and provides much of the tourism and visitors to this area.

Due to the fault block geology, the Sangre de Cristo Wilderness is crisscrossed east to west by short and narrow drainages that are terminated by impassable ridges and cliffs. Many, if not all of the hiking trails in the Wilderness follow these drainages to high altitude lakes or the several 14,000-foot high peaks—Crestone Needle, Crestone Peak, and Humboldt Peak are three of the ten peaks that exceed this height.

Crestone Needle

Hike Distance: 8.2 miles to Lower South Colony Lake and 4.9 miles to Crestone Needle. Total 13.1 miles each way.

Hiking Time: Day 1: 186 minutes to Lower South Colony Lake. Day 2: To the summit in 163 minutes. Down to Lower South Colony Lake in 140 minutes. Lake to trailhead in 150 minutes.

Starting Elevation: 8,820 feet

Highest Elevation: 14,197 feet

Elevation Gain: 5,777 feet (includes 200 extra feet each way)

Day 1: 2,930 feet

Day 2: 2,847 feet

Trail: All the way with some gaps between lake and low point of the ridge

Difficulty: Most difficult (considerable easy hand work needed up the final 0.5 mile)

Relevant Maps: Trails Illustrated 138; Crestone Peak 7½ minute; Beck Mountain 7½ minute; Custer County Number One; San Isabel National Forest

Views from the Summit:

NNE to Upper South Colony Lake

NE to Humboldt Peak and Lower South Colony Lake

ESE to Broken Hand Peak

SSW to the San Luis Valley

SW to Pico Asilado

W to Crestone Peak

WNW to Kit Carson Peak and Challenger Point

Getting There: From the intersection of Colorado 69 and Colorado 96 in the town of Westcliffe, drive southeast on Colorado 69 for 4.7 miles. Then turn right onto Road 119, which is also called Colfax Lane. Continue 5.4 miles on this straight, level road to a T. Turn right (west) on Road 120 and continue straight and park off the road at 1.5 miles from the T before the road becomes too rough for regular cars and is blocked for the 6.3 miles to the road end.

Comment: Crestone Needle is one of the more dangerous fourteeners. The final ascent gully is very exposed to falling rock and when wet it can be treacherous. In 1982, seven hikers were killed on this peak. Crestone Needle forms part of the boundary between Custer and Saguache Counties and the San Isabel and Rio Grande National Forests.

The Hike: Begin west up the rough road. In 1.5 miles you will pass the national forest boundary and 0.7 mile farther you cross an intersection with the Rainbow Trail.

In 0.6 mile farther cross South Colony Creek as you continue southwest along the creek, staying on the main road. After 5.4 miles from the trailhead, keep left on the road and avoid the trail to your right that leads to the Upper South Colony Lake. Cross the creek again and continue up to the end of the road beneath Broken Hand Peak. The trail to the Lower South Colony Lake proceeds northwest from the parking area for just over 0.5 mile to some good campsites near the lake.

The ascent from Lower South Colony Lake begins west-southwest to the left of the lake and a pool. The trail is clear as you ascend to the low point of the ridge, but becomes less visible close to the ridge.

Some easy hand work may be needed just before the saddle is reached. Broken Hand Peak will be on your left and the pinnacles of Crestone Needle on your right. It will be about 2 miles from the lake to this point. Then continue northwest up the south side of the ridge on a clear trail. In about 0.3 mile, the first of a series of cairns appear to supplement the trail. 0.5 mile lose about 50 feet of elevation and turn right to ascend a wide, long, rocky gully that leads to the summit. Some flowing water will likely be present in this gully. Ascend northwest keeping the water on your left. The rock is firm and there are many foot and handholds when necessary. Cairns mark the way at intervals. After about 2 miles ascending this gully, you will reach a ridge. Turn left (west-southwest) and the high point is 150 feet farther. A small cairn and register cylinder mark the small summit. Be careful to retrace your ascent route. It is easy to lose your route and either descend too low into the wide gully or to stray too far north near the ridge.

Crestone Needle and Peak

Crestone Needle and Peak

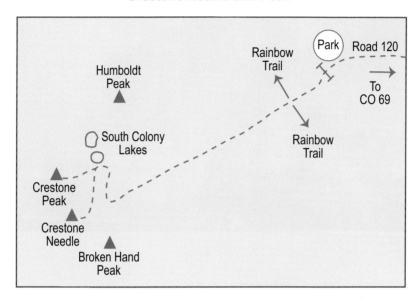

Crestone Peak

Hike Distance: 6.1 miles each way
Hiking Time: Up in 280 minutes. Down in 195 minutes.
Starting Elevation: 11,045 feet (reached on four-wheel drive road)
Highest Elevation: 14,294 feet
Elevation Gain: 4,504 feet (includes 1,255 extra feet)
Trail: Virtually all the way—faint in spots
Difficulty: Most difficult
Relevant Maps: Trails Illustrated Number 138; Crestone Peak 7½ minute;
    Custer County Number One; San Isabel National Forest
Views from the Summit:
    NNE to Humboldt Peak
    NNW to Colony Baldy
    NW to Mount Adams
    E to Crestone Needle
    SE to Mount Lindsey, Ellingwood Point, Blanca Peak, and Little Bear Peak
    WNW to Kit Carson Peak

Getting There: From the town of Westcliffe at the intersection with Colorado
96, drive south on Colorado 69 for 4.5 miles and turn right on Colfax Lane (Road
119). Follow Colfax Lane for 5.4 miles to a T. Turn right here on Road 120 and set

Crestone Peak

your odometer to zero. Continue straight up the valley and park on your right at mile 1.5.

Comment: Many consider the valley of the South Colony Lakes to be the most beautiful in Colorado. Access is by a very rough, blocked, four-wheel drive road that brings you to a high trailhead. The lakes are ringed by four 14,000-foot peaks: Humboldt Peak, Crestone Needle, Crestone Peak, and farther west and out of view, Kit Carson Peak. Despite the difficult access, this area is very popular, especially on weekends.

The Hike: After hiking 5.2 miles up the rough road to the trailhead, begin hiking west on a narrow trail and soon pass a trail register and a Sangre de Cristo Wilderness sign. Follow this trail as it rises and falls, crosses a talus field, and passes above Lower South Colony Lake where you take a right fork. At 1.8 miles from the trailhead you reach a trail fork in a clearing before and above Upper South Colony Lake. Ascend the newly improved trail on the right (north) to a ridge at 12,860 feet. Humboldt Peak towers above on your right. You can continue left (west) on the ridge and follow either of two trails which are faint at times and rise and fall along the ridge and connect to reach a large, fairly level grassy area known as the Bear's Playground. Keep to the left of this area and continue south and gradually upward on another faint trail with occasional cairns. After 0.75 mile, several cairn-marked routes will lead you into the long northwest couloir of Crestone Peak. Generally take the highest entry point and traverse into this trough as you continue south-southwest. The high peak looming above on your left is a false summit. A small keyhole crack in the rocks is one negotiable access route to this northwest couloir.

Once in the northwest couloir, follow it directly up to the so-called "Red Notch" between the false summit on the left and your target on the right. Snow and ice linger in this couloir until late summer. The rock that remains after the melt off is reasonably good and requires lots of easy, steep handwork.

Once at the saddle, continue southwest on a cairn-marked, easy trail to reach the top of Crestone Peak in 0.25 mile. A cairn and register cylinder denote the high point. As is the case on these high summits, the views are awe-inspiring. Enjoy your accomplishment before returning by your long ascent route. Be especially careful as you down climb in the northwest couloir and be sure to exit where you entered it on the ascent.

Horn Peak

Hike Distance: 6.5 miles each way
Hiking Time: Up in 227 minutes. Down in 175 minutes.
Starting Elevation: 9,125 feet
Highest Elevation: 13,450 feet
Elevation Gain: 4,779 feet (includes 227 extra feet each way)
Trail: All the way
Difficulty: More difficult
Relevant Maps: Trails Illustrated Number 138; Horn Peak 7½ minute; Custer County Number One; San Isabel National Forest
Views from the Summit:
  NE to Westcliffe
  NW to Rita Alto Peak
  S to Crestone Peak
  SSE to the Dry Lakes and Little Horn Peak
  SSW to Mount Adams
  SE to Humboldt Peak
  SW to Fluted Peak

Getting There: From Colorado 96 in Westcliffe drive south on Colorado 69 for 3.4 miles and turn right on Schoolfield Road. Set your odometer to zero. At mile 1.7 turn left onto Road 129. At mile 3.6 turn right onto Road 130. At mile 6 turn right at a four-way intersection. Continue straight at mile 6.2 and park on the right at mile 6.4 near a sign and trail to the Rainbow Trail in 0.25 mile. (The Horn Creek Trailhead lies 0.2 mile farther up the road.)

Comment: Colorado offers many fine mountain vistas from its towns and cities. One of the most spectacular is across the Wet Mountain Valley toward the Sangre

Horn Peak from Comanche Peak

Horn Peak

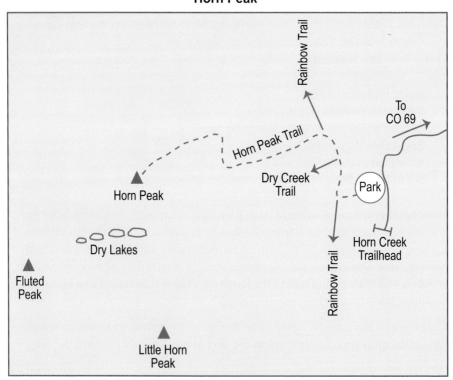

de Cristo Mountain range from Westcliffe. One of the most striking peaks in this range is Horn Peak. A good trail off the Rainbow Trail leads to its summit.

The Hike: Begin on the Horn Creek Spur Trail, which connects with the Rainbow Trail after an easy 0.25 mile. Turn right and stay on the Rainbow Trail another 0.9 mile until you reach the Horn Peak Trail on the left. The sign says it is 3 miles to the top but it's farther. Ascend to the left (southwest) past a trail register on a wide rocky road that will become a narrower trail. After 1.8 miles from the Rainbow Trail cross Hennequin Creek and enter the Sangre de Cristo Wilderness at two signs along the trail. Two more miles brings you to treeline and some wood poles to mark the rocky trail up the ridge to a cairn and some wonderful vistas at the Horn Peak summit. Rejoice, relax, and enjoy your perch before retracing the ascent route.

Humboldt Peak

Hike Distance: 8.4 miles on the ascent. 7.3 miles on the descent (loop)
Hiking Time: Up in 280 minutes. Down 220 minutes.
Starting Elevation: 8,600 feet
Highest Elevation: 14,064 feet
Elevation Gain: 6,058 feet (includes an extra 594 feet)
Trail: All the way on the ascent
Difficulty: More Difficult
Relevant Maps: Trails Illustrated Number 138; Beck Mountain 7½ minute; Crestone Peak 7½ minute; Custer County Number One; San Isabel National Forest
Views from the Summit:
S to Broken Hand Peak
SW to Crestone Needle and Crestone Peak
WNW to Mount Adams
WSW to Kit Carson Peak

Getting There: From the intersection of Colorado 96 and Colorado 69 in West-cliffe, drive south on Colorado 69 for 4.6 miles and turn right onto Road 119 (also called Colfax Lane). Continue straight on this road for 5.4 miles until it reaches a T. Turn right and continue for 1.5 miles and park off the road.

Comment: This outing takes you to the lovely South Colony Lakes. Four four-teeners surround this scenic valley and Humboldt Peak is the easiest to ascend. It resembles a large anthill. A lengthy hike is necessary to access this special place. An overnight camp in the upper valley can make this a less strenuous outing and is recommended.

The Hike: Begin west up the rough road that winds up the valley parallel to South Colony Creek. Follow the main road as it crosses the Rainbow Trail after 2.6 miles and crosses the creek in another 0.4 mile. In 2.6 more miles past the creek crossing, leave the road and take the South Colony Creek Trail on your right. This trail

Humboldt Peak from the Bears Playground

Humboldt Peak

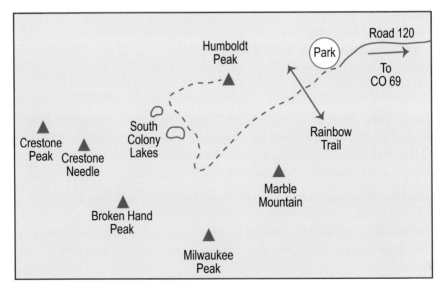

leads to a Lower and then an Upper South Colony Lake in 1.6 miles. Just before the trail reaches the upper lake, take a right fork and follow the steep trail up north-northwest to the ridge. En route to the ridge take the right fork as the trail splits. At the ridge turn right and follow the ridge trail ascending northeast. The summit lies at the northeast edge of a flat area and is marked by a rock shelter. The views from here are spectacular when there is good visibility. The best descent is directly south toward the Lower South Colony Lake over talus and tundra farther down. Continue south to regain the trail and return to the rough road that takes you back to your vehicle.

Medano Lake

Hike Distance: 3.3 miles each way
Hiking Time: Up in 104 minutes. Down in 73 minutes.
Starting Elevation: 9,590 feet
Highest Elevation: 11,530 feet
Elevation Gain: 2,210 feet (includes 135 extra feet each way)
Trail: All the way
Difficulty: Moderate
Relevant Maps: Trails Illustrated Number 138; Medano Pass 7½ minute; Saguache County Number Five; Rio Grande National Forest

Getting There: From Westcliffe and Colorado 96, drive south on Colorado 69 for 23.7 miles. Turn right onto Road 559 at a sign to Medano Pass. At mile 7.1 from Colorado 69 keep right at a fork as the road becomes rougher. At mile 7.2 take the left fork at a sign directing toward Medano Pass. Four-wheel drive is required from here. At mile 9.1 reach tree-covered Medano Pass and descend another 0.5 mile where a sign directs you to the right another 0.2 mile to the Medano Lake Trailhead.

Medano Lake

Medano Lake

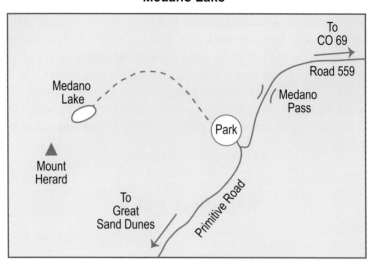

Comment: Not many hikers get to Medano Lake. Although the length and eleva-tion gain are relatively modest, the trailhead lies in a remote area of the Sangre de Cristo Wilderness, accessible only to four-wheel drive vehicles. The route follows Medano Creek and flowing water is frequently in view, with many creek crossings. The heavy aspen forest makes this a great mid-September hike when golden leaves abound. Medano Creek eventually flows into the Sand Dunes. Medano in Spanish means "sand hill."

The Hike: Start out hiking to the west from the trailhead parking area. Make the first of many creek crossings and continue up the well-defined trail. While the trail mostly traverses forest, you will pass through a few scenic meadows. In the higher sections of the trail, high peaks come into view. Medano Lake is modest in size and lies in a rocky cirque around treeline. Good fishing in the lake has been reported. Mount Herard (formerly called Mount Seven) is visible to the southwest and can be climbed from a saddle to the right of the summit. Return as you ascended.

Megan Lake

Hike Distance: 4.4 miles each way
Hiking Time: Up in 145 minutes. Down in 103 minutes.
Starting Elevation: 9,500 feet
Highest Elevation: 11,572 feet
Elevation Gain: 2,418 feet (includes 346 extra feet)
Trail: All the way
Difficulty: Moderate

Megan Lake

Megan Lake

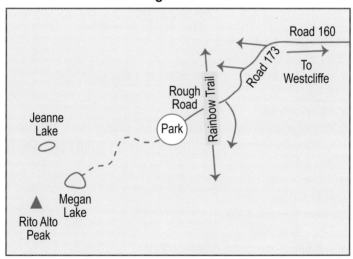

Relevant Maps: Trails Illustrated Number 138; Horn Peak 7½ minute; Rito Alto Peak 7½ minute; Custer County; San Isabel National Forest

Getting There: From Colorado 69 in Westcliffe, drive west on Hermit Road (County 160). After 7.4 miles turn left and again at 7.6 miles. Follow signs to North Taylor Trailhead. At mile 8.7 pass the Rainbow Trail on the right. When the rough road reaches a sign on the left (stating the North Taylor Trailhead is 0.75 mile up the road), park unless you have four-wheel drive and high clearance.

Comment: The trail to Megan Lake runs alongside North Taylor Creek. Two creek crossings can be difficult with high, rushing water. Therefore the best time to make this hike is from mid-August to late September when the water is low and the aspen will be turning.

The Hike: Continue up the road 0.9 mile to road end at a sign for Trail 1348 stating (erroneously) that it is 2.5 miles to Megan Lake. Pass a trail register and signboard and soon thereafter the Wilderness boundary. The steep rocky trail continues across the creek twice and reaches a scenic valley. Finally after crossing a field marked by cairns at each end, persist upward to reach an open area, with Megan Lake on the left. Rito Alto is the high peak to the west-southwest. Jeanne Lake is 0.4 mile above to the northwest if you have the energy, time, and weather. Return as you ascended.

Mount Lindsey

Hike Distance: 5.3 miles each way
Hiking Time: Up in 204 minutes. Down in 177 minutes.
Starting Elevation: 10,600 feet
Highest Elevation: 14,042 feet
Elevation Gain: 4,498 feet (includes 528 extra feet each way)
Trail: All the way
Difficulty: More difficult
Relevant Maps: Trails Illustrated Number 138; Blanca Peak 7½ minute;
  Huerfano County Number One; Costilla County Number One; San Isabel
  National Forest
Views from the Summit:
  NW to Iron Nipple
  ESE to West Spanish Peak
  SW to Little Bear Pek
  WSW to Blanca Peak and Ellingwood Point

Getting There: From Walsenburg at the north end of town, drive on Colorado 69 for 24.8 miles into Gardner. Turn left and after 0.7 mile turn left toward Redwing. Avoid roads on the left at miles 30.6 and 32.6 from Walsenburg. The road becomes unpaved at mile 32.7. At mile 37.4 turn left at a fork onto Road 580 and set your odometer to zero. After 4.6 miles on Road 580, pass the Singing River Ranch and the Aspen River Ranch at mile 4.9. Pass the National Forest boundary at mile 8.3

and the Zapata Trail on the right at mile 9.1. The road ends at a parking area and the trailhead at mile 10.3. The road for the final 7 miles is rough and narrow but regular cars with good clearance can reach this trailhead.

Comment: Mount Lindsey is one of Colorado's fifty-four 14,000-foot peaks. The demanding and scenic hike to the summit passes through the Sangre de Cristo Wilderness to the boundary between Huerfano County and Castilla County. Mount Lindsey lies on private land in Castilla County but there are no restrictions to this access from Huerfano County.

The Hike: Begin south from the Huerfano Trailhead on the Lily Lake Trail. Pass a signboard and trail register and soon thereafter cross the Huerfano River on logs. After 1 mile from the trailhead, go left (south) at a fork with the Lily Lake Trail leading to the right. Soon the trail becomes rougher and steeper as it rises,

The route up Mount Lindsey

past a talus slope on the left, to finally reach a clearing with Nipple Creek below on the right. Eventually cross the creek and ascend to a bench with good views of Blanca Peak and Mount Lindsey.

From here the trail descends about 100 feet and then gradually rises over grassy slopes to reach the first of two saddles. The trail then curves left to a saddle at 13,130 feet between the Iron Nipple on the left and Mount Lindsey on the right. Continue to the southeast on a rough trail that leads up the left side of the peak. Pick one of two couloirs that eventually lead up to the right and the summit ridge. Cross over a false summit another 300 yards to a rock pile and register cylinder at the Mount Lindsey summit. If weather permits, enjoy the views and refresh before the long retracing of the ascent route.

Mount Lindsey

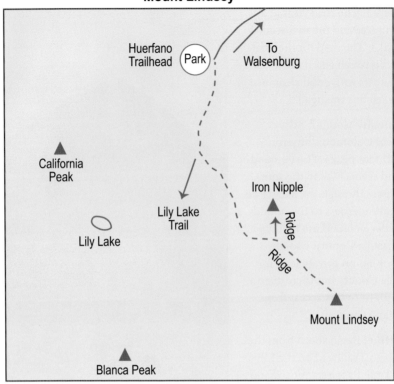

Music Pass

Hike Distance: 4.1 miles each way

Hiking Time: Up in 102 minutes. Down in 84 minutes.

Starting Elevation: 9,240 feet

Highest Elevation: 11,400 feet

Elevation Gain: 2,520 feet (includes 180 extra feet each way)

Trail: All the way

Difficulty: Moderate

Relevant Maps: Trails Illustrated Number 138; Crestone Peak 7½ minute;
Custer County Number One; San Isabel National Forest

Views from the Summit:
WNW to Pico Asilado, Milwaukee Peak, and Crestone Needle
WSW to Tijeras Peak and Music Mountain

Getting There: From the junction with Colorado 96 in Westcliffe, drive south on Colorado 69 for 4.3 miles and turn right onto Colfax Lane (Road 119). Drive 5.4 miles on this straight road and turn left at a T and a Music Pass sign. Follow this dirt road for 4.9 miles and park near another Music Pass sign. Four-wheel drive is advised beyond this point.

Comment: Music Pass, southwest of Westcliffe, is less frequented than many other destinations in the Sangre de Cristo Wilderness. It is not a route to any of the four-teeners and the rough four-wheel drive road is blocked 1.3 miles on the eastern side of the pass. The redeeming fact, however, is that the view to the west from Music Pass is one of the grandest in Colorado. There are a series of lovely, high peaks surrounding a bowl of trees and the hidden Upper and Lower Sand Creek Lakes.

The Hike: From the parking area and the southern trailhead for the Rainbow Trail, begin hiking to the south on the road, which becomes rougher as it ascends through heavy forest. It will be 2.8 miles and 1,500 feet of elevation gain on this main road before it is blocked to four-wheel drive traffic. Continue southwest past the blockade and then a trail register up the last 1.3 miles to Music Pass, with a fence and signs on its western side. Take some pictures and enjoy the scene before returning back to the trailhead.

Music Pass

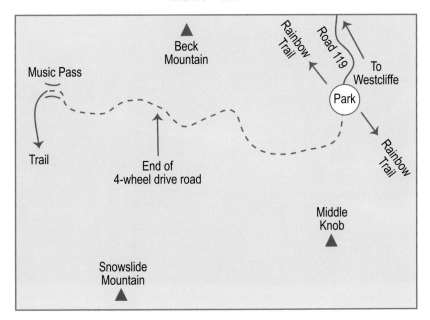

South Colony Lakes

Hike Distance: 7.2 miles each way
Hiking Time: Up in 190 minutes. Down in 165 minutes.
Starting Elevation: 8,600 feet
Highest Elevation: 12,030 feet
Elevation Gain: 3,880 feet (includes an extra 225 feet each way)
Trail: All the way
Difficulty: More difficult
Relevant Maps: Trails Illustrated Number 138; Beck Mountain 7½ minute;
    Crestone Peak 7½ minute; Custer County; San Isabel National Forest

Getting There: From the intersection of Colorado 96 and Colorado 69 in West-cliffe, drive south on Colorado 69 for 4.6 miles and turn right onto Road 119 (also called Colfax Lane). Continue straight for 5.4 miles on this road to a T. Turn right and continue another 1.5 miles. Park off the road where Road 121 forks off to the left. The road farther in is blocked. It is a very difficult road for a vehicle.

Upper South Colony Lake

Comment: The South Colony Lakes lie in one of Colorado's most scenic and popular basins. Three 14,000-foot peaks rim the basin and a fourth lies nearby a ridge to the west. The usage of this valley would be even more extensive if it were not for the very rough and long access road and the distance from larger population areas.

The Hike: Begin west up the rough road, which eventually bends to the southwest, crosses the Rainbow Trail at mile 2.6, and South Colony Creek at mile 3. Follow the road as it continues up the valley through the forest. At mile 5.7 from where you parked, leave the road and take the South Colony Lakes Trail on the right. Ascend the final mile past timberline to the lower lake on your left at 11,670 feet, with the upper lake another 0.5 mile west at 12,030 feet. You will be surrounded by alpine beauty. Crestone Needle and Crestone Peak lie to the southwest and west, with Broken Hand Peak to the south-southeast. Humboldt Peak, the easiest fourteener to climb from this basin, is the gigantic anthill to the north. Kit Carson Peak cannot be seen from these lakes but lies west over the ridge at the head of the valley.

South Colony Lakes

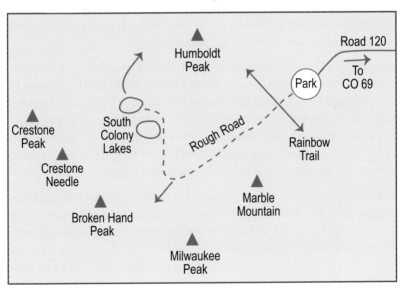

South Crestone Lake

Hike Distance: 5 miles each way
Hiking Time: Up in 170 minutes. Down in 132 minutes.
Starting Elevation: 8,800 feet
Highest Elevation: 11,800 feet
Elevation Gain: 3,435 feet (includes 435 extra feet)
Trail: All the way
Difficulty: More difficult
Relevant Maps: Trails Illustrated Number 138; Crestone 7½ minute; Rito Alto Peak 7½ minute; Horn Peak 7½ minute; Saguache County Number Five; Rio Grande National Forest

Getting There: From Colorado 17 in the San Luis Valley, between Alamosa to the south and Poncha Pass to the north, turn east at Moffat onto T Road and drive 12.4 miles to the intersection of Alder Street and Galena Avenue in central Crestone. Turn right onto Galena Avenue and drive for 2.2 more miles to the parking area at road end. En route to this trailhead, stay on the main road and keep right at mile 1 and mile 1.6. Regular cars can reach this parking area.

Comment: The Sangre de Cristo Wilderness is full of good hiking destinations and can be accessed from the east or west. The hike to beautiful South Crestone Lake proceeds eastward from a trailhead outside of the town of Crestone. The demanding route follows South Crestone Creek up to the lake with great, jagged peaks circling above. The good trail is alternately steep and gradual as it traverses lush terrain. Despite the considerable length and elevation gain, this is one of the easier lake hikes on the western side of the Sangre de Cristo range.

The Hike: From the parking area, begin hiking to the northeast and quickly pass a register on the left and the trail to Willow Lake on the right. Continue straight along South Crestone Creek and soon ascend a series of switchbacks and enter the Wilderness at a sign. Pass by some lovely meadows and cascading water as the route curves to the right. Higher up, the trail rises along the left side of a meadow and then through a talus slope and gains a more level area, just before the lake. The rocky spires above are impressive and a subpeak of Mount Adams lies to the east. Return as you ascended.

South Crestone Lake

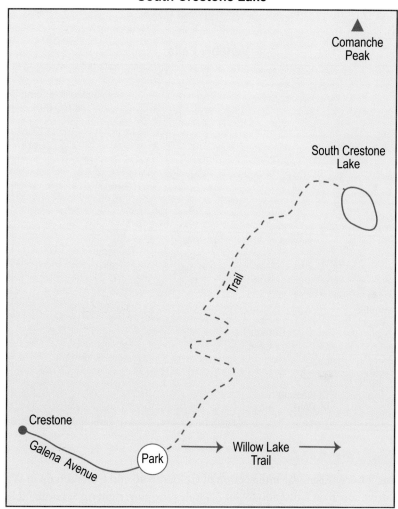

Venable Falls

Hike Distance: 2.6 miles each way
Hiking Time: Up in 85 minutes. Down in 59 minutes.
Starting Elevation: 9,020 feet
Highest Elevation: 10,400 feet
Elevation Gain: 1,450 feet (includes 70 extra feet)
Trail: All the way
Difficulty: Moderate

Relevant Maps: Trails Illustrated Number 138; Horn Peak 7½ minute; Custer County Number One; San Isabel National Forest

Venable Falls

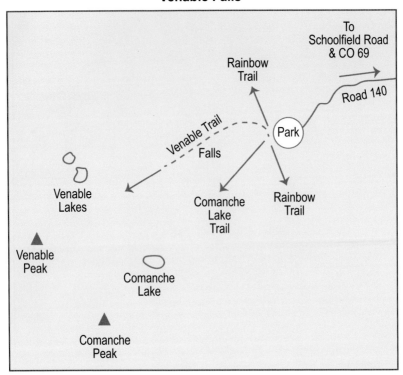

Getting There: From the intersection of Colorado 96 and Colorado 69 in West-cliffe, drive south on Colorado 69 for 3.4 miles and turn right on Schoolfield Road. Drive for 4.4 miles to a T. Go left and stay left after 0.8 mile. From this junction it is 1.1 miles to the turnoff on the right to the Comanche-Venable Trailhead, which is another 0.4 mile. Regular cars can reach this trailhead.

Comment: There are many wonderful hikes from the Rainbow Trail, which runs north to south west of Westcliffe, alongside the Sangre de Cristo Wilderness. These are mostly steep treks of some length. One of the easier outings is the hike to Venable Falls. Rising through aspen and spruce forest, the rock-strewn trail affords few vistas. But Horn Peak can be seen on the left (south) earlier in this hike and Spring Mountain higher up in the basin.

The Hike: Start walking north from the parking area toward the Venable Trail. A steep 0.5 mile brings you to the Rainbow Trail. Hike to the right fifty yards and then ascend the Venable Trail on the left (south-southwest) past a register and Wilderness signs. With Venable Creek always on your left, ascend the clear trail almost 2 more miles to a fork and trail sign, just before the second sharp switchback to the right. It is less than 100 yards down the left (south) fork to the cascading waters of Venable Falls. There are several vantage points as Venable Creek rushes down a rocky chute. For heavy water flow, try this hike in June. For aspen gold, wait until mid-September. The Venable Trail continues up to the Venable Lakes, Phantom Terrace, Venable Pass, and Venable Peak

Venable Falls

Neighboring towns: Pagosa Springs, South Fork,
   Del Norte, Monte Vista, Summitville
Size: 158,790 acres
Elevation: 8,000 to 13,000+ feet
Miles of trails: 180

Wild and rugged, the San Juan Mountains stretch in an arc over a hundred miles long from southwestern Colorado into northern New Mexico. The South San Juan Wilderness is in a remote part of the San Juan range, just to the north of the New Mexico state line. It is in this place that the San Juan Mountains remain yet untouched by man and where the wanderer can find solitude from the crowded avenues of the city.

The South San Juan area is special for its rugged scenery, large expanses of forest, and high altitude trails that offer a sense of remoteness difficult to find elsewhere. High ridges, pinnacles, and deep canyons—carved by the headwaters of the San Juan, Conejos, and Blancos Rivers—characterize the geography of the Wilderness. Pristine spruce, fir, and ponderosa forest make the Wilderness a sanctuary for deer, elk, bear, and other wildlife that thrives unmolested by human activity. It comes as no surprise then that it was in this place that the last Colorado grizzly was shot in 1979.

Some would argue that the best backpacking in the state is here. In the autumn, the area is popular with hunting parties looking for trophy elk. But outside of the autumn hunting season, solitude can be more readily found here for the soul who is willing to seek it out.

Bear Lake

Bear Lake

Hike Distance: 4.1 miles each way
Hiking Time: Up in 122 minutes. Down in 95 minutes (senior time).
Starting Elevation: 9,900 feet
Lowest Elevation: 9,800 feet
Highest Elevation: 11,590 feet
Elevation Gain: 2,240 feet (includes 450 extra feet)
Trail: All the way
Difficulty: Moderate
Relevant Maps: Trails Illustrated 142; Platoro 7½ minute; Red Mountain 7½
minute; Conejos County; Rio Grande National Forest

Getting There: From Monte Vista on U.S. 160, drive south on Colorado 15 for
12 miles and turn right onto Road 250. Follow this good dirt road 40 miles and
turn right on Road 105. After 2 miles turn left and park at the Bear Lake Trailhead,
a sign, and a register.

Comment: Of the many Bear Lakes in Colorado, this is the South San Juan Wilderness version. Unlike the Bear Lake in Rocky Mountain National Park, this Bear
Lake is reached by relatively few visitors.

The Hike: Begin hiking down to the south-southeast and quickly cross Bear Creek
and enter the South San Juan Wilderness. With many switchbacks, the good trail

rises to a high point at 11,590 feet. An unnamed 12,555-foot peak looms above on the left as a trail leads left at a cairn and traverses the south flank of the unnamed peak and heads toward Tobacco Lake and Conejos Peak. You continue straight and reach the highest point of this hike with Bear Lake visible ahead after a short descent. The lake water looks green and the lake is the size of two football fields. I saw no evidence of fish in the lake.

Bear Lake

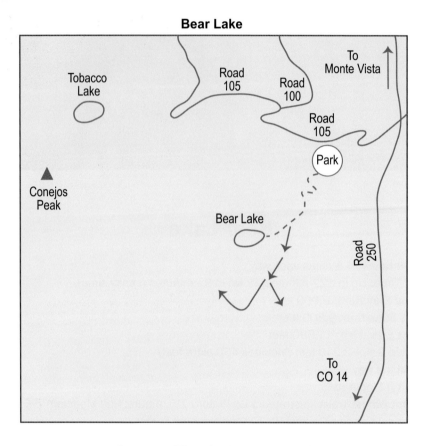

Long Trek Mountain

Hike Distance: 3.6 miles each way
Hiking Time: Up in 112 minutes. Down in 88 minutes (senior time).
Starting Elevation: 11,600 feet
Highest Elevation: 12,866 feet
Elevation Gain: 1,712 feet (includes 223 extra feet each way)
Trail: Initial 80%
Difficulty: More difficult

Rick Clark and Paul Barrett below Long Trek Mountain

Long Trek Mountain

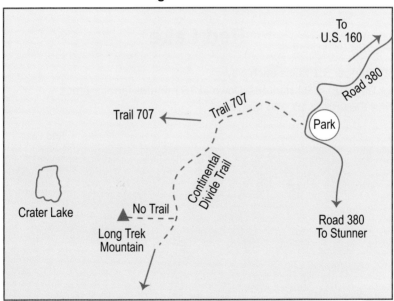

Relevant Maps: Trails Illustrated Number 142; Elwood Pass 7½ minute; Rio
    Grande County, Conejos County, and Archuleta County; Rio Grande National
    Forest
Views from the Summit:
    S to Summit Peak and Montezuma Peak
    W to Crater Lake

Getting There: From U.S. 160 between South Fork and Wolf Creek Pass, drive south on Park Creek Road, which is Road 380. Follow Road 380, which is wide and well graded, for 19.1 miles and park near Trail 707, the Crater Lake Trail—0.8 mile before reaching the trailhead. Pass the Elwood Cabin on the left. This cabin can be rented.

Comment: The beautiful high meadows and striking peaks make this hike especially memorable as you use part of the Continental Divide Trail.

The Hike: Begin hiking up Trail 707 to the west and rise above treeline. Within 0.5 mile the Continental Divide Trail joins Trail 707 from above on the right. After 0.8 mile on Trail 707, take the Continental Divide Trail on the left and gently descend briefly and follow the trail and periodic cairns. Head directly toward Long Trek Mountain before the trail curves left along the foot of the peak. When you are parallel to the left end of the summit ridge, leave the trail and ascend the grassy slopes on the right to reach a small cairn and magnificent vistas on the summit. Enjoy your high perch before retracing the ascent route back to the trailhead.

Red Lake

Hike Distance: 3.1 miles each way
Hiking Time: Up in 94 minutes. Down in 78 minutes (senior time).
Starting Elevation: 10,980 feet

Red Lake

Highest Elevation: 11,735 feet
Elevation Gain: 1,100 feet (includes 345 extra feet)
Trail: All the way
Difficulty: Easy
Relevant Maps: Trails Illustrated Number 142; Cumbres 7½ minute; Conejos
    County; Rio Grande National Forest

Getting There: From Colorado 17, 0.3 mile south of La Manga Pass, turn right on
Road 624 and follow it for 4.1 miles to the Red Lake Trailhead.

Comment: This lake lies in the southern section of the South San Juan Wilderness
and is an easier hike than to the other lakes in the Wilderness. The lake's name may
come from the red earth around it.

The Hike: Begin hiking west on the trail by the register. Ascend an old road on a
moderate grade through the forest until you reach the first of several benches that
rise through open country. Cairns help to clarify the trail. At the 1.3-mile mark pass
a sign and enter the South San Juan Wilderness. Pass a few ponds. Upon reaching
the highest bench you will see Red Lake below. Descend over 100 feet to the lake,
which is the size of three football fields and full of fish. Conejos Peak can be seen to
the northwest. Return by your outgoing route.

Red Lake

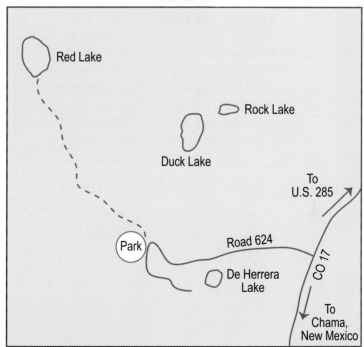

Neighboring towns: Ouray, Ridgeway, Lake City, Gunnison
Size: 102,721 acres
Elevation: 8,400 to 14,300 feet
Miles of trails: 110

The name comes from a Ute Indian word with one of the translations being "dirty water." This Wilderness is located in the north-central region of the San Juan Mountains in Colorado. There are two fourteeners and at least twenty-five 13,000-foot peaks in the Uncompahgre Wilderness. Big Blue Creek flows off Uncompahgre Peak (14,309 feet) in this rough and majestic section of the San Juan Mountains, which was formerly known as Big Blue Wilderness Area.

Uncompahgre Peak's unusual broad, flat, tilted summit falls away almost vertically on three sides for as much as 1,500 feet, a landmark visible from far away. Its fourth side lies gentle and inviting to many climbers. Below Uncompahgre Peak, the Wilderness is a mountainous land of towering rock castles and sweeping ridges that some claim is the most splendid scenery in the state. Technical climbers find endless routes to challenge their skills. Wetterhorn Peak (14,015 feet) stands not far southwest of Uncompahgre Peak. Numerous forks of the Cimarron River rush out of the central section of this Wilderness, flowing north to eventually become one. You'll find a few small lakes with trout, and many trout in the numerous streams.

Uncompahgre Peak

Hike Distance: 8.1 miles each way (without four-wheel drive), 4.2 miles each way (with four-wheel drive)

Hiking Time: Up in 260 minutes. Down in 190 minutes (without four-wheel drive); Up in 140 minutes. Down in 100 minutes (with four-wheel drive).

Starting Elevation: 9,310 feet (without four-wheel drive); 11,400 feet (with four-wheel drive).

Highest Elevation: 14,309 feet

Elevation Gain: 5,929 (without four-wheel drive, includes 465 extra feet each way); 3,339 feet (with four-wheel drive, includes 465 extra feet each way)

Trail: All the way

Difficulty: Most difficult (without four-wheel drive); More difficult (with four-wheel drive)

Relevant Maps: Trails Illustrated Number 141; Uncompahgre Peak 7½ minute; Hinsdale County Number One; Uncompahgre National Forest

Views from the Summit:

NW to LaSalle Mountains (Utah)

SE to Handies Peak

SW to Lizard Head, El Diente Peak, and Mount Wilson

WNW to Coxcomb Peak

WSW to Wetterhorn Peak, Mount Sneffels, and Matterhorn Peak

Uncompahgre Peak

Uncompahgre Peak

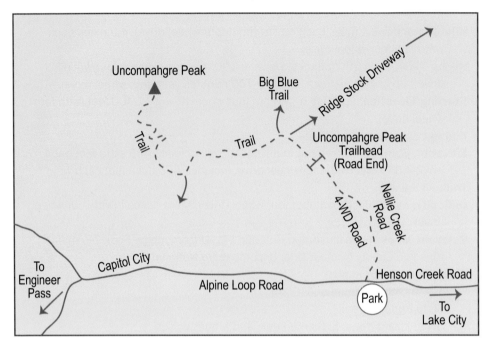

Getting There: In Lake City from Colorado Road 149, turn west on Second Avenue and set your odometer to zero. After two blocks go left at a T. You are now on the Henson Creek Road. Follow this good, wide, unpaved road through many mine remnants at mile 3.6 and reach the Nellie Creek Road on your right at a sign 4.9 miles from Colorado 149. Park off the road here unless you have a high clearance, four-wheel drive vehicle that will take you the 3.9 miles up the Nellie Creek Road to the trailhead.

Comment: Uncompahgre Peak, Colorado's sixth highest, has a distinctive and striking summit. The trail begins at the end of a four-wheel drive road up Nellie Creek, enters the Uncompahgre Wilderness, and quickly moves above treeline. The trail is a good one and your target can be seen throughout the upper 90 percent of the hike.

If you are able to four-wheel drive the almost 4 miles up the Nellie Creek Road, you will save considerable time and 2,590 feet in elevation gain. The hike will be described from the lower end of the four-wheel drive (Nellie Creek) road.

The Hike: Walk up the Nellie Creek Road, which provides few vistas. Make at least two big creek crossings before passing through an open meadow shortly before reaching the trailhead and road end at mile 3.9.

Continue to the north past the trail register and enter the Uncompahgre Wilderness a few hundred feet below timberline. The trail rises into a beautiful valley with lots of grassy, rounded slopes and curves to the left. Soon the mighty prow of Uncompaghre Peak comes into view. At mile 4.9 from the Henson Creek Road you reach a fork and take the trail on the left (the right fork leads to Big Blue Creek). With your destination in full view, continue up to another fork at a ridge at mile 6.7. Keep to the right (west-northwest) and follow a ridge past several cuts on the left with great views of Wetterhorn Peak on your left. Soon reach a series of switchbacks that lead clockwise around the left corner of the summit block. Here there are two possible routes up a short rocky segment to the lengthy summit plateau. One of these routes is marked with cairns and each ascends about 50 yards. There are enough firm rocks that can be readily negotiated.

Once on the lower plateau, continue by trail the easy final 0.25 mile to the summit. A cement block, a trail register, and great scenery greeted me at the top. Many notable peaks can be seen from here on a clear day.

Try to stay on the trail on your return and avoid the temptation to short-cut. An endangered species (butterfly) protection area lies nearby off the trail.

Wetterhorn Peak

Hike Distance: 4.3 miles each way
Hiking Time: Up in 172 minutes. Down in 119 minutes.
Starting Elevation: 10,770 feet
Highest Elevation: 14,017 feet
Elevation Gain: 3,545 feet (includes 150 extra feet each way)
Trail: All the way
Difficulty: More difficult
Relevant Maps: Trails Illustrated Number 141; Wetterhorn Peak 7½ minute; Uncompahgre Peak 7½ minute; Hinsdale County Number One; Uncompahgre National Forest
Views from the Summit:
    NW to Coxcomb Peak
    ENE to Uncompahgre Peak
    SSE to Handies Peak
    SE to Redcloud Peak and Sunshine Peak

Getting There: From Gunnison Avenue (Colorado 149) in Lake City, drive west on Second Street and after 0.2 mile turn left on Engineer Pass Road. Continue on this good road for 8.8 miles to an intersection at the site of the former Capitol City. Turn right and ascend the North Henson Road, setting your odometer to zero.

Avoid roads on the right after 0.2 and 0.9 mile from Capitol City. Take the right fork at mile 1.4 and another right fork at mile 1.9. Four-wheel drive can take you 0.7 mile farther to the trail register and signboard just below a road barrier at the trailhead.

Comment: Wetterhorn Peak stands like a ship's prow in the Uncompahgre Wilderness. Considered the most difficult of the five fourteeners between Lake City and Ouray, it requires some exposure and occasional handwork. The clear trail ascends the beautiful Matterhorn Creek Basin and follows cairns above treeline all the way to the summit.

The Hike: Start out to the north around a road barrier on a wide, rocky road. After 0.7 mile pass the Matterhorn Cutoff Trail on the left (this trail leads west). Ascend a switchback, pass Wilderness signs and reach a signed fork after 2 miles from the trailhead. Take the left (west) fork, cross two small creeks, and traverse a vast, open meadow over tundra. Continue through a boulder field before ascending a ridge to the left.

Wetterhorn Peak

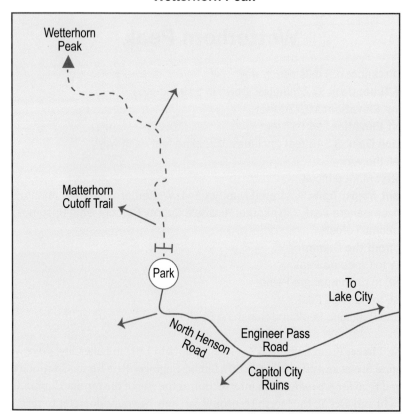

You are now above 13,000 feet and the steepness increases over the final 1,000 feet. Ascend the ridge to the right (west), initially to the left and later on the right side of the ridge. Eventually pass through a narrow slit between rocks. Nearing the top, pass through a gap to the right of a large fin-shaped rock. Then descend 10 feet to a ledge at the base of an 80-foot rocky chute on the right. There are good footholds as you rise to the small flat summit and a modest rock pile. Enjoy the vistas and your accomplishment before carefully following the cairns back to the trailhead.

Wetterhorn Peak

Neighboring towns: Winter Park, Georgetown, Dillon
Size: 12,986 acres
Elevation: 8,600 to 12,700 feet
Miles of trails: 17

The Wilderness consists of that portion of the Vasquez Mountains west of Berthoud Pass and south of Winter Park Ski Area. Dropping in elevation, the tundra gives way first to krummholz and then forests of Engelmann spruce, subalpine fir, and finally lodgepole pine. Krummholz, a German word meaning "twisted wood," aptly describes the forest survivors at timberline. Because of the severe environment and bone-chilling winds above treeline, Engelmann spruce and subalpine fir are unable to grow upright. Instead, they grow as clumps of prostrate, shrubby trees spreading downwind in gnarled and twisted shapes, with their upwind branches killed off by the desiccating winds.

Vasquez Creek flows heavily off Vasquez Peak to form the main drainage of the area. A deep indentation in the Wilderness boundary from the north maintains Vasquez Creek as non-Wilderness to allow for a collection system that sends much of the water toward Denver.

With much of the 17-mile-long trail system above timberline, sudden summer thunderstorms can make exposure to lightning in the Vasquez Mountains a dangerous risk. You should plan on hiking early and dropping into the trees before afternoon storms break. In winter, avalanches are common.

McQueary Lake Loop

Hike Distance: 7.7 miles (total loop); 2.3 miles to McQuery Lake
Hiking Time: Out in 72 minutes. Back in 169 minutes.
Starting Elevation: 12,451 feet (Jones Pass)
Highest Elevation: 12,780 feet
Lowest Elevation: 10,400 feet
Elevation Gain: 2,443 feet (includes 63 extra feet)
Trail: Initial 0.6 mile and final 4 miles
Difficulty: More difficult
Relevant Maps: Trails Illustrated Number 103; Byers Peak 7½ minute;
Grand County Number Four; Arapaho National Forest

Getting There: From the stoplight in Empire, drive west on U.S. 40 for 7.3 miles and turn left onto the road to the Henderson Mine and set your odometer to zero. Avoid a road on the left after 0.4 mile and turn right onto a rough road at mile 1.7. Follow this main road as it ascends to Jones Pass at mile 5.8 and park off the road. Most regular cars can reach Jones Pass.

Comment: This counter-clockwise loop leads to little visited McQueary Lake within the Vasquez Peak Wilderness. Jones Pass is often blocked by snow into August, preventing a closer start to the lake from the bottom of the western end of Jones Pass Road. Several McQueary brothers settled in this area many years ago.

McQueary Lake from the Continental Divide Trail

The Hike: From Jones Pass begin north on the Continental Divide Trail. Ascend to a ridge and a Vasquez Peak Wilderness sign. Leave the trail and descend the ridge west toward an unnamed 12,410-foot peak. When you reach the low point of this ridge, descend north (right) toward McQueary Lake over mostly grassy slopes. Be careful with this 1,230-foot loss of elevation. The lake is surrounded by a grassy area with the Continental Divide above to the east and northeast.

To continue the loop, leave the lake and descend the valley to the south. There are only occasional suggestions of a trail. Stay close to McQueary Creek and reach a dam after 1.3 miles from the lake. Then follow an aqueduct road to the south-southwest. Keep left at a junction. This road takes you past various water facilities to a roadblock at a fork. Ascend east (left) on the Jones Pass Road, which leads you back to Jones Pass in 2.6 miles to complete the loop. Avoid a right fork halfway up en route to the pass.

McQueary Lake Loop

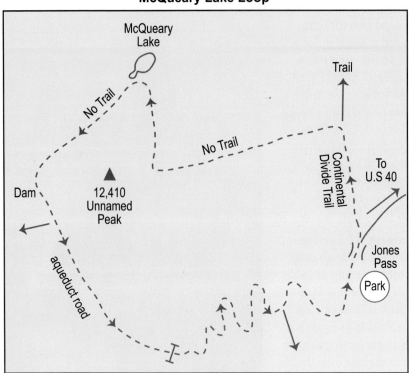

Mount Nystrom

Hike Distance: 3.5 miles each way
Hiking Time: Up in 107 minutes. Down in 90 minutes.
Starting Elevation: 11,600 feet
Highest Elevation: 12,652 feet
Elevation Gain: 1,832 feet (includes 780 extra feet)
Trail: Intermittent
Difficulty: Moderate
Relevant Maps: Trails Illustrated Number 103; Berthoud Pass 7½ minute;
Byers Peak 7½ minute; Arapaho National Forest

Views from the Summit:
NW to Bills Peak and Byers Peak
ESE to Vasquez Peak
SW to Saint Louis Peak
SE to Torreys Peak

Left: Mount Nystrom

Below: View from the Continental
Divide Trail down to Jones Pass Road

Mount Nystrom

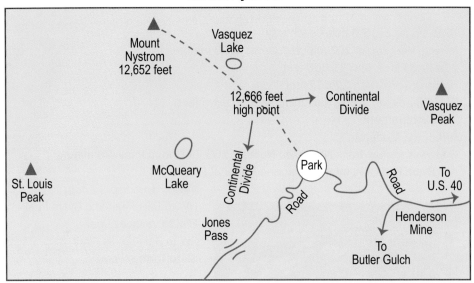

Getting There: From the stoplight in Empire, drive west on U.S. 40 for 7.3 miles and turn left onto the road to the Henderson Mine and the Big Bend Picnic Area as U.S. 40 curves sharply to the right. Keep straight at 0.4 mile and take the right fork at 1.7 miles from U.S. 40, with the Henderson Mine on your left. You are now on the Jones Pass Road. Drive up this road for 2.8 miles and park at timberline. Regular cars with good clearance can usually come this far. To reach this point stay on the main Jones Pass Road, take the right fork at 0.2 mile from the Henderson Mine and keep left on the main road at 1.6 miles.

Comment: There are several ways to hike to the top of Mount Nystrom. This route from the southeast is closest to Denver and can be hiked in half a day. The Jones Pass Road allows you ready access to timberline. You then ascend to the highest point of the hike on the Continental Divide and walk up and down the ridge for 1.75 miles to Mount Nystrom's summit, which overlooks four valleys within the Vasquez Peak Wilderness.

The Hike: Start northwest from the Jones Pass Road and cross the tundra to reach the ridge to the right of an unnamed high point at the head of the valley. An intermittent trail appears en route to the ridge. Join the Continental Divide Trail and then go right along the ridge. From the ridge high point, which lies on the Continental Divide, proceed north on a ridge trail and leave the Continental Divide Trail. Mount Nystrom will be visible north-northwest at the ridge high point. The top of Mount Nystrom is marked by a wooden pole and a nearby rock pile. Mountaintops can be seen in every direction. Return by your ascent route, but be careful and use your compass since many of these ridges resemble each other.

Stanley Mountain (eastern approach)

Hike Distance: 4.2 miles each way
Hiking Time: Up in 139 minutes. Down in 107 minutes (senior time).
Starting Elevation: 11,315 feet (Berthoud Pass)
Highest Elevation: 12,521 feet
Elevation Gain: 1,906 feet (includes 350 extra feet each way)
Trail: All the way (Continental Divide Trail)
Difficulty: Moderate
Relevant Maps: Trails Illustrated Number 103; Berthoud Pass 7½ minute;
    Clear Creek County; Arapaho National Forest
Views from the Summit:
    N to Longs Peak
    NE to James Peak
    ENE to Colorado Mines Peak
    ESE to Engelmann Peak
    SW to Pettingell Peak
    WNW to Vasquez Peak

Stanley Mountain (eastern approach)

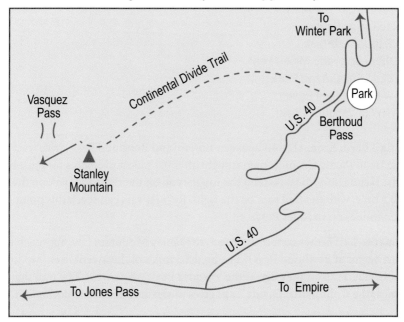

Getting There: Drive on U.S. 40 to Berthoud Pass and park in the lot to the east.
The pass lies between Empire to the southeast and Winter Park to the north.

Comment: There are three main routes to the top of Stanley Mountain. This one provides lots of ridge walking above treeline with great scenery.

The Hike: Cross U.S. 40 carefully and begin west on the clear, good trail that enters the forest and rises above treeline. After 2.3 miles pass a Vasquez Peak Wilderness sign and reach the ridge and continue generally southwest over open terrain to the rocky summit of Stanley Mountain, 10 yards off the main trail.

Stanley Mountain (western approach)

Hike Distance: 3.5 miles each way
Hiking Time: Up in 130 minutes. Down in 92 minutes.
Starting Elevation: 10,280 feet
Highest Elevation: 12,521 feet
Elevation Gain: 2,677 feet (includes 218 extra feet each way)
Trail: All the way
Difficulty: Moderate
Relevant Maps: Trails Illustrated Number 103; Berthoud Pass 7½ minute;
 Clear Creek County; Arapaho National Forest
Views from the Summit:
 N to Longs Peak
 NE to James Peak
 ENE to Colorado Mines Peak
 ESE to Engelmann Peak
 SW to Pettingell Peak
 WNW to Vasquez Peak

Getting There: From U.S. 40 between Empire and Berthoud Pass, drive west past the Big Bend Picnic Ground, keep straight after 0.4 mile and reach a fork just before the Henderson Mine. Ascend the rough road on the right and park on the left after 0.5 mile, with the trail sign on the right. Regular cars can reach this point. This road continues up to Jones Pass.

Comment: This is the western approach to Stanley Mountain (the approach from the east begins at Berthoud Pass). The final 2.3 miles of the ascent uses the Continental Divide Trail on the edge of the Vasquez Peak Wilderness. The trail sign as you reach the Continental Divide Trail gives misleading distance information.

The Hike: Begin on the trail to the northeast and briskly ascend with many switchbacks 1.2 miles to a junction with the Continental Divide Trail. Continue to the right (northeast) and reach a sharp trail curve to the right below Vasquez Pass.

Stanley Mountain (western approach)

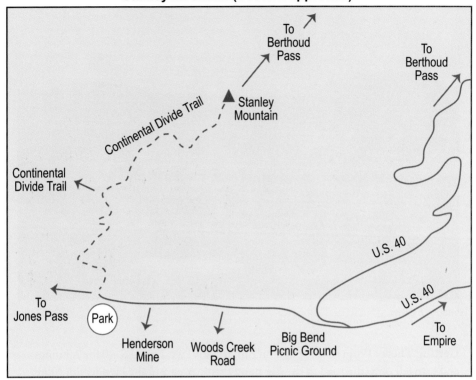

Then rise through the trees to treeline and continue up to a large cairn atop Stanley Mountain above the trail on the right.

Vasquez Lake

Hike Distance: 3.5 miles each way
Hiking Time: Out in 103 minutes. Back in 109 minutes.
Starting Elevation: 12,451 feet (Jones Pass)
Highest Elevation: 12,782 feet
Lowest Elevation: 11,785 feet (Vasquez Lake)
Elevation Gain: 1,698 feet (includes 701 extra feet)
Trail: All the way until the final 0.5 mile to the lake
Difficulty: More difficult
Relevant Maps: Trails Illustrated Number 103; Byers Peak 7½ minute; Grand County Number Four; Arapaho National Forest

Vasquez Lake

Getting There: From the stoplight in Empire drive west on U.S. 40 for 7.3 miles and turn left onto the road to the Big Bend Picnic Area and the Henderson Mine. Set your odometer to zero. Avoid a road on the left after 0.5 mile and turn right on an unpaved road at mile 1.8. Follow this main road up to Jones Pass at mile 5.8 and park. Most regular cars can reach Jones Pass.

Comment: From a high starting point at Jones Pass (12,451 feet), this hike uses the well-defined Continental Divide Trail for 3 miles before the final 0.5 mile without a trail to remote, small Vasquez Lake in the Vasquez Peak Wilderness.

The Hike: Start out to the north-northwest from a trail sign and ascend over 300 feet in 0.2 mile to a Vasquez Peak Wilderness sign. Continue along the ridge and note McQueary Lake below on your left. Ascend to a high point at 12,666 feet and then descend almost 1,000 feet on the good trail, with Vasquez Lake visible on the left. When you arrive at a ridge point roughly parallel to Vasquez Lake, leave the trail and descend northwest over rocks and then scree, talus, and tundra to the small lake. Mount Nystrom lies above to the west and Vasquez Peak can be seen to the east-southeast.

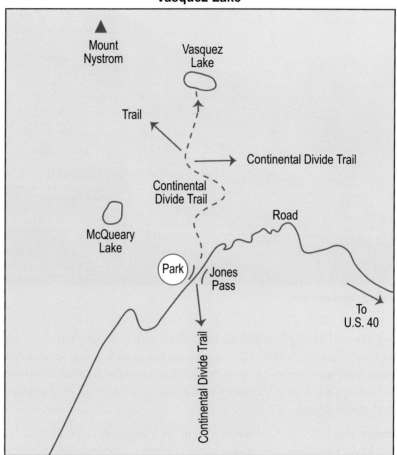

Vasquez Lake

Mount Nystrom

Vasquez Lake

Trail

Continental Divide Trail

Continental Divide Trail

Road

McQueary Lake

Park

Jones Pass

To U.S. 40

Continental Divide Trail

Vasquez Pass

Hike Distance: 7 miles each way

Hiking Time: Up in 200 minutes. Down in 155 minutes.

Starting Elevation: 9,450 feet

Highest Elevation: 11,700 feet

Elevation Gain: 2,730 feet (includes 240 extra feet each way)

Trail: All the way

Difficulty: More difficult

Relevant Maps: Trails Illustrated Number 103; Berthoud Pass 7½ minute; Grand County Number Four; Arapaho National Forest

View toward Vasquez Pass

Getting There: Drive to Winter Park on U.S. 40, turn west onto Vasquez Road and set your odometer to zero. Continue up the valley on Vasquez Road for a total of 4.6 miles to a road barrier and park nearby. Keep straight as various roads connect to Vasquez Road, with Vasquez Creek always nearby on the left. Regular cars can reach this trailhead.

Comment: Few hikers go to Vasquez Pass in the Vasquez Peak Wilderness. The pass can be accessed from several directions. This hike description details the northern route from Winter Park and Vasquez Road. The trail is mostly gradual and there are few distractions other than the natural beauty of the Wilderness. On the day I took this hike, I encountered a moose. Deer are more frequently seen.

The Hike: Begin to the south on the road that is blocked to cars but not bicycles. As you continue up the valley, there will be several creek crossings. After 2.8 miles, a sign directs you to the left and off the road. Descend to a signboard and a creek crossing. Soon you enter the Vasquez Peak Wilderness where bicycles are forbidden. Follow the trail as it meanders upward, sometimes it is less distinct, and finally breaks out of the forest at a boulder and talus field, where cairns help you find the trail up southeast to Vasquez Pass at 11,700 feet on the Continental Divide. Stanley Mountain lies above the pass on the left (east) and Vasquez Peak is the third summit on the right (west). Return as you ascended.

Vasquez Pass

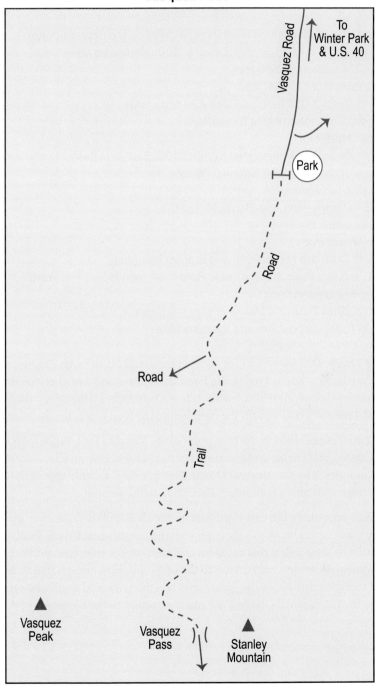

Vasquez Peak

Hike Distance: 4.6 miles on the ascent. 4 miles on the descent (loop).
Hiking Time: Up in 164 minutes. Down in 100 minutes (loop).
Starting Elevation: 10,280 feet
Highest Elevation: 12,947 feet
Elevation Gain: 3,087 feet (includes 420 extra feet)
Trail: Initial 75%, intermittent thereafter
Difficulty: Moderate
Relevant Maps: Trails Illustrated Number 103; Berthoud Pass 7½ minute; Clear
    Creek County; Arapaho National Forest
Views from the Summit:
    NNE to Longs Peak and Mount Meeker
    NE to James Peak
    E to Mount Eva
    ESE to Colorado Mines Peak and Stanley Mountain
    SSE to Grays Peak, Torreys Peak, Bard Peak, and Mount Parnassus
    SE to Engelmann Peak
    SW to Jones Pass and Mount of the Holy Cross
    WNW to Mount Nystrom and Vasquez Lake

Getting There: Drive west on U.S. 40 from Interstate 70, through Empire, for 9.6 miles. Turn left on the road to the Big Bend Picnic Area and a road on the left after 0.4 mile from U.S. 40. At mile 1.7 from U.S. 40, turn right off the paved road and ascend 0.4 mile to a trail sign on the right before the road enters the forest and park.

Comment: Vasquez Peak is the high point of the Vasquez Peak Wilderness. It lies on the Continental Divide and forms part of the border between Clear Creek and Grand Counties. The Continental Divide Trail provides a scenic approach to the summit ridge with only a faint intermittent trail to the summit.

The Hike: Start out to the east-northeast on the clear trail that takes you up 1.3 miles by many switchbacks to a junction with the Continental Divide Trail. Go left (northeast) and follow this excellent trail another 2.5 miles to a saddle. Leave the Continental Divide Trail and rise to the east on an intermittent trail to an unmarked summit cairn. Enjoy the great views and then descend south and southeast to regain the Continental Divide Trail and your return to the trailhead.

Vasquez Peak

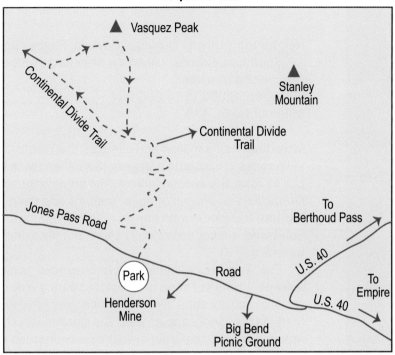

Neighboring towns: Durango, Bayfield, Pagosa Springs, Southfork, Creede, Lake City, Silverton, Ouray
Size: 492,418 acres
Elevation: 8,000 to 14,000 feet
Miles of trails: 475

More than half a million acres in size, the Weminuche Wilderness is Colorado's largest, more than twice the size of Flat Tops, the second largest. The area contains the headwaters of dozens of major streams and rivers, feeding both the Rio Grande and San Juan Rivers, two of the Southwest's most ecologically and culturally significant waterways.

The Weminuche Wilderness (pronounced "why-meh-nuke-ee") consists of an area uplifted during a period of volcanic activity eons ago. Recent ice ages have left their mark on the landscape as well. The glaciers left sharp turrets and jagged peaks separated by lake-studded alpine valleys. The western portion contains the Needle Mountain range and is extremely rugged, with tall granite peaks and deep ravines and river gorges. The area's three fourteeners (Eolus, Sunlight, and Windom Peaks) are all located here. The eastern end of the Weminuche stretches nearly to the Rio Grande headwaters near the town of Creede. Here the Continental Divide snakes along from east to west with large areas above treeline and immense views.

The Durango-Silverton narrow gauge railroad is a popular option for hikers and sightseers wanting to visit the western end of the area.

Columbine Lake

Hike Distance: 6.2 miles up to Lower Chicago Basin. 2.9 more miles to Columbine Lake

Hiking Time: 230 minutes to Lower Chicago Basin. 105 minutes more to Columbine Lake. Down to Lower Chicago Basin in 70 minutes. 165 minutes more down to Needleton.

Starting Elevation: 8,212 feet

Highest Elevation: 12,700 feet

Elevation Gain: 5,728 feet (includes 1,240 extra feet)

Trail: All the way

Difficulty: More difficult

Relevant Maps: Trails Illustrated Number 140; Columbine Pass 7½ minute; Mountain View Crest 7½ minute; La Plata County Number Three; San Juan National Forest

Columbine Lake from Columbine Pass

Getting There: Take the Durango Silverton Narrow Gauge Train and get off at Needleton. (Call 970-247-2733 for information about this popular, historic, tourist attraction.)

Comment: Every Colorado hiker should try to get up into Chicago Basin once in his or her lifetime. Although the trek is complicated and strenuous, the scenic rewards are far greater.

After the train drops you off at Needleton, the hike, with an ample backpack, up the Needle Creek Trail into the Weminuche Wilderness requires stamina. Once in Lower Chicago Basin, around 11,200 feet, you select a campsite with dazzling peaks, wild goats, and flowing water all around you. The Needle

Creek Trail then continues around to the right through numerous switchbacks and two vast meadows to lofty Columbine Pass and then down to Columbine Lake. The trail is exceptionally clear and well graded.

The Hike: Begin across the bridge over the Animas River at Needleton and follow the wide Needle Creek Trail for 6.2 miles up into lovely Lower Chicago Basin, with Needle Creek always on your right.

At Lower Chicago Basin, most parties will camp. To continue up to Columbine Pass, follow the main Needle Creek Trail and avoid the left fork, which ascends northwest up to Twin Lakes. This main trail curves right and crosses Needle Creek at the head of Lower Chicago Basin. Then ascend past mine tailings up into the trees. Pass an old mining tunnel and cabin and continue up through two high, grassy meadows to a series of switchbacks leading to Columbine Pass. From here, descend left 350 feet on the Johnson Creek Trail to beautiful Columbine Lake. Enjoy all the wild beauty before retracing your steps.

Columbine Lake (La Plata County)

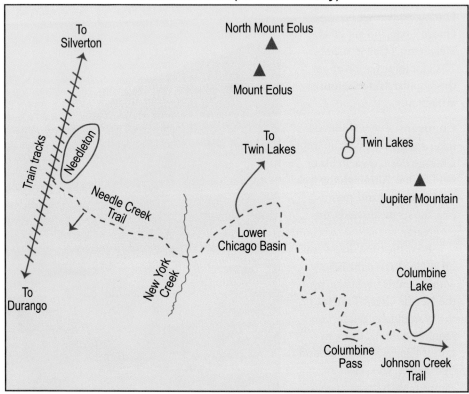

The author, Diane Gimber, and Frank Beghtel below Fourmile Falls

Fourmile Lake

Hike Distance: Up in 6.2 miles (Fourmile Trail). Down in 7.8 miles (Anderson Trail).

Hiking Time: Up in 186 minutes. Down in 207 minutes.

Starting Elevation: 9,040 feet

Highest Elevation: 11,185 feet

Elevation Gain: 3,303 feet (includes 1,158 extra feet)

Trail: All the way

Difficulty: More difficult

Relevant Maps: Trails Illustrated Number 140 or 145; Pagosa Peak 7½ minute; Mineral County; San Juan National Forest

Fourmile Lake

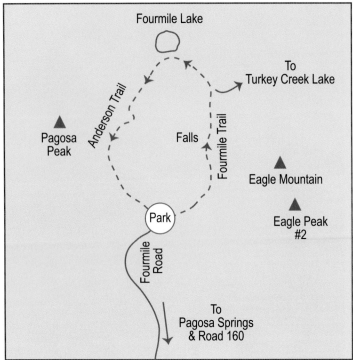

Getting There: From Highway 160 in central Pagosa Springs, drive north on 5th Street and then on the Fourmile Road for a total of 13 miles to the Fourmile Lake Trailhead at the end of the road.

Comment: The trek up the Fourmile Trail in Weminuche Wilderness is 6.2 miles and not the 4 miles one might expect. After 3 miles, as lovely waterfalls come into view, the trail steepens until the last mile before the lake. There are many creek crossings. The counterclockwise return on the Anderson Trail is more gradual and there are no waterfalls.

The Hike: Begin on the right fork from the trailhead register and signboard. Lose some elevation before the trail begins to ascend. Eagle Peak Number Two can be seen on the right. Around the midway point of your ascent, a series of waterfalls are passed. Continue steeply through the forest to a signed fork in a clearing 5 miles from the trailhead. Turkey Creek lies 3 miles farther to the right. Take the left fork for the final 1.2 miles to Fourmile Lake with the drainage on the left.

At the large, serene lake, an unnamed "twelver" towers over the lake to the west-northwest. To descend on the Anderson Trail and make this a loop hike, ascend from a trail sign before the long, meandering hike that takes you past impressive Pagosa Peak on the right, before a series of descending switchbacks.

Mount Eolus

Hike Distance: 9.2 miles each way

Hiking Time: Up to Lower Chicago Basin in 230 minutes. To Mount Eolus in 210 more minutes. Down to Lower Chicago Basin in 125 minutes. To Needleton in 165 more minutes. (This hike is usually done over two days. Day one ends with a camp in Chicago Basin. Day two gains the summit and returns to the train at Needleton.)

Starting Elevation: 8,212 feet

Highest Elevation: 14,083 feet

Elevation Gain: 6,911 feet (includes 570 extra feet each way)

Trail: All the way

Difficulty: Most difficult

Relevant Maps: Trails Illustrated Number 140; Mountain View Crest 7½ minute; Columbine Pass 7½ minute; La Plata County Number Three; San Juan National Forest

Views from the Summit:
 N to North Mount Eolus
 NNW to Wetterhorn Peak
 E to Windom Peak
 ENE to Sunlight Peak and Twin Lakes
 ESE to Jupiter Peak
 SE to Columbine Pass
 SW to La Sal Mountians
 WNW to Mount Wilson, Turret Peak, and Pigeon Peak

Getting There: Take the Durango Silverton Narrow Gauge Train and get off at Needleton. (Call 970-247-2733 for more information.)

Comment: The rewards of this long trek to Mount Eolus far outweigh the hard work required. From Needleton you will ascend the Needle Creek Trail for 6.2 miles to the Lower Chicago Basin and camp. This basin is full of alpine beauty with soaring peaks, roaring waterfalls, blankets of wildflowers, and even a herd of Rocky Mountain goats. Besides Mount Eolus, two other fourteeners, Windom Peak and Sunlight Peak, can also be climbed from Chicago Basin.

The Hike: From the train hike east across the bridge over the Animas River. Reach a fork after 0.5 mile and keep left past a register and signboard. After 1.75 miles, cross New York Creek on a bridge. Around mile 4.5 you enter magnificent Chicago Basin. A good campsite higher in the basin is near a fork at 11,200 feet.

To reach Mount Eolus, ascend the left fork to the north-northwest on a rough, steep trail past treeline to the Twin Lakes at 12,500 feet. Just before the lakes, leave the main trail and go west to a trail that leads west-southwest. Higher in the basin cairns mark the trail as it curves to the right at a rocky wall and leads counterclockwise up to a saddle between Mount Eolus and North Mount Eolus. Continue south over a narrow rocky terrace, known as "The Sidewalk in the Sky." It is easier than it looks. Continue up the left side of the summit ridge. Ascend a series of ledges clockwise to a notch to the south of the summit. Then ascend the ridge to the right for 30 yards to a trail register and gorgeous summit views. As you retrace your route back down you may want to "bag" North Mount Eolus by an easy side trip after crossing "The Sidewalk in the Sky."

Mount Eolus

Mount Eolus from Twin Lakes

Mount Eolus

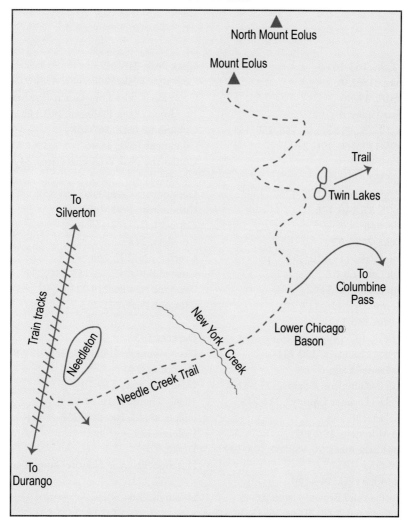

Index

About the Author

Now eighty years old, Dave Muller continues weekly hiking, cross-country skiing, and snowshoeing in the Colorado high country. From Washington D.C., he was educated at Gerzaga College High School and Georgetown University. A psychiatrist who continues to practice and explore the difficulties of human existence, he rejoices in the beauty and climate of Colorado.